$12.50

E4

FROM DESERTS
THE PROPHETS COME

The Creative Spirit in Australia 1788-1972

GEOFFREY SERLE

HEINEMANN MELBOURNE

William Heinemann Australia Pty Ltd Melbourne

© Geoffrey Serle 1973

First published 1973

National Library of Australia Card Service Number
and International Standard Book Number 0 85561 029 8
Library of Congress Catalog Card Number 72-97325

Printed in Australia by John Sands Pty Ltd Halstead Press Division

Registered at the GPO Melbourne for transmission by post as a book

Hoping, if still from deserts the prophets come,
Such savage and scarlet as no green hills dare
Springs in this waste. . . .

A. D. Hope

CONTENTS

ACKNOWLEDGEMENTS

For permission to use copyright material acknowledgement is made to the following:

Robin Boyd, 'Artificial Australia', *Boyer Lectures 1967*, to the Australian Broadcasting Commission;
The Australian Ugliness, to Cheshire Publishing.

Van Wyck Brooks, *The Writer in America*, to E.P. Dutton and Co. Inc.

Vincent Buckley, *Essays in Poetry*, to Melbourne University Press.

C.M.H. Clark, 'Faith', in P. Coleman (ed), *Australian Civilization*, to Cheshire Publishing.

Roger Covell, *Australia's Music*, to Sun Books.

R.M. Crawford, *An Australian Perspective*, to Melbourne University Press.

K.S. Cunningham, 'Education', in C. Hartley Grattan (ed), *Australia*, to University of California Press.

F. Dalby Davison, 'Vance Palmer and his Writing', to *Meanjin Quarterly*.

Flora Eldershaw, 'The Landscape Writers', to *Meanjin Quarterly*.

B. Elliott, 'The Colonial Poets', in G. Dutton (ed), *The Literature of Australia*, to Penguin Books Australia;
The Landscape of Australian Poetry, to Oxford University Press.

J.M. Freeland, *Architecture in Australia*, to Cheshire Publishing.

Mary Gilmore, 'Nationality', to Angus and Robertson.

Percy Grainger, from notes to 'Colonial Song', to Schott and Co; from preface to 'Marching Song', to G.S. Schirmer; from the author's letters, to Mrs Grainger.

H.M. Green, *A History of Australian Literature*, to Angus and Robertson.

Tyrone Guthrie, *A Life in the Theatre*, to Hamish Hamilton.

Arnold Haskell, *Waltzing Matilda*, to Adam and Charles Black.

Harry Heseltine, 'Australian Fiction Since 1920', in G. Dutton (ed), *The Literature of Australia*, to Penguin Books Australia.

ACKNOWLEDGEMENTS

Ursula Hoff, 'Reflections on the Heidelberg School', to *Meanjin Quarterly*.

A.D. Hope, 'Australian Literature and the Universities', to *Meanjin Quarterly*.

Robert Hughes, *The Art of Australia*, to Penguin Books Australia.

H.M. Jones, *The Theory of American Literature*, to Cornell University Press.

H.G. Kippax, 'Drama' in A.F. Davies and S. Encel (eds), *Australian Society*, to Cheshire Publishing; from introduction to *Three Australian Plays*, to Penguin Books Australia.

T. Inglis Moore, *Social Patterns in Australian Literature*, to Angus and Robertson.

Alan Moorehead, *Cooper's Creek*, and *Rum Jungle*, to the author and Hamish Hamilton.

Vance Palmer, 'Battle', and *Louis Esson and the Australian Theatre*, to *Meanjin Quarterly*.

A.A. Phillips, *The Australian Tradition*, to the author.

K.S. Prichard, 'Some Perceptions and Aspirations' in *Southerly*, to Angus and Robertson.

M. Roe, *Quest for Authority in Eastern Australia 1835-1851*, to Melbourne University Press.

Bernard Smith, 'Architecture in Australia', in *Historical Studies*, to School of History, University of Melbourne; *Australian Painting*, and *European Vision in the South Pacific*, to Oxford University Press.

Hugh Stretton, *Ideas for Australian Cities*, to Georgian House.

Ian Turner, 'The Social Setting' in G. Dutton (ed), *The Literature of Australia*, to Penguin Books Australia.

Clive Turnbull, *Art Now*, to Hawthorn Press.

Patrick White, 'The Prodigal Returns' in *Australian Letters*, to the author.

Judith Wright, *Preoccupations in Australian Poetry*, to Oxford University Press.

Every effort has been made to trace owners of copyright material, but in some cases this has not proved possible. The publishers would be interested to hear from any copyright holders not here acknowledged.

PREFACE

This book is about literature, art, music, theatre and architecture in their Australian context, about 'high' culture, culture in the sense of what the creative spirit has achieved in terms of Art. It also attempts briefly to cover science and scholarship (in so far as is permitted by the lamentable state of historical research in these fields), but does not pretend to be intellectual history or to cover the ideas which have shaped Australia. It is frankly élitist: except incidentally, it does not discuss either 'popular' culture or the sociology of culture (on which there are great books to be written).

This is the revised version of lectures I gave at Monash University in 1971 in an experimental course in Australian cultural history. I was aiming to cut a new path for teaching and research in Australian history, to bring cultural history into the general discourse of Australian historians, and to bridge the gap between general history and the major works in literary, art, musical and architectural history which have appeared in recent years. Historians are frequently critical of the lack of understanding of general historical context which art-historians or literary critics often display; the latter sometimes deplore historians' ignorance of the arts. It is time a general historian reached out towards the specialists.

Another reason for teaching the course and writing the book is that I deplore the attitude of nearly all teachers in Arts faculties at universities who happily tolerate a situation in which more than 95 per cent of their graduates depart without more than a nodding acquaintance with the life and work of one or two of Australia's best writers and painters, and without having read or even heard of the major works of scholarship which have been written around them. And most of these graduates become teachers! In this, as in other fields, the universities are still too preoccupied with their great task of transmitting the world's learning and are paying inadequate attention to their additional duty to study the immediate civilization to which they belong.

I cannot claim expert knowledge in any of the major cultural fields (except, perhaps, to a limited extent in literature). Much of this book is a summary presentation of the distinguished works of Bernard Smith (*European Vision and the South Pacific* and *Aus-*

tralian Painting), H. M. Green (*A History of Australian Literature*), Judith Wright (*Preoccupations in Australian Poetry*), A. A. Phillips (*The Australian Tradition*), Roger Covell (*Australia's Music*), Leslie Rees (*Towards an Australian Drama*), J. M. Freeland (*Architecture in Australia*) and Robin Boyd (*Australia's Home* and *The Australian Ugliness*), and others from which I have quoted freely. I hope that one consequence of this book will be that readers will be led to consult some of these works. But I may claim that almost exactly half of this book is entirely original —not so much in its juxtaposition of what was happening in the different arts in various periods, or in its provision of a general context, but in the rudimentary attempt at a theory of cultural growth.

My father, Percival Serle, started me on this track by encouraging me to read 'The Loaded Dog' and 'The Geebung Polo Club' as well as *Stalky & Co.* and *Treasure Island*. I would probably not have made a book of it but for the enthusiastic encouragement of David Callaghan, Larry Jagan, Mark Taft and the other volunteers at Monash in 1971 and 1972 whose company I so much enjoyed. And I have to thank Arthur Phillips especially, Clem Christesen, Bruce Grant, Kenneth Hince, Phyllis and John Murphy, Stephen Murray-Smith, Bernard Smith, and my wife Jessie, both for suggestions and for eliminating many stupidities.

G.S.

1

James Tuckey, Lieutenant on the ship which brought the unwilling convict settlers to Port Phillip Bay and Hobart Town in 1803-4, mused on future possibilities: 'I beheld a second Rome, rising from a coalition of banditti. I beheld it giving laws to the world, and superlative in arms and in arts, looking down with proud superiority upon the barbarous nations of the northern hemisphere.'[1]

Such fancies were to be commonplace among young idealistic patriots late in the nineteenth century before disillusion set in. But intellect and the arts, until very recent times at least, have been almost the last things a European has associated with Australia. To the educated Englishman, the Australian colonies were mercifully faraway places to which to dismiss convicts, black-sheep remittance-men, and the redundant poor and others who were nuisances; camps of brawling goldminers from which rich, uncouth uncles turned up unexpectedly; valuable suppliers of wool; a country which produced jolly good cricketers; on the whole a handy part of the Empire whose undisciplined soldiers were useful to have around—as Angela Thirkell remarked, a marvellous country for the warrant-officer type; but certainly not a continent whose intellectual and cultural contributions to civilization, leaving aside freaks like Nellie Melba, were worthy of remark.

There is little, certainly, to remark in the first half-century after the foundation at Port Jackson. It would be ludicrous to expect, and it is unnecessary to attempt to explain the absence of many or any good writers or artists in early colonial society, composed as it was of such unpromising elements; moreover it was numerically tiny and the infant free society was overwhelmingly dominated by lust for material gain. 'The first object of young societies is bread and covering,' said Thomas Jefferson. 'Science [or culture or learning] is but secondary and subsequent.' In an obvious sense, culture and everything else begins from scratch in a new country, despite the inheritance of the whole of European and English culture. Nevertheless, not all of early Australian history was squalid and brutish. Australia was not entirely cut off from civilization.

Consider for a start the intellectual quality of many of the official class and the earnestness with which they strove to transplant the fine fruits of old-world civilization. As a group the early Governors were remarkable all-rounders. Bligh had distinguished scientific attainments; Sir Thomas Brisbane was a good astronomer and like Bligh was a Fellow of the Royal Society; Sir John Franklin was a great explorer and talented scientist; Sir Richard Bourke, when he retired, edited the correspondence of his kinsman, Edmund Burke; and C. J. La Trobe was a cultural virtuoso. Alexander Macleay, Colonial Secretary of New South Wales, was an outstanding zoologist, and Sir Thomas Mitchell, the Surveyor-General, was extraordinary in the range of his talents. The explorers were mainly the pick of the British Army, often men of scientific accomplishment and sometimes of considerable sensitivity. A high proportion of the first elected members of the Legislative Council of New South Wales in the 1840s were men with first-rate minds and first-rate education in the classical mould. James Macarthur was a sophisticated political theorist; William Charles Wentworth was capable of constructing an ideology for his class and generation; Robert Lowe, later Gladstone's Chancellor of the Exchequer, was a man of sheerly commanding intellect, by English standards let alone colonial; J. A. Froude, the English historian, considered James Martin would have been a great Chief Justice of England; Sir Terence Aubrey Murray was the father of Gilbert Murray, the classical scholar, and of Hubert Murray of Papua; Sir Charles Nicholson was no mean classical scholar; and William Forster was a minor poet and dramatist. No Victorian ministry is ever likely to rival the educational qualifications of the first, which was composed of three Cambridge and two Trinity College, Dublin graduates and two Army officers who became Generals. Admittedly, this ruling group of the official, gentleman class was only tiny, and perhaps left little permanent cultural mark.

We should not look for cultural quality only in the conventional forms. In literature, for example, there is almost nothing of worth in the novel, poetry or drama before 1850. We need not trouble ourselves on literary grounds with the verse of Michael Massey Robinson, Governor Macquarie's laureate, or with Wentworth's second-prize Cambridge poem of 1823, or with Judge Barron Field's evocation:

> Kangaroo, Kangaroo!
> Thou Spirit of Australia,
> That redeems from utter failure,

From perfect desolation,
And warrants the creation
Of this fifth part of the Earth,
Which would seem an after-birth . . .

Similarly the early novels like Savery's *Quintus Servinton*, Tucker's *Memoirs of Ralph Rashleigh*, or Rowcroft's *Tales of the Colonies* are usually no more than thinly disguised autobiography by men who were really not much more than amateur immigration agents or compilers of guide-books to the colonies. H. M. Green has remarked that 'it has often been asserted that the early literature of a colony is bound to be a literature of exile, weak and homeward-looking, a feeble reflection of life and literary forms and conventions that are remote in space and time . . . a thin shadow spun out of books and memories by weaklings and third-raters dreaming of home.' But, Green goes on, there is another strand 'spun out of native material and personal experience', usually uncultivated but 'infinitely more robust . . . a by-product of action'.[2] The real literature of the period, by far the best writing, is to be found in the journals of men such as Watkin Tench of the First Fleet—observant, contemplative, witty and a stylist; or in *Settlers and Convicts* by An Emigrant Mechanic (Alexander Harris)—so vivid and downright and honest an observer, except when he preaches; or in the journals of explorers such as Sturt, Grey and Giles, or in the despatches of Governors like Bourke, Gipps and La Trobe. This was a period when there was no split between the two cultures, and men brought up on the Bible, whose training was military or scientific, could often write superbly well. Perhaps the most freakish literary production of all was the weekly *Atlas* (1844-48) edited by Lowe and Martin, full of political polemic and urbane satire, comparable with the highest current English literary standards and reflecting classical culture at its best.

However, the chief importance of early Australia in intellectual and cultural terms was as a field for science. The discovery and settlement of a new continent naturally caused immense excitement to geographers, botanists and zoologists especially, and also to geologists and astronomers. To educated men everywhere the chief interest of Australia was its widening of scientific horizons. Scores of able, educated men were attracted to early Australia by scientific interest; the main preoccupation of a high proportion of the educated and cultured settlers was with scientific matters.[3]

The Pacific became a great school for scientists, whose investigations had an immense impact on biological thought—on the whole study of man and nature. The figure of Sir Joseph Banks, president of the Royal Society for more than forty years, looms large over the first thirty years of Australian history. He and Daniel Solander had brought back a large collection of specimens from Cook's Tahitian-Australian voyage, and he then developed at Kew the Royal Gardens' collection of exotic plants. The early Governors had to report to Banks, the colonies' great patron, as well as to their official superiors, about the state of their colony and the progress of scientific observation. Banks sponsored Flinders' voyages of coastal exploration and sent out the young botanist, Robert Brown, to accompany him; he also despatched botanists or collectors such as George Caley, Allan Cunningham and George Suttor, most of whom had been employed at Kew. He maintained correspondence with a regiment of naturalists who stacked returning ships with plants and animals. 'Our ship', wrote J. H. Vaux, was 'literally crowded, so as to resemble Noah's Ark. There were kangaroos, black swans, a noble emu, and cockatoos, parrots and smaller birds without number. . . .'[4] Bennelong and one or two other Aborigines were also sent off as 'specimens'.

Botanical and zoological discoveries in Australia excited interest because of the problems they introduced as well as their novelty. Solander's notebooks classifying the plants he collected at Botany Bay are full of erasures and revisions. J. E. Smith, founder and president of the Linnean Society, wrote in 1793:

> When a botanist first enters on the investigation of so remote a country as New Holland, he finds himself as it were in a new world. He can scarcely meet with any certain fixed points from whence to draw his analogies; and even those that appear most promising, are frequently in danger of misleading . . . him. Whole tribes of plants, which at first sight seem familiar to his acquaintance, as occupying links in Nature's chain . . . prove, on a nearer examination, total strangers, with other configurations, other oeconomy, and other qualities; not only the species themselves are new, but most of the genera, and even natural orders.[5]

Robert Brown, having brought back more than 3,000 mostly unknown specimens from his voyages with Flinders, in 1810 published the first volume of the first definitive work of Australian botany, *Prodromus Florae Novae Hollandiae*, which was not in any sense replaced until Bentham's work of the 1860s. Brown kept up close links with Australia and Australian botany throughout his distinguished later career. The French also shared in the excitement: Baudin's voyage in command of the *Géographe* and the *Naturaliste* from 1800 to 1804 produced a zoological collection equivalent to Brown's in botany. J. W. Lewin was assisted by patrons of science to migrate to New South Wales in 1800 and published the first major works on birds and insects. The Macleays—Alexander and his son, William, both Fellows of the Royal Society before migrating—were other notable contributors in the biological area.

The major significance of biological observation in the Australian region was the contribution it made to demolishing traditional views about man and the universe. Bernard Smith in his *European Vision and the South Pacific* remarks that 'the wealth of new material which arrived in such abundance . . . exposed not only the systematics of the biological sciences but also traditional European ideas concerning the nature of the universe to novel and difficult questions, and was one of the factors which led to the collapse in scientific circles of the chain of being as an acceptable explanation of universal nature.'[6] Ultimately, after several preparatory works like Lyell's *Principles of Geology*, in 1859 Charles Darwin produced his revolutionary synthesis, *On the Origin of Species by means of Natural Selection*. It is not the least significant fact in Australian history (though it is rarely mentioned in the short histories) that Darwin, T. H. Huxley and J. D. Hooker all carried out early scientific work in Australia. Darwin was naturalist on the *Beagle* during its voyage from 1831 to 1836 and was in Australia for two months early in 1836. Beyond the Blue Mountains, he wrote in his diary one day:

> I had been lying on a sunny bank and was reflecting on the strange character of the animals of this country as compared to the rest of the world. An unbeliever in everything beyond his own reason might exclaim, 'surely two distinct Creators must have been at work'; their object, however, has been the same and certainly the end in each case is complete.[7]

His observations reinforced his developing views; he ultimately used many Australian examples in his great work and maintained a long correspondence with Australian scientists. Huxley was naturalist under Owen Stanley on the *Rattlesnake*, voyaging mainly in northern Australian waters between 1846 and 1850, when he produced the paper which made a major contribution to study of the morphology of the animal kingdom. Australia meant much to him—if only because he courted and won his wife in Sydney. If the infant University of Sydney had carried out its intention to have a chair in natural history, it is known that Huxley would have applied and must have been appointed. Hooker was naturalist on the Ross Antarctic expedition of 1839-43, spent several months in Van Diemen's Land, and in 1859 published *The Flora of Tasmania*.

Before Darwin, who made anthropology possible, scientists were in no position to develop study of the Aborigine. Among educated and enlightened men late in the eighteenth century there was a strong Rousseauian cult of the noble savage, living an estimable life in a state of primitive nature. Cook himself, who for the most part observed accurately and acutely, remarked: 'These people may truly be said to be in the pure state of Nature, and may appear to some to be the most wretched upon Earth; but in reality they are far happier than . . . we Europeans. . . .' He admired their courage and endurance, the simplicity of their material needs, the 'hard' primitiveness and virtue of their life. Governor Phillip—witness his naming of Manly—and Governor Macquarie had a similar attitude. But few convicts or settlers saw much nobility in the Australian savage. The enlightened Tench was revolted by his contacts; M. F. Péron, the medical naturalist on Baudin's expedition, had a violent reaction of disgust. The evangelical missionary view came to prevail. These were the lowest orders of humanity (and the Tasmanians were the lowest of the low), licentious sinners living in a degraded spiritual condition; throughout the beautiful Pacific, only man was vile. Providence had designed them to pass away, to die out—a view which fitted the needs of pastoral settlers. The most sympathetic observers of the Aborigines and their main defenders were some of the explorers who had seen something of tribal life—especially Eyre and Grey, also Sturt and Mitchell. The impressions of visiting scientists in the 30s and 40s helped to build up a fair mass of detailed study by mid-century; but even the best of it was superficial and haphazard, and it included much speculative rubbish by Fundamentalists. The great inhibiting factor was the assumed Biblical time-span—6,000 years since Adam. Few Europeans in the nineteenth century began even to sense the cultural depth and sophistication of Aboriginal music, dancing, art and story.[8]

Ernest Giles, with some justification, wrote that 'Exploration of one thousand miles in Australia is equal to ten thousand miles in any other part of the earth's surface, always excepting Arctic and Antarctic travels.'[9] Great distances, lack of water, the problem of food supply, scurvy, extremes of temperature, and danger from Aborigines were the reasons why it took ninety years for the last outlines to be drawn. It was a perennial irritating intellectual problem: simply, what was *there*, at the heart of the continent, in the 'ghastly blank' in the centre? Apart from the need to find new pastures, the explorers were driven on by the ignominy of not knowing; Sturt and Mitchell were obsessed with their respective visions of a huge inland sea and a vast northern river-system. Moreover, it was a popular problem, understood to some extent by everyone, because in a sense it was so simple. The geographical problem was central in the Australian imagination for nearly half our history and aroused passionate popular interest. The long drawn-out drama of Burke and Wills, with its intense mass public involvement in Victoria, is one example; similarly, controversy about what happened to Leichhardt and his ability as an explorer went on and on through the later nineteenth century. The explorers were heroic enough, but the public's passionate involvement made them either super-heroes or super-fools.

To measure their achievements against their difficulties is impossible. Perhaps, as explorers, they were on the whole a middling lot, none of them winning quite outstanding distinction. Of necessity they were mostly slightly odd: as Alan Moorehead says, they

> profess to love the desert, they find a kind of exhilaration there, a sense of freedom, of physical cleanliness, perhaps even a spiritual regeneration, and no matter how they are reduced by their hardships they return again and again . . . these men elevate their trials almost into a mystique, a cult of barrenness and asceticism.[10]

Patrick White, Francis Webb, Sidney Nolan and others have found in them fruitful subjects. They were nearly all army men, surveyors or scientists. Sturt and Mitchell are among the more interesting—men who though mainly concerned to add to knowledge were also men of sensibility who could convey their great experiences in appropriate literary terms. Sturt, for example, described the occasion when his thermometer burst at 127° in the shade and his matches ignited when they fell to the ground:

> the blasts of heat were so terrific, that I wondered the very grass did not take fire. . . . every thing, both animate and

7

inanimate, gave way before it; the horses stood with their backs to the wind, and their noses to the ground, without the muscular strength to raise their heads; the birds were mute, and the leaves of the trees, under which we were sitting, fell like a snow shower around us.[11]

Mitchell could also react aesthetically to new scenes, usually in the current romantic convention. He described one of the great Australian visual experiences—a dry inland river in first flood—as follows:

a murmuring sound like that of a distant waterfall . . . drew our attention. . . . Still no flood appeared, although its approach was indicated by the occasional rending of trees with a loud noise. . . . At length the rushing sound of waters and loud cracking of timber announced that the flood was in the next bend. It rushed into our sight, glittering in the moonbeams, a moving cataract, tossing before it ancient trees, and snapping them against its banks. It was preceded by a point of meandering water, picking its way like a thing of life, through the deepest parts of the dark, dry, and shady bed of what thus again became a flowing river.[12]

Mitchell, it must be said, was perhaps the greatest all-rounder of his day: surveyor and mapmaker, mathematician, inventor of a new type of screw propeller, author of textbooks on drill, geography and winegrowing, translator of Camoens' *Lusiad*, an artist and a writer of ability—men are not so educated, or so educate themselves, today. But he was also an unhappy and cranky man who, among other things, took part in the last recorded duel in Australia in 1851.

By the 1840s Hobart had become the major centre of scientific activity, largely because of energetic patronage by Governor Sir John and Lady Franklin and by Franklin's secretary, Alexander Maconochie, who had been secretary of the Royal Geographical Society and first professor of geography at the University of London. Franklin founded the Van Diemen's Land Natural History Society, which became the Scientific Society, and when the Colonial Office vetoed his plan for a museum supported by public money Lady Franklin founded and organised a museum herself as a temple of science. The Society published the *Tasmanian Journal of Natural Science*, which was of astonishing competence and made the Society the focus of scientific endeavour in all the colonies. At primitive Port Phillip, C. J. La Trobe clung to it as a lifeline of civilization. Specimens in numerous fields were sent to the experts in Britain; Richard Owen, the comparative anatomist, for example, for years worked mainly on Tasmanian and Australian material. The *Journal* maintained its standard well with pioneer local studies in meteorology, ornithology, herpetology, conchology, and so on. Unfortunately, there was a ludicrous split, reflecting the political divisions of Franklin's time, when Sir John Eardley-Wilmot succeeded him as Governor and founded the Royal Society of Tasmania, an informal branch of the Royal Society in London. The offended Scientific Society moved its headquarters to Launceston and rightly regarded the activities of the new society as a travesty of proper scientific behaviour. The following Governor, Sir William Denison, brought about a reconciliation and a merger in 1848, but in the 50s scientific initiative inevitably moved to Melbourne.[13] There are further grounds for arguing, as many Tasmanians nostalgically have, that before it was swamped by mainland progress the tiny island community saw a fine cultural flowering in the 30s and 40s, within and despite the penal society. As an unusual claim to distinction, in T. G. Wainewright it had one of the most remarkable convicts of all: he had been an early admirer of William Blake and was 'a writer of real originality, but deeply neurotic', on whom Oscar Wilde was to write an essay, 'Pen, Pencil and Poison'; in Van Diemen's Land he became an excellent portraitist. Sir John Franklin had the better of Governors Bourke and Gipps in developing education; his friendship with Dr Arnold of Rugby led to the foundation of two fine secondary schools, Hutchins' and Launceston Grammar. Tasmanian educational development was carried further by Arnold's son, Thomas (Matthew's brother and grandfather of Julian and Aldous Huxley), as inspector of schools from 1850 to 1856.

Most of the considerable body of painting of the first half-century was a by-product of scientific work, in a period when the scientist was his own illustrator or worked closely with professional artists.[14] An immense quantity of graphic records was produced— of flora, fauna, topography, Aborigines and the general progress of the colony. Descriptive scientists frequently relied on the care and accuracy of the draughtsmen assisting them in depicting specimens. Bernard Smith has displayed how, from close association with scientists, artists tended to become more empirical and realist in approach. Landscapists became more inclined to place primitive peoples, animals and plants in appropriate environmental settings, rather than use some remote fancy drawn from

9

neo-classical thought. The notion of the typical landscape, reflecting the scientist's interests in types, became part of nineteenth century artistic theory. In painting, as in science, Christian assumptions and the inspiration of the classical world tended to give way to empiricism and evolutionary thought.

Sir Joseph Banks held sway from the start and Governor Phillip was careful to mobilize the limited artistic talents of the founding party. One of the most entertaining of Australian artists is the unidentified primitive 'Port Jackson painter', who produced at least 250 water-colours between 1788 and 1792. At the other extreme is probably the finest product of the association between science and art—Gould's *Birds of Australia*. John Gould was already a world-famous ornithologist when he decided to cover the Australian field and arrived in Van Diemen's Land in 1838. In two years of travel round the colonies he identified some 300 new species, doubling the known number. On his return to England he published in thirty-six quarterly parts until 1848, with a later supplement. His wife, Elizabeth, drew many of the illustrations which, after her death in 1841, were continued by Edward Lear (the nonsense man) and others. The end-product remains one of the classic works of Australiana (and the most expensive). Between the Port Jackson painter and the Goulds was a host of topographical and illustrative artists. Surveyors, especially, practised landscape painting and drawing as well as their professional panoramas. Mitchell was very active; so were Robert Hoddle and Robert Russell, the Melbourne surveyors, and W. R. Govett in the Blue Mountains area. Artists often accompanied exploring expeditions to provide visual records of the journeys; the products by S. T. Gill, G. F. Angas, Ludwig Becker and others are among the most prized possessions of State libraries and galleries. The artists attached to the numerous visiting scientific expeditions added a great deal. The close relationship between science and art ended with the invention of photography and its wide use from the 1850s. Over the previous seventy years Art had acquired from Science a basic habit of analytic naturalism, and together they had gone far towards describing the new world of Australia and the Pacific.

Nevertheless, the roll-call of talented artists attracted to Australia independently of the service of science is not unimpressive. Augustus Earle, world traveller and former Royal Academy trainee, spent 1825 to 1828 in New South Wales, opened an art school, and painted two governors, many leading citizens and landscapes full of noble savages and noble frontiersmen; he also held an exhibition which, according to the Sydney *Gazette*, was 'much visited by the youth of the Colony, and must have a considerable influence in promoting good taste among the rising generation'.[15] John Glover, after a very successful painting career in England, migrated to Van Diemen's Land in 1831 at the age of sixty-four and continued happily for years to paint the Tasmanian countryside, in the eighteenth century manner but with some local character. John Skinner Prout travelled the colonies for eight years in the 1840s as a picturesque painter. The young George French Angas, son of one of the leading promoters of South Australia, illustrated that colony and New Zealand with great skill. The South Australian work in the 1840s of the water-colourist and lithographer, S. T. Gill, was of higher artistic value than the later goldfields sketches for which he is more widely known. The most important and prolific of the early artists was Conrad Martens (1801-78), artist on the *Beagle* with Darwin and his lifelong friend, who settled in Sydney. He was a fine topographical artist but also very much a product of the romantic revival who came to specialize in studies of Sydney Harbour. He is perhaps most significant as a painter who managed to live by his art for twenty-five years, maintaining a family by sales and teaching.[16]

New South Wales and Tasmania are fortunate to have been founded in the great days still of Georgian taste, in the closing years of a century and a half of glorious British architecture associated with the names of Wren, Vanbrugh, Hawksmoor, Gibbs, the Adams, Nash, Soane and others; an architecture which reflected the age of reason in its simplicity, restraint, symmetry and emphasis on proportion.[17] Lachlan Macquarie, the builder, and Mrs Macquarie (with her book of plans) were children of the age, both well aware of what good architecture was. Wherever he went, Macquarie insisted on basic building standards and brick or stone when possible. Francis Greenway (1777-1837), who had tried to forge his way out of bankruptcy, was his agent, who in six years from 1816 built an extraordinary number of churches, schools, courthouses, barracks, hospitals and other public buildings. However did this minor Bristol architect, who was little more than a spec builder, blossom out so nobly to meet the challenge of supplying a new country's first public buildings? The architectural historians agree that he was a great architect, but interpret him variously. One believes he was essentially original and gave a purely Australian soul to his buildings; another claims that his real distinction lies in the range of his stylistic models stretching back to Wren and in the originality of his Baroque revivalism.[18]

The Macquarie Street barracks, St James's church and the Windsor church were among his finest works, few of which survive and not one in its original state; only in very recent years has it been possible to mobilize strong forces to preserve what remains.

The verandah—a transmission from India and other tropical imperial possessions, familiar to military officers in the colony—was the first local characteristic to develop. It was adopted initially as an external means of access, to avoid traversing each room of these simple Georgian box houses, but its general cooling effect and advantages as a shady living-area soon came to be recognized. (This was long before the days when galvanized iron roofing often made the verandah the only tolerable living area, in country houses especially.) A second characteristic, where for 'lack of room or imagination' verandahs were not adopted, came to be wide, overhanging eaves as an answer to generally poor bricks and mortar. J. M. Freeland argues that long, low buildings emerged very early, 'earth-hugging and horizontal, perfectly in harmony with the landscape', characterized by the verandah or the 'aesthetic richness that came from the deep shadow cast by the overhang on the brick walls'. He claims the 1820s and 30s as the rich time of colonial architecture, with the 30s as high summer: 'Macquarie's reign had prepared the ground, the twenties saw his seed grow lustily and luxuriantly and the thirties brought it to its full and finest flowering.' It was 'an all too short-lived indigenous architecture'—as well as the prevalent good Georgian taste and the beauty of the local vernacular, the workmen were of high quality and bricks, lime and cedar came to be on the whole good and cheap. Entrance doorways and graceful elliptical fanlights—'veritable cobwebs of delight'—were features of substantial and modest houses alike. Both, he claims, were built to the same standards of taste and style—simple, honest, direct. 'When the Colonial Style came to full flower, naive though it was in many ways, it was distinguished by an exemplary regard for an economy of resources and materials used in the best of taste. In this lay its modest glory and supremacy in Australian architectural history.'[19] Hardy Wilson's drawings, *Old Colonial Architecture* (1923), were a notable pioneer commemoration of the period.

The first major variation, but only for substantial housing, came in the 1830s with the introduction of the Regency style. The aim was to impress: the style was large, formal, imposing, often with bold classical elements, frequently displaying a portico or at least a porch and rarely a verandah. The chief agent was

John Verge, who migrated to become a pastoralist, failed, and fell back on building. The new pastoral aristocracy flocked to him for design of imposing mansions in the latest English fashion. Some of the finest examples are Camden Park, Elizabeth Bay House, and Panshanger in Tasmania.[20]

Tasmania developed much less of a colonial style than New South Wales, partly because of the climatic lack of need for the verandah. Tasmania was also just too late to be predominantly Georgian, or for that style to flower as it did so magnificently in the eastern United States. Its architecture reflected England much more closely, and its more English climate and visual appearance encouraged the colonists to reproduce 'home' more than elsewhere by systematic cutting-out of native trees and planting of oaks, elms, beeches, hawthorns, poplars. An abundant amount of Tasmania's early architecture has at least survived, because of relative lack of 'progress', and much of great beauty remains intact. Melbourne and Adelaide of course could not share the Georgian or Regency heritage, were too late to take part in the 'one coherent phase of Australian architectural development',[21] though St James' Old Cathedral in Melbourne, begun in 1839, is more or less Regency.

From about 1840 imported fashion dictated public and private town building in some variety of revivalist style—classical or medieval. In addition, Freeland argues, the building regulations adopted in Sydney in 1837 in themselves 'spelled doom to the Colonial style'. The main purpose was fire control, but the wholesale adoption of London regulations, shaped to a very different climate, had immense visual effects. Verandahs, temporarily, and window-shutters were eliminated, and parapets replaced roof overhangs (to protect passers-by from falling snow). Almost identical regulations were adopted in most of the other capitals, with important inhibitory effect on variation from English models.[22]

Lieutenant William Dawes and Governor Phillip planned Sydney and Parramatta with rudimentary nobility, but in the succeeding years of hardship and weak government the towns were permitted to grow higgledy-piggledy. The crucial legislation, which set the pattern for nearly all the new towns of eastern Australia for the rest of the century, was inspired by Governor Darling in 1829. He settled for modest, attainable principles: the street patterns had to be rectilinear and main streets at least 100 feet wide, but no provision was made for squares or parklands in inner areas. Russell and Hoddle accordingly laid out Melbourne's square mile. Only the provision for three-chain stock-routes which became inner suburban boulevards, and La Trobe's determined reservation of parklands outside the town proper, partially redeemed the uninspired 'plan'. At Adelaide, however, Colonel William Light was free to produce an individual plan which in its noble quality was unrivalled until W. B. Griffin conceived Canberra. Generations later, Hugh Stretton has remarked, 'his planning is still blessed, and used as he intended'. On the step between coast and hills he laid down 'two patches of city grid around six generous squares, within a figure eight' of broad half-mile-wide parklands, including the Torrens valley—a great gesture of courageous enlightenment. His general principles conformed to the latest thinking in town-planning; boldness of execution in the use of the valley and the lavishness of his green-belt vision raised the plan to brilliance.[23]

From about 1840 local painting and the other arts had acquired a small audience. In the 40s there was a market for the lithographic views and engravings of Sydney and Hobart by Prout, Joseph Fowles, James Maclehose, Martens and others. There is evidence in Hobart especially of the development of an appreciative group of patrons of paintings executed for the pleasure of local residents rather than as exotic works for Europeans in Europe. Amateur painting became a frequent pastime, art exhibitions became viable in economic terms, Prout gave successful lectures on painting at the Mechanics' Institutes; and indeed in 1849 there was a series of lectures at the Hobart Institute 'On the Perception of the Beautiful, the Principles of Taste, Expression as Applied to the Fine Arts, etc.'. A tiny cultural élite was gathering and recognizing itself.[24]

Surgeon John White of the First Fleet described New South Wales as 'a country and place so forbidding and so hateful as only to merit execration and curses'.[25] Few Europeans have reacted quite so violently but nearly all have found the natural environment awesome and forbidding. The native-born, knowing no better, have simply found it natural. Settlers fighting and taming or retreating in defeat from the land, European man against the Australian continent, has been a leading theme of Australian history. Both the strangeness or special character of the land and the conflict between man and land have been central in the Australian imagination and major inspirations for the creative artist.

There were frequent early references to the picturesque 'park like' quality (like an English nobleman's open park) of some of the country around Sydney and some of the better pastoral country. But overwhelmingly, as Bernard Smith has so thoroughly documented it, the general impression of the country was of oddity, monotony, melancholy, sterility and hostility.

Oddity, eccentricity, the inversion of Nature at the Antipodes —the notion cropped up again and again. Even the pleasant park country was deceptive, not at all what it seemed—on the one hand the brilliant appearance of plants, birds and insects, on the other the barrenness of the soil, the violent variation of climate and the difficulty of cultivation. Péron in his *Voyage of Discovery* drew attention to the frequent 'whimsical freaks of Nature': 'New Holland defies our conclusions from comparisons, mocks our studies, and shakes to their foundations the most firmly established and most universally admitted of our scientific opinions.' James O'Hara wrote in his *History of New South Wales* (1817):

> Nature may be said to have in this country indulged in whim. . . . animals were discovered which might at first sight be considered monstrous productions, such as an aquatic quadruped, about the size of a rabbit, with the eyes, colour and skin of a mole, and the bill and web-feet of a duck, a parrot with the slender legs of a sea-gull, a skate with a head like that of a shark. . . . The whole animal creation appeared to be different from that of every other region: nor less so the vegetable; every tree and shrub, perhaps without exception, was of a species peculiar to the soil, and another Flora diffused an endless variety of unknown tints and forms.

Barron Field found Australia a topsy-turvy land where all things were exceptional and inverted; so extraordinary a country could never have formed part of the original creation, the kangaroo was its one redeeming feature. Botanists were amazed at eucalypts shedding bark seasonally and retaining their leaves.[26]

Monotony and sombre melancholy: the reaction was almost standard. Darwin remarked on the 'extreme uniformity in the character of the vegetation', the 'desolate and untidy' appearance of the woods;[27] Mrs Meredith flagged through the 'heavy, weary monotony' of the Bathurst plains;[28] Surgeon Cunningham found 'one dull green uniformity of foliage existing from year's end to year's end'.[29] Oxley wrote in his journal: 'One tree, one soil, one water, and one description of bird, fish, or animal prevails alike for ten miles and for one hundred. A variety of wretchedness is at all times preferable to one unvarying cause of pain and distress.'[30] H. M. Hyndman made the classic denunciation of the gum tree from experience about 1870:

> I can imagine nothing more depressing than a long ride or drive through the Australian bush. . . . To this day I never look upon a blue gum-tree without a mournful feeling coming over me. I see again the long rows of these forbidding trees which I passed through . . . as I rode down from Armidale to Grafton. . . . The intolerable weariness of those woeful gums oppressed me. They are the most dissipated-looking trees I ever beheld. Dante could well have represented them in his Inferno, in the shape of drunken men, as trees, standing around in sempiternal penitence for their orgies of the past. And the wretched things with their blotchy trunks and bare foliage give no shade. . . .[31]

By this time the melancholic convention was deeply entrenched among artists and writers. Marcus Clarke could refer to the 'funereal, secret, stern' forests. 'In Australia alone is to be found the Grotesque, the Weird, the strange scribblings of nature learning how to write.' 'All is fear-inspiring and gloomy.' The dominant note of the scenery was 'Weird Melancholy'.[32] And Adam Lindsay Gordon had made his monstrous misobservation (which he really did not mean, but which was frequently to be quoted against him) of the land 'where bright blossoms are scentless, And songless bright birds'.

Sterility and desolation: 'The dismayed and astonished navigator', wrote Péron, 'can scarcely conceive how so vast a sterility could be produced in the neighbourhood of such fecundity' in Asia.[33] Hostility—symbolized by the Blue Mountains, impenetrable for twenty-five years, hemming in the settlers, tending to make them feel intruders; hostility, best seen in the many accounts of explorers forced to the limits of endurance against what they often saw as an implacable foe.

We must give full weight to the strangeness of the Australian environment in the eyes of migrants—the immensity of the continent, its aridity, its sameness, its haggardness, the silence of the bush, the unfamiliarity of the night sky—and recognize the frequently violent reaction.[34] We need to remember the struggle throughout the nineteenth century to occupy and domesticate the land, shown in the history of pastoralism and agriculture—the vicissitudes of the pastoral industry which produced insolvency as often as wealth, the constant failure of Europeans on marginal agricultural lands. So much of the content of nineteenth century Australian history is the story of coming to terms with the environment, of migrants and their children beginning to understand what they were doing here, of recognizing and accepting themselves as Australians, of beginning to feel at home.

For there was another side. As the invaders spread out from their beach-heads and domesticated the nearer interior and brought it to order, so affection grew. When the Blue Mountains were crossed and the Bathurst plains were settled, observers delighted in the homely scenes of rural contentment. Mitchell described the Victorian Western District as 'Australia Felix', gentler landscapes were discovered, and the myth of the hardy adventurous pioneer frontiersman buoyed up the squatters as they made their tracks. As early as the late 1820s, idyllic scenes began to be painted of the bivouac, the campfire and boiling the billy.[35] The Aborigines retreated or, where they stood, were eliminated. The squatters made their terms but, although most originally intended only to plunder the land and retire, many eventually lived out their lives in affectionate relationship with the environment. Tasmanian settlers, naturally enough, came to terms much earlier with scenery and climate and gained considerable aesthetic pleasure from their surroundings—if only it were not for the convicts, deforming the wilds and stigmatizing the plains, as Wentworth had it. Landscapists in the 1830s and 40s found plenty which was picturesque. Marcus Clarke had the vision to counterpoise an alternative to the melancholy:

> Some see no beauty. . . . But the dweller in the wilderness . . . becomes familiar with the beauty of loneliness . . . learns the language of the barren and the uncouth, and can read the hieroglyphs of haggard gum-trees . . . and the Poet of our desolation begins to comprehend why free Esau loved his heritage of desert sand better than all the bountiful richness of Egypt.[36]

The process of migrant acclimatization and growth of harmony between man and land was nevertheless slow and painful.

It was easier for the native-born. But it took a century before the melancholic convention lost its dominance, at least for the tamed country on the coastal side of the Dividing Range—a century before Roberts and Streeton and Paterson emerged to display understanding warmth and affection, and joyful, optimistic patriotism.

TRANSPLANTATION

2

Australia, for its first century, was overwhelmingly a society of British migrants; although the native-born became a majority in the 1870s, adult native-born did not clearly predominate until the last decade of the century. Essentially it was a transplanted society, a new province (or group of provinces) of the United Kingdom, a rapidly expanding component of the British Empire. Bound by the various assumptions they had acquired in their British youth, community leaders strove to recreate British society, either totally or in modified form.

C. Hartley Grattan has defined the process of transplanting a culture from an old country to a new as the 'intricate process of establishing continuities, accepting discontinuities, and engendering original contributions', from which a 'palpably original synthesis' evolves.[1] The continuities are clear enough: Australia grew up as in part a product of the American and French Revolutions, in the age of liberalism and the challenge by democracy and the overthrow of religious certitude and authority, and in the Victorian age when the doctrines of self-help and self-improvement flourished. The Australian colonies inherited and reproduced British law, parliamentary government (bicameralism, cabinet government, etc.), the British versions of Christianity, prevailing ideas in economics, politics, education and culture. Almost every institution and voluntary organisation was recreated —friendly societies, trade unions, mechanics' institutes, temperance societies, savings banks, and innumerable others. There were also major discontinuities which indicate the speedy triumph of secular liberalism: the rapid exclusion of both conservative-aristocratic and church-dominated structures of society.[2]

The conservatism of an agrarian gentry and an established Anglicanism in an ordered hierarchical society was rejected, once for all, within a generation. In New South Wales and Van Diemen's Land before 1850 a landowning gentry, with high aristocratic claims, made a determined attempt to recreate the classes and graces of old England. The Macarthurs and a few score others, mostly from the fringes of the English gentry, sometimes succeeded in gathering a deferential farming tenantry around them; as pseudo-squires led village communities; built and endowed churches; as magistrates made much of the law in practice; founded élitist schools for their children; formed aristocratic circles round those few Tory governors who were inclined to favour them; gathered convivially at clubs like the Australian in Sydney and the Union in Hobart; and rode to hounds with their few social equals. The best of them, like James Macarthur, were decent and conscientious Tories with a strong sense of duty. In a petition of 1841 they hoped that 'as in the old world, wealth will produce leisure, and the union of the two will be followed by steady advancement in art, science, and all the elegancies of prosperous and well-peopled cities.'[3] With their pastoral allies and a few of the official class, a handful of merchants and a few lawyers and doctors, they made their great attempt to perpetuate their position in drafting the new constitutions in the 1850s—and failed, though it was a close-run thing.

The squatting explosion of the late 30s and 40s gravely damaged the conservative cause. Squatters and landowners had a basic clash of economic interest, and the gentry were appalled at the squatters' near-revolutionary attitude to government. When they won their tenure, the squatters quickly became politically reactionary and in fact absorbed the gentry. As they became reconciled to the country and built their mansions they began to play a semi-aristocratic part, almost automatically taking the chair at shire council meetings. But they had been numerically swamped during the gold rushes; more important, they were so discredited and detested by the mass of the populace for their ruthless drive for and locking of the land that as a class they could carry little authority. On the whole, as Anthony Trollope found, they had something in common with the eighteenth century squirearchy—were no more cultivated than the squires in *Tom Jones*.[4] A very few built up fine private libraries. With rare exceptions like Francis Ormond, they were not noted for philanthropy or support of education and cultural causes. So one classical source of patronage for the artist was to be absent: there were to be no great houses with great ladies presiding over salons and adopting and nurturing young talent. Over the years a distinctive style of life with some graciousness did, however, develop; but only a small minority of pastoral families survived for more than a couple of generations. It should be noted that descendants of those few families include Judith Wright, Patrick White, Russell Drysdale, John Manifold and

Geoffrey Dutton—which may lend some credence to an association between aristocracy and the arts. Similarly there has been a tiny persistent strain based on a few old official and professional gentlemanly families with claims to be a cultural élite—the old Toorak before it was swamped by bourgeois wealth—about whom Martin Boyd wrote in his novels and from whom the Boyd family descends.

In the long run there was no chance whatsoever of there being a state church in Australia or of the Christian churches having any marked political or cultural authority. The state had to be neutral, there had to be religious equality and toleration, simply because of the strength of Roman Catholicism, Presbyterianism and Nonconformity. The mid-nineteenth century was an age of passionate religious controversy which was fully reflected in Australia—such as the Tractarian High Church movement in the Church of England and the disruption of Presbyterianism. Catholicism and liberalism were at each other's throats throughout Europe; then Darwinism destroyed the literalness of the Bible. Australian historians on the whole have underestimated the degree of churchgoing and church-membership in the mid-nineteenth century and later. Nevertheless, in the overriding liberal atmosphere, 'Religion became at best a thing of the spirit, of the private man born into his denomination, and not of the common weal.'[5] The Protestant clergy lost most of their authority as general guides and instructors to their flocks. One Presbyterian clergyman lamented in the mid 40s:

> Times are widely different from the last Century. Then the church and pulpit were the vehicles of knowledge, now it is the daily Press. Men are less evangelic for Religion. They hear a Sermon, but read Six newspapers weekly, the Bible never. The voice of the people was echoed by the Minister, now the Editor is the organ of politics and liberty.[6]

The churches had little to offer in terms of high culture and relatively little intellectually, mainly because of the strength of Nonconformism, the growing evangelical dominance over the Church of England, and the confined missionary outlook of Catholicism with its largely uneducated laity.

The gold-rush migrants of the 1850s, who more than doubled the population, confirmed the already strong liberal and democratic trends. Australia was to develop within the dominant framework of secular liberalism—the loose system of ideas which among other things implies some belief in human perfectibility and in the power of reason and education to make men behave better. Australian culture was to be mainly urban bourgeois, though not without some fillip from the 'real' Australia, outback.

Michael Roe in *Quest for Authority in Eastern Australia 1835-1851* and George Nadel in *Australia's Colonial Culture* have delineated the remarkable cultural missionary work by idealistic reformers in mid-nineteenth century Australia. They reflected, in exaggerated strength, liberal principles, the determination for self-improvement of large sections of the middle and artisan classes of early Victorian England, and the general movement of perfectionist reform which was so strong in the United States and England in the earlier nineteenth century. Roe sees the idea of moral enlightenment—the phrase was coined by Charles Harpur, the radical poet—as the binding-force of society.

> A growth from eighteenth-century thought, this faith mingled Romantic, Protestant, and liberal attitudes. It was developed especially by upholders of secular culture and of the Temperance movement, who urged that everyone could, indeed must, become good, wise, prosperous, and responsible. All aspects of human personality—reason, will, instinct, imagination, spirit—might help towards this end. Perception of so happy a fate, and striving towards it, would impregnate society and bind it together.[7]

As expressed in the 1840s and 50s, this philosophy is a remarkable illustration of the idealist utopian strand in Australian history. It took in such diverse campaigns as the anti-transportation movement—the cleansing of Australia—and attempts to reform the savage state of the criminal law; it included the temperance movement, in an age when it can convincingly be argued that drink was the curse of the working classes, and agencies of thrift like the savings banks; but, most important, it promoted the campaign for education for all, and especially popular adult education—the diffusion of knowledge. Learning, culture, knowledge were the weapons and tools which would build the ideal society. This noble cause deserves some attention.

One of the first and most important civilizers of the frontier was the stormy Presbyterian cleric, John Dunmore Lang, who on his ten trips home over the years directly recruited several thousand migrants, including many Scottish artisans. Lang and many of his migrants were conscious cultural missionaries, who brought with them the superior attainments of Scottish education. In 1830-31 Lang chartered the *Stirling Castle* on which he brought out several teachers for his Australian College and fifty-two Scottish mechanics and their families. On the four months' voyage the mechanics were morally and intellectually enlightened by classes in arithmetic and geometry and concentrated study of Adam Smith's *Wealth of Nations*. The social and political impact of these migrants and others whom Lang brought out in the 40s, in Sydney, Brisbane, Geelong and elsewhere, would make a fascinating study. Lang's leading recruit was Henry Carmichael, a graduate of St Andrew's University, an acquaintance and correspondent of Jeremy Bentham, and strongly influenced by the great reformer of education, Pestalozzi. Carmichael (as usually happened) fell out with Lang and conducted his own school, and was a major educational influence for another quarter-century. He became the leading anti-clerical propagandist for secular education and—rather pathetically—devoted his life to Australia as a new field for educational experiment, buoyed by the great faith that (in Nadel's words) 'all of man's propensities, all of his affections, social and moral, could be developed by proper systems of training'.[8]

Much of the missionary zeal went into the Mechanics' Institute movement, like so much else a reflection of England. The first Schools of Arts or Institutes had been founded in Edinburgh in 1821 and London in 1823; by 1841 there were 200 in England and by 1853 nearly 700. Hobart Town led the way in 1827, Sydney followed in 1833, Newcastle in 1835 and Melbourne in 1839, and in the next half century hundreds more Institutes or Schools of Arts were formed in almost every township, nearly all of which wrote the aims of intellectual, social and moral improvement into their constitutions. In Sydney the main functions were the library, instruction classes, debates (rigidly excluding politics and religion), and tuition in essay-writing. Lectures and classes on science, engineering and mechanics usually had the leading purpose of teaching artisans the theory underlying their crafts, but could not have been very relevant to the particular colonial needs of the time. There was clearly some response, but many proud artisans were repelled by the patronage of middle class worthies imposing their standards; and there was continual difficulty in finding lecturers who could pitch their material at an appropriate level. Workingmen needed elementary education of a much more practical kind than the Institutes provided. Within a few years of their foundation, the purely recreational element usually came to dominate, the classes dwindled away, and while the libraries remained useful (and may have supplied vital nourishment for more untrained talent than we realize), the halls became merely town meeting-centres and dance- and billiard-rooms.

Many of these cultural missionaries had a sublime faith in the power of the arts and sciences and especially literature to incline men towards a superior morality. John Woolley, first principal of the University of Sydney, was perhaps the most distinguished advocate of a secular religion based on the dif-fusion of knowledge. Barzillai Quaife, Congregationalist and Presbyterian minister and teacher, and author of *The Intellectual Sciences* (1872), the first important work of philosophy published in Australia, was another major figure. By schools and learning, by art exhibitions and the like, 'the ardent minds of the sons of the soil may be prevented from running to waste, may be raised above the unsatisfying pursuit of sensual enjoyments to revel in the lofty and inexhaustible pleasures of the intellect,' said the *Atlas* in 1845. Literature, the great civilizer, would best promote harmony, unity, patriotism, national character, a sense of nation-ality, and definition of the meaning of Australian life. A Shakespeare or a Milton—culture not politics—made a nation.[9]

The great enemy was usually seen to be Mammon, especially during the gold rushes. Henry Parkes frequently used to orate about the deadening effects of high prosperity on finer moral and intellectual feelings. It was usually assumed that materialism and culture were antipathetic, that culture was a social remedy in a materially preoccupied society, that the colonists needed to be educated so that they could be, as it were, something better than atheists in their social relations. A great deal of cant was expressed on this subject, dismay at the working classes being comfortably off. But some realised that adult educational and cultural possibilities for the farmer or artisan or labourer could begin only with the leisure, free from exhaustion, which came from relative material prosperity and shorter hours of work. Material improvement was perhaps a prerequisite for moral enlightenment.

The general cultural results were of course very disappointing, a poor return for such faith and idealism. But there was some spread of literary culture. 'Everybody reads,' one observer exaggerated in 1845.[10] The absence of social life in rural areas certainly encouraged study; gatherings of shepherds to hear readings of the latest Dickens novel were not unusual. And there was a reasonable supply of books: the library of the Sydney Mechanics' Institute held 3,000 volumes in 1840 and the Australian Subscription Library had 13,000 in 1844; 23 booksellers in Sydney in 1855 and 10 in Melbourne in 1851 made fair livings. Like the Americans, the Australian colonists soon became avid readers of newspapers. The staple reading and chief educative influence were the British digests of the day, such as Constable's *Miscellany*, the *Penny Magazine*, the *Mechanics' Magazine*, *Household Words*, and the publications of the Society for the Diffusion of Useful Knowledge. As in Britain, however, the bad drove out the good. This was also the period of the spread of the popular trashy novel; and the public displayed an obstinate preference for popular fiction over works of self-improvement and moral elevation. The *Illustrated Australian Magazine* denounced the confirmed novel-reader as a 'mental drunkard',[11] and improvers were very worried that cheap novels were inflaming the passions which it was the task of education to subdue.

Given the nature of the population before the gold rushes—predominantly illiterate or near-illiterate convicts and unskilled labourers—it was hardly likely that the moral enlighteners could make a very wide impact. But the small, aware and responsive artisan class was strongly reinforced from the 1850s. With the flux of social fortunes during the gold rushes and the spreading-out of population, the outback also gained a strong leavening of more or less educated men. The morally enlightened artisan for the rest of the century may be claimed as one kind of élite in the van of political and cultural progress—member of a benefit society or lodge or trade union, a co-operator in a building society, a pledged abstainer or temperant, mechanics' institute member, voracious consumer of newspapers, a moderate radical political activist, and earnest debater of philosophy, political economy and literature. But there is no doubt that the mass of the labouring classes remained unregenerate.

One of the decisive consequences of the gold rushes was that the swamping of the existing population by free migrants removed most doubts about the respectability of Australia. Right-thinking and proper people could now migrate in peace of mind. The 1850s migrants, in terms of education, were probably better than a cross-section of the population of the British Isles. The upper classes and the labouring classes—and certainly the depressed and poverty-stricken—were under-represented; the professional class, the middle-classes and the artisan class almost certainly migrated in disproportionate numbers.[12] And we might bear in mind, with whatever scepticism, that Lord Macaulay believed this to be the most enlightened generation of the most enlightened people that had ever existed.

For most of the rest of the century—disregarding for the moment the 'native' element—the Australian colonies were each very like Scotland or Ulster or Yorkshire or Kent, in relation to England. In a very real sense the dominant majority of Australian colonists regarded themselves as being part of England or Britain still; assumed it was the virtues of British civilization which were making their successful colonisation possible; and certainly thought of creating, not just another, but a better England—without the faults, but still another England. To illustrate the dominance of the migrants by Victorian examples, 85 per cent of members of parliament before 1900 were migrants and the proportion would be about the same in the professions and the business world. All the headmasters of the leading secondary schools and the top officials in the Education Department before 1900, all the Anglican and Catholic bishops and at least three-quarters of the clergy were migrants. (The proportions would not be quite so high for any of the other colonies.) They named suburbs and towns after British towns and villages and famous men, such as Kew, Malvern, Sandringham, Footscray, Fitzroy and Collingwood (but occasionally adopted such native names as Prahran, Kooyong and Dandenong). In urban districts they stripped nearly all the gums and planted their gardens with oaks, elms, beeches and planes (but also an occasional Moreton Bay fig, palm or pepper tree), and introduced as much English wild life as they could.*

* The acclimatization movement—the attempt to introduce exotic, mainly English, animals, plants, birds and fish—is the subject of *They All Ran Wild*, a learned and entertaining work by E. C. Rolls. The movement reached its peak in the 1860s, but deer had been inroduced by 1803 and game for sport in the 20s. There followed attempts to introduce blackbirds, thrushes, starlings, robins, pheasants, partridges and especially skylarks and nightingales; rabbits, hares and foxes; trout, salmon and carp; blackberry and prickly

They also reconstructed every possible British or old-world cultural institution. Many learned and gifted men felt it to be their first duty to transmit all they could of the European cultural heritage to Australia. It was a noble gesture of faith to found the universities of Sydney and Melbourne so soon—'to enlighten the mind, to refine the understanding, to elevate their fellow men',[13] as W. C. Wentworth, Sydney's prime mover, put it. A select committee of the N.S.W. Legislative Council reported in 1849 on the best means of 'instituting a University for the promotion of literature and science':

> The University of Harvard, to our shame be it mentioned, was established by the Pilgrim Fathers of New England, in less than twenty years after its settlement; and this monument of the piety, the learning and the wisdom of its founders has produced its fruit in some of the greatest names of America. Nearly sixty-two years have elapsed since the British standard was first unfurled on these shores in token of their permanent subjection to British rule. And yet for all beyond the mere rudiments of learning, we have still to send our sons to some British and foreign University, at the distance of half the globe from all parental or family control; and as might be predicted, in most cases with certain detriment to their morals; in few, with any compensating improvements to their minds.[14]

Unfortunately, in the first fifteen years an annual average of only about a dozen matriculated students enrolled at the University of Sydney; Melbourne fared little better in its early years. However, generous salaries attracted professors of high quality, like W. E. Hearn, the economist, and Charles Badham, the classical scholar (probably because he was too unorthodox in religion to be appointed to an English university). In the 1880s six of Melbourne's professors were or were to become Fellows of the Royal Society.

Sir Redmond Barry, a Supreme Court judge, was chancellor of Melbourne University and chairman of trustees of the Public Library and National Museum (and later of the National

---

pear; for economic reasons, donkeys, alpacas, angora goats, llamas, ostriches, camels and zebu cattle; even boa constrictors. That is, to introduce them to run wild, not just as specimens in zoos. Rolls is scathing about well-meaning fools doing incalculable damage to the balance of nature. His account of which importations could adapt, and which could not, is fascinating.

Gallery) from their foundation in the 1850s until his death in 1880, three weeks after sentencing Ned Kelly. An Anglo-Irishman, he identified himself with the colony and had nothing in common with the fortune-hunters who were plundering the land; his mission was to transplant the values of civilized Europe. In the early 1840s, like J. P. Fawkner, he threw open his private library to anyone who cared to use it. He intended the Public Library to contain 'the glorious deeds of Her Majesty's illustrious ancestors and the achievements of men who enabled us to achieve enlightened moderation and liberty'. The Library and its sister institutions 'would be filled with the presence of those august sages who have enunciated the immutable precepts on which depend the social, moral and religious welfare of the human race'. The Library was not for the idle and frivolous, but was intended to stimulate 'intellectual culture' and help students to appreciate 'the pure, the beautiful and the true'. It was open to any well-behaved person over the age of fourteen, at the time a remarkable absence of restriction. Barry made the famous order for every work referred to by Gibbon in his *Decline and Fall of the Roman Empire*. In the early days, when books arrived from overseas, he would take off his coat and help to sort, shelve and catalogue them. He drove and bullied his colleagues, agents, suppliers and contacts in the leading libraries of the world with unflagging zeal. It was mainly he who in his time made the Melbourne Library one of the great libraries of the world, 'almost a Texas among collectors', whose recondite holdings still amaze scholars, and the organizing centre of more public lending libraries than existed in England.[15] The dominance of the classics in his thinking was illustrated when it was decided in 1859 to begin an art collection—not of paintings, contemporary or not, but casts, busts, photographs, friezes, medals, coins and gems, mainly reproductions of ancient classical works. The London Committee was to aim at an illustrated history of the development of art:

> commence with a few specimens of the most salient productions of Nineveh, Egypt, Etruria and Aegina . . . the Grecian schools of Phidias and Praxitiles might be liberally represented. [Guard] those whom you may employ against the notion that anything is good enough for a colony. . . .[16]

In 1863 a standing Commission on the Fine Arts was appointed with Barry as chairman, and the acrimonious wrangling over buying policy during the following century began; the new National Gallery was opened the following year.[17] New South Wales established its Gallery in 1876, South Australia in 1881 and Queensland in 1895.

Melbourne and Sydney (which lagged some distance behind until the 1880s) were developing into major cities by world standards, by the late 80s ranking about thirtieth in population (relatively larger than today) and among the top ten in terms of area. Culturally they were almost replicas of British provincial cities of similar population like Birmingham, Liverpool, Glasgow or Leeds, neither very much better or worse in sophisticated taste, and also very much on a par with Chicago or San Francisco. Many visitors were surprised and impressed. H. M. Hyndman looked back to about 1870:

> I have been a great deal about the world and I have moved freely in many societies, but I have never lived in any city where the people at large, as well as the educated class, took so keen an interest in all the activities of human life, as in Melbourne at the time I visited it. Art, the drama, music, literature, journalism, wit, oratory, all found ready appreciation. The life and vivacity of the place were astonishing.[18]

(Can this really be true?) Sir Charles Dilke in the 80s believed that, relatively, Australians read more, bought more books and had more private libraries than the English. 'In many of the factories of Victoria and New South Wales we find not only the excellent bands of musicians which some English factories can show, but debating societies admirably managed, concerts of good music given by the men in evening dress. . . .'[19] Francis Adams, despite his criticisms of Melbourne's banality and philistinism, was so impressed with the 'general sense of movement, of progress, of conscious power' that he considered that, given higher education, the Melbourne middle class would far outstrip the English in intellect and knowledge within thirty years or so.[20] J. A. Froude was so struck by men like Sir James Martin and James Service that he concluded that 'in respect of intellectual eminence the mother country has no advantage'; indeed the colonies, 'in proportion to their population, have more eminent men than we have'.[21]

The level of thought in the intellectual world is best indicated by the high quality of newspapers and periodicals. There is little doubt that the Melbourne *Argus* was one of the best newspapers in the world, though the frequent claim that it was second only to *The Times* is questionable. The *Melbourne Review* (1876-85) and the *Victorian Review* (1879-86) were primarily media for debate of religious, political and economic ideas; as Asa Briggs has remarked, they are 'fascinating repositories of Victoriana'.[22] The illustrated press was strong; journals like the *Australasian Sketcher* and the *Illustrated Journal of Australasia* were adaptations of the *Illustrated London News* and other English journals. Similarly, there were at least five variants on London *Punch*; only Melbourne *Punch*, which lasted for seventy years, was successful. The mails were crammed with copies of English journals and newspapers. Australia as a whole took nearly half British book-exports. Shakespeare societies waxed and waned; loyal Scots built so many statues of Rabbie Burns that there may possibly be more than those of Queen Victoria. Melbourne in the 1860s even had an alleged Bohemia centred on the Yorick Club.

This was at least a fairly sophisticated migrant provincial culture, in close touch with the intellectual issues of the day although of course it contributed little to them. It may be that, in terms of awareness of intellectual issues and general appreciation of the arts, there was a considerable decline in the first half of the twentieth century. There had been a cultural time-lag— overseas debates tended to be reflected in Australia a year or five years or ten years later. The gold rush migrants were on the whole 'a hard-reading lot' who strove to keep up with currents of thought at home but inevitably dropped increasingly out of touch. The cultural time-lag possibly widened, perhaps because succeeding groups of migrants included fewer well-educated men and women.

But this was a derivative culture, dependent on the next mail from home, drawing almost no inspiration from its immediate environment. Until late in the century, there was a striking contrast between the sophisticated veneer of appreciation for intellect and the arts and the sheer poverty of creative achievement.

Judith Wright has discerned a duality which is reflected in a large part of Australian literature: firstly, 'the reality of exile'; secondly, 'the reality of newness and freedom'. Australia has been both a society of transplanted Europeans and a new country with a novel contribution to make to the world. The conservative has seen it as a country to escape from or at best endure; the radical has seen it as a country of hope, of liberty and a new chance. The one literary tradition began with the 'violent response of the European consciousness' to the Australian scene; the cry of the exile, of the second-hand European on alien shores, has continued down to Richardson's *Fortunes of Richard Mahony*, Martin Boyd's novels and Patrick White's *Voss*. The other tradition of radical optimism may be said to begin with Harpur's poetry, flourished in the *Bulletin* school and continued in such writers as Vance Palmer.[1]

Cecil Hadgraft makes the striking statement—for the sake of argument, but asserting it can be broadly maintained—that poets in Australia may be divided chronologically into English poets, Australian poets, and poets.[2] The derivative note was inevitable for a start; it would be long before the literary English manner of describing Australia gave way to a natural Australian manner. The first natural model was the eighteenth century; the Romantics were slow to make their way, but nearly all the later nineteenth century poets may fairly be described as colonial Romantics. And nearly all their work may be described as a 'poetry of exiles'; as H. M. Green says, 'it still hovered between the old and the new worlds, trying to sing of one in terms of the other and finding unnatural what was unexpected'.[3] Some of it was nostalgic for Old England, but much of it, while it necessarily followed English models, earnestly strove to describe and interpret the local scene—and often with pride and affection.

It was not literally a poetry of exile if only because the two best colonial poets, Harpur and Kendall, were native-born. Charles Harpur (1813-68), son of a convict schoolmaster, was a clerk, teacher, farmer and goldfields commissioner. He probably had a fair basic education and went on so to educate himself that he eventually published translations of the *Iliad*. Harpur has been generally accepted as a minor poet, though significant because he made the great effort to see without the inherited spectacles. He owed much to Wordsworth (especially his attitude to Nature), Milton and Shelley. It is commonly said that he failed to break away from the spirit and diction of the English masters he studied, that his verse had some marked qualities but was bookish, antiquated, abstract, artificial. He is also accepted as a man with the noble but crazy ambition to be the first authentic voice of Australia, a national laureate, who lived the life of a poet and hated the petty materialism around him, who with great dedication tried to lay the basis of an Australian poetry and compelled the attention of at least a few to the phenomenon of poetry in a new country. He was also a radical political pamphleteer and activist who dreamed of Australia as a cradle of liberty. 'Proud, impulsive, and hyper-sensitive,' writes T. Inglis Moore, 'he felt deeply the humiliations suffered through being the son of convict parents as well as being native-born at a time when currency lads were scorned by immigrant critics, of struggling as a poverty-stricken farmer, and of meeting either neglect as a poet or the venomous hostility of [journalists]'.[4] Judith Wright has made a case for according him more recognition than he has usually received. Much of his best work has never been published; his attempts to depict the landscape, especially his stress on the light and the solitude, have been under-appreciated; he had a splendid ear and appreciation of language; and he recognized the problems of being an Australian poet, seeing himself as drawing on the English tradition while striving to find an Australian voice. And what was his audience, where was it? Wright sees him as the first and one of the most illuminating examples of the Australian split-consciousness—and as faced with the impossibility of acceptance as an Australian poet in a period when Europe (and therefore Australia) derided the possibility even of an American poet. As he bitterly and ironically wrote:

> While others dip their fleecy flocks, and store
> Bright gold, I've only so much *verse* the more . . . .
> A vagrant, and the cause still, all along,
> This damned unconquerable love of song.[5]

Henry Kendall (1839-82) admired and respected Harpur as the founder of a tradition. Modern critics are usually hard on

Kendall. His talent is admitted, but he is regarded as having seen Australia almost wholly in terms of the English poetry in which he had saturated himself, especially Shelley and Tennyson. His verse is full of Romantic diction—dell, brook, lea, rill, glen, vale and so on. Nevertheless, he tried desperately to assimilate the local scene and wrote some semi-colloquial ballads. His descriptive lyric poetry, 'channels of coolness' full of mountains and waterfalls and 'woodland music', is a product of coastal New South Wales, though he also wrote much about the hell of the Inland, of which he knew nothing. As H. M. Green says, his *Leaves from an Australian Forest* (1869) may be claimed as an Australian work as no other had yet been; he did unveil part of the face.[6] He even won some recognition as a national poet; many people believed he was describing Australia well. He was limited in range, according to Brian Elliott, with

> no formed philosophy, no conspicuous intellect, only an abundance of poetic feeling. . . . He came too late in the colonial period to be able to rest at ease upon inherited tradition, yet as a native poet he was born too early to find support in a cultural system based upon local experience. He was of the generation which failed because it possessed neither a clear inheritance nor an established confidence.[7]

It remains to be said that he was probably the best nineteenth century Australian poet, who earned inclusion in Palgrave's *Golden Treasury* and *The Oxford Book of English Verse*.[8]

Adam Lindsay Gordon (1833-70) is a very different type, the poet of action who had been a boxer, mounted trooper, horse-breaker and famous rider. He was indeed a migrant exile and very derivative—especially from Byron, Swinburne, Tennyson and Browning—so much so that there are elements of plagiarism in his work. He has been a worry to the critics, mainly because he was two poets—one serious and one popular. His serious work was little known, met with little response, and is generally held to be mediocre. Yet over the years a few critics have judged 'The Rhyme of the Joyous Garde' (about Lancelot), an example of his search for a refuge in medieval idealism, to be very good indeed. His popular verse is just that—pleasant jingling—but significant in that it introduced the bush-ballad, from which so much sprang. And whatever the quality of the verse, Brian Elliott stresses his original use of landscape imagery:

Nothing in all Colonial poetry matches in importance Gordon's signal achievement, the fixation of the Australian image. Emotionally, he simply spoke as he felt: the mood of his best work is conversational; its philosophy stoically grim, but spontaneously articulate; its visionary content based upon a broad impressionism; the keynote brightness and sunlight, starlight, a high luminosity in the air.[9]

The fascinating question is why, after his suicide, he became in a real sense the national poet, almost the mouthpiece of a generation. It seems odd, as so much of his popular verse is so English —even 'How We Beat the Favourite' is set in England—seems odd if we forget how many of this generation were English migrants. The extraordinary culmination of his posthumous career was the enshrinement of his bust in Westminster Abbey in 1934 as Australia's National Poet. There are many explanations. His personal story made him a legend, 'a kind of second-hand Byron'. He was the poet of the horse—and the horse was all-important in nineteenth century Australia. 'The Sick Stock-rider', though stilted and derivative in some respects, was also highly original. He reached a mass audience through the sporting press in which much of his verse was first published. And his moralizing struck a common chord. Some elements of the bush frame of mind were reflected in platitudinous verses like 'Life is mostly froth and bubble,/Two things stand like stone,/Kindness in another's trouble,/Courage in your own', or 'For good undone and gifts misspent and resolutions vain,/'Tis somewhat late to trouble. This I know—I should live the same life over, if I had to live again;/And the chances are I go where most men go.' And he had twenty years start on 'Banjo' Paterson, who was a greatly superior popular poet and exponent of the bush ethos. He appealed to the homestead as well as the men's quarters, and he fitted in closely with what the Anglo-Australian thought an Australian poet should be like. He was the popular poet Australia needed at the time.[10]

Of the scores of other verse-writers, perhaps only Brunton Stephens deserves mention as a poet. In 1888, cashing in on the centennial and new British interest in the Empire, D. B. W. Sladen published no fewer than three anthologies of Australasian verse, all full of rubbish. One reviewer was Oscar Wilde, who remarked that it was 'interesting to read about poets who lie under the shadow of the gum-tree, gather wattle blossoms and buddawong and sarsaparilla for their loves, and wander through the glades of Mount Baw-baw listening to the careless raptures of the mopoke'. Wilde found a 'depressing provinciality of mood and manner', but warmly praised Kendall and Gordon.[11]

The few colonial novelists up to the 1850s usually wrote fictionalized autobiography and—Catherine Spence apart, perhaps —were quite lacking in creative imagination. The popular English novelists, Charles Reade and Bulwer Lytton, wrote celebrated novels about Australia without ever having been there, and Dickens introduced Australia several times into his novels. In the 70s Anthony Trollope wrote the lightweight *Harry Heathcote of Gangoil* and *John Caldigate* after a visit which also produced his very fine *Australia and New Zealand*. The three outstanding colonial novelists were Kingsley, Clarke and Boldrewood. The subjects of their three famous books were pastoral life, the convict system and bushranging, which were indeed the staple subject-matter of the great bulk of colonial novels.

Henry Kingsley (1830-76), brother of the clergyman, novelist and reformer, Charles Kingsley, spent five years in Victoria as a gold-digger, mounted policeman and guest of gentlemanly squatters. On his return to England he published in 1859 *Geoffry Hamlyn*, which he had possibly begun in Australia. It is a romantic adventure story 'for boys of all ages', a very readable melodramatic yarn and no more, but full of vigour and zest. There is little attempt at realism or serious observation; the novel was skilfully written for the popular English market to make money he desperately needed, in the conventions set by Reade, Dickens and Lytton. His attitudes are those of the English landed gentry; his characters mostly stem from good county families; his muscular Christian heroes all achieve happiness while the villains die. Young gentlemen go to the colonies to make their fortunes, have exciting adventures and return with their hopes fulfilled; Kingsley himself knew better. Joseph Furphy in *Such Is Life* could not stomach 'the slender-witted, virgin-souled overgrown schoolboys who fill Henry Kingsley's exceedingly trashy and misleading novel'. It is difficult to see how anyone could who demands any reasonable degree of reality in novels. But what Kingsley did do was to display all the properties of the pastoral novel—a bushfire, attack by Aborigines, a fight with bushrangers, a lost child—which ultimately became clichés. He did incidentally include some genuine atmosphere and depicted at least one Dinkum Aussie quite well. *Geoffry Hamlyn* immediately became and long remained a popular Australian classic and was praised in the highest terms by Clarke and Boldrewood.[12]

Marcus Clarke (1846-81) migrated to Victoria at the age of seventeen and soon became a brilliant journalist. *His Natural Life*—written by the age of twenty-five, it should be noticed—was published as a serial in 1870-71 in 280,000 words, nearly 900 pages in the recent Penguin edition. He then heavily cut and altered for the book version usually published. It is a powerful exposure of the convict-system, a study in unrelieved brutality, full of suspense and horror, rambling, verbose and melodramatic. But he could write; he was strong on characterization; he had a plot, however improbable; he had compassion and savage awareness. He was a serious writer as none of the other colonial novelists were; this was a major study in injustice and evil. It stood far above anything contemporary, and triumphed over its glaring faults. Clarke had intellect, and something to say. He is one of the many examples in Australian literature of great talent without the opportunity or peace of mind to fully realize that talent—but at least he had sufficient determination to produce one work which borders on greatness.[13]

'Rolf Boldrewood' (T. A. Browne, 1826-1915) emigrated as a four-year-old; Australia was always home to him. He was a squatter for twenty-five years through the golden age of pastoralism, then a mining warden and magistrate. The first of his dozen or so novels was published locally in 1878; *Robbery Under Arms* appeared as a serial in 1882-3 and as a book in 1888; and he wrote on past 1900. But he looked back to the great days of his youth and did not reflect at all the vast changes in life and literature late in the century of which he disapproved. He was a born story-teller who owed a large debt to Sir Walter Scott and the English romantic novel of adventure, but, strong on action, weak on character, he had no depth. *Robbery Under Arms*, his only important work, is essentially a good thriller, though Hadgraft perhaps depreciates it too much in describing it as 'the best Australian counterpart of the good American Western'. In his squatting novels (though less so in *Robbery Under Arms*), Boldrewood writes from the viewpoint of the pastoral aristocracy, as one who defended patriarchal order and detested democracy. And yet, his commonest theme is the successful migrant, he is extremely proud of Australia as the land of opportunity, and implicitly condemns English upper-class values and the injustices of that class-ridden society. Despite his romantic conventions, he is something of a realist and naturalist, with an obtrusive element of guidebook justification of Australia. He wrote both for Australian and English readers, as an Australian patriot. His are the first entirely recognizable native-born Australians in Australian fiction; he uses many colloquialisms and comes close to catching the tone of popular speech (in so far as we can judge what it was then like). Boldrewood's works provide the key-study of the transition between migrant and native writers.[14]

Almost the only other notable novelists of the colonial period were three ladies writing very popular Anglo-Australian romances in the 80s and 90s. Ada Cambridge (1844-1926), an Anglican clergyman's wife, wrote nineteen novels, of which *The Three Miss Kings* is perhaps the best. 'She was at the same time', says Green, 'a conservative and prejudiced aristocrat, a hater of shams and injustice, and a sincere and sympathetic humanitarian';[15] her poetry also shows her as a bold rebel on some social questions. The prolific Mrs Campbell Praed (1851-1935), who was born in Queensland but left for Europe in 1876, wrote more than forty novels of which nearly half relate to Australia.[16] *Policy and Passion*, on bush life and politics, stands out as the best of her works. 'Tasma', Jessie Couvreur (1848-97), also left for Europe as a young woman and subsequently drew on her experiences, notably in *Uncle Piper of Piper's Hill*, which is witty, excellent in characterization and a classic portrait of the self-made colonial tycoon. All three authors were Anglo-Australians between two worlds, writing for the English market and tending to explain and justify colonials, and also, perhaps, writing mainly for women. All three are more interesting as people and as women than as novelists, for they are infuriating in the contrast between their acute intelligence and intellectual depth, displayed in excellent passages of insight, and their romantic tripy plots. They were bound, however, by the conventions of polite female fiction and were, perhaps, more satirical than we know.

Thus, the literary achievement of the first century amounted to very little, and the 70s and early 80s seems to be a disappointing marking-time period, especially in poetry. The only native-born novelist of the slightest consequence was Mrs Praed, and she was living in Europe. One curious aspect of the novels as a whole is how backward-looking they were, how little they reflected contemporary life, and how little of Australian spirit or idealism they showed, how the *Bulletin* school was almost totally unanticipated. In particular, it was odd that there had been so little attempt to create fiction from mining life, despite all its excitement and fascinating reversal of accustomed social relationships.

The 1860s and 70s were similarly disappointing in painting achievement, although the 80s were to be very different. Robert Hughes has unkindly remarked that 'no country in the West ... was less endowed with talent'.[17] After Martens and Gill there are only a handful of painters worth remark in the 1850-80 period, although one could wish that more paintings by Thomas Clark, Thomas Wright and others had survived so that informed judgments might be made.[18]

William Strutt (1825-1915), who had been extensively trained in Paris, spent eleven years in Victoria from 1850 and produced several notable history paintings—social documents, such as *Black Thursday* and *Bushrangers on the St Kilda Road*. He was attempting to depict the outstanding features of colonial life, and in choosing bushfires, droughts and deaths of explorers he was both paralleling the melancholic sentiment of Adam Lindsay Gordon and Marcus Clarke and anticipating the treatment of the outback by some modern painters. Nicholas Chevalier (1828-1902), a Swiss who was in Victoria from 1855 to 1869, was perhaps a more successful painter in water-colours than oils. *The Buffalo Ranges*, the first local painting bought by the Victorian Gallery, typified many of his rather laboured grandiose paintings of alpine scenery in late Romantic style. Chevalier was also a leading cartoonist on *Punch*. More important was Eugene von Guerard (1811-1901), if only for the range and quantity of his landscape painting and his appointment from 1870 to 1881 as first head of the Victorian Gallery and Art School. He was a precise topographical painter whose most successful works were depictions of domesticated settings of Western District homesteads. In Tasmania, W. C. Piguenit (1836-1914), native-born of French descent, retired from surveying in 1872 and in late Romantic vein sought dramatic effect, mainly in Tasmanian mountain scenery. A note of gloom and melancholy pervades his paintings of natural bush and mountains. After Martens, New South Wales seems to have been bereft of worthy painters.

Louis Buvelot (1814-88), who is often seen as the bridge between colonial and Heidelberg painting, was a Swiss who after eighteen years in Brazil arrived in Melbourne in 1865 at the age of fifty-one, to begin twenty years of sustained work. Buvelot's chief interests were light and atmosphere, late afternoon light especially; and his usual subjects were the settled countryside, outer suburban farms, not the cities, the country proper, the inland, or exotic Australia generally. He was a mid-century painter close to the Barbizon school, who tried to adapt to the local scenery and light. Bernard Smith stresses that his landscapes were more 'European' than those by some of his early predecessors like Lewin, Earle and Glover; much as he enjoyed gum-trees, he saw them 'against a background of European recollections',[19] so that they often appear as much like oaks or poplars as gums. There is a resemblance between Buvelot's (and Martens') paintings and Harpur's poetry: an emphasis, not on the difference between the Australian landscape and the European, but on the similarity—especially when 'blurred and generalized' by distance and evening light.[20] But he introduced the *plein-air* practice of the Barbizon school, he made a great advance in catching colour, he was a true professional, a major influence on young local painters. Frederick McCubbin wrote of him:

> Where von Guerard and Chevalier went in search of mountains and waterfalls for their subjects, Buvelot interested himself in the life around him; he sympathized with it and painted it. There was no one before him to point out the way. He possessed therefore in himself the genius to catch and understand the salient living features of this country. In a sense he was a forerunner: all his pictures are reminiscent of Australian life as we know it.[21]

Most of these artists were continental Europeans (and there were to be more—Italians, a German and a Portuguese—in the 80s). Painting was one field in which British taste and influence were not entirely dominant. But of course British standards dominated public taste, and colonial public taste necessarily was more doctrinaire and less flexible than the British. Evangelical assumptions held sway, in particular Ruskin's view that a painting was good in proportion to the number of uplifting truths it contained. The taste was for genre, the historical or religious motif, the fine moral act. G. F. Folingsby, who came out from England in 1880 and took charge of the Melbourne Gallery School in 1882, was best known for his *Bunyan in Prison* and the *First Meeting between Henry VIII and Anne Boleyn.* 'Sentimental and narrative genre, grandiose canvases both in history and landscape deriving from the Munich and Düsseldorf schools, and the melodrama and linear naturalism of the Pre-Raphaelites were the order of the day,' writes Bernard Smith.[22] James Smith, who for fifty years was Melbourne's leading literary and art critic, believed the chief function of the National Gallery was to stimulate the moral and spiritual faculties: 'The special field of the operation of painting is the expression of spiritual ideas.'[23] The first travelling scholarship from the Gallery school was won in 1887 by John Longstaff for his *Breaking the News,* based on a mining disaster. Two of the works bought by the Gallery from the visiting art section of the International Exhibition of 1888 were the statue, now outside the State Library, *St George and the Dragon,* signifying the triumph of good over evil, and a painting depicting a dying Christian martyr-gladiator scratching a cross on the ground. The cellars of the Gallery are full of early purchases of works by forgotten Royal Academy artists, mostly 'factory seconds'. But in England taste was fast changing to accept contemporary life as a proper subject for the painter. And, at least in Melbourne, where in the mid-70s nearly 200 students were attending the Gallery's painting and drawing classes, a new generation was emerging.

That relatively recent invention, the piano, arrived in the First Fleet. Presumably, in the early years, Handel and tunes from the *Beggar's Opera,* Arne's 'Rule Britannia', folksongs, and Wesley's hymns were frequently played and sung. Sixty years later, 'Home, Sweet Home', Schubert's and Weber's songs, Liszt's piano-pieces, German sonatas and Italian arias were popular; for by this time, in a period when Vienna held sway, British musical taste varied only slightly from that of central Europe.[24]

By the 1840s there was a reasonably lively musical life in Sydney, given the size and nature of the population. In Melbourne the first public concert in 1839 just pre-dated the first race-meeting, and, by a wider margin, the first dramatic performance. William Vincent Wallace migrated to Sydney in 1835, opened the first music school in 1836, was tagged as the 'Australian Paganini' when he gave recitals in 1837, and organised the first music festival in 1838. He then departed, leaving large debts, and subsequently became famous as author of the opera, *Maritana*. Isaac Nathan was of much more lasting importance. He arrived in 1841 and stayed for the remaining twenty-three years of his life. He opened an academy of singing, became cathedral choirmaster, organised sacred concerts, and became a sort of musical laureate—composing an elegiac ode on 'Leichhardt's Grave', patriotic anthems, songs such as 'The Currency Lasses' and an opera, *Don John of Austria*.

The gold rushes brought many musicians and large audiences. There was always music on the diggings at night—fiddles, flutes, accordions, bugles, banjos, even brass bands; and singing of hymns, or general favourites like 'The Last Rose of Summer' or 'Ben Bolt' or traditional English, Irish, Scottish, German or American ballads—and sometimes Australian, when Charles Thatcher, 'the Colonial Minstrel', had made his topical songs wildly popular. In this period the great agency of musical progress, inherited from England and especially the north country, was the choral society. In 1853 forty members of the Melbourne Philharmonic Society gave their first performance of *The Messiah*. In 1854 they gave eleven concerts, including three performances of Haydn's *Creation*, and by 1860 had given 200 concerts.[25] From 1870 the Brisbane Musical Union was outstanding for its performances of oratorios; choral singing was also strong in Nonconformist Adelaide. Sydney held its first major music festival in 1859. Opera was well established in 1855 and the world's best performers made the Australian colonies part of the run. Until the depression of the 90s, Melbourne had at least one season every year (which was not to happen for most of the twentieth century). From 1861 W. S. Lyster dominated the operatic scene. His company, which had thirty-three operas in its repertoire, played continuously for most of 1861, added the works of Verdi to the staple fare of Donizetti, Bellini and Rossini, and later introduced Offenbach.[26] From 1872 Lyster was reinforced by Alberto Zelman who, undeterred by having only the pianoforte score, worked out the orchestration for a performance of Wagner's *Lohengrin*.

The German minorities in Victoria and South Australia introduced through their Liedertafel groups rather different tastes and conventions to the prevailing English. But tastes in drawing-room entertainment were almost purely English, in a period when any well-educated person, a lady especially, was presumed to be able to play or sing a part when called on. Sales of pianos and sheet music were extraordinarily high by European standards. One informed but obviously inflated estimate in 1888 was that 700,000 pianos had been shipped to Australia in the previous century. Roger Covell remarks:

> for many settlers the piano embodied the essence of the civilization they were leaving behind them in Europe, and particularly in the British Isles. It was an emblem of gentility and cultivated aspiration, a sacred object from the curtained shrine of the Victorian parlour. . . . Middle-class values have rarely expressed themselves with more touching gallantry and tenacity than in the sacrifices and discomforts endured by countless families in order to bring this cumbersome symbol of higher values to their chosen home in small, unstable ships and on grinding bullock drays.[27]

We might note the remark of R. E. N. Twopeny in 1883, that in few parts of the world was so much music to be heard, and in no part so much bad music.[28] But in most of the capital cities there was a core of competent professionals, about half of them German, who provided instrumental and vocal concerts of fairly high standard. Orchestral work was rare before the Melbourne Exhibition of 1888, which was in part a cultural festival. The Exhibition Commissioners engaged the leading English conductor, Frederick Cowen, at the astounding fee of £5,000 for six months. Cowen brought out fifteen instrumentalists, combined them with the best local talent, and drilled the orchestra and a choir of 708 singers for a month. They then launched on an astonishing programme, which may never have been equalled anywhere, of more than 260 concerts, averaging ten concerts and three or four rehearsals a week, and covering the whole standard repertoire. About 11,000 people attended every Saturday; the Beethoven symphonies and Wagner became immensely popular. Cowen thought the soloists and choir excellent, while the orchestra, though patchy in quality, showed 'great precision of ensemble and technique'.[29] An attempt was made to found a permanent orchestra, but the venture died. On the other hand, Francis Ormond, a squatter, had endowed a chair of music at the University of Melbourne in 1887. And the eisteddfod movement in the Ballarat district and the South Street competitions from 1879 were beginning to discover a chain of promising singers. Brilliant instrumental prodigies were appearing as early as the 70s, and of course were sent overseas for further training as quickly as possible. One of them, John Kruse, who left at the age of sixteen in 1875, became one of the most famous violinists of the day as a member of the Joachim Quartet and a professor at the Berlin Hochschule.

Nineteenth century musical composition was of negligble importance. There was a fair bulk of composition, largely of songs and cantatas, but none of it has survived in anyone's repertoire (except 'Advance Australia Fair' and 'Song of Australia'!) Judgment is difficult, however, since so little was printed or remains in manuscript. Kenneth Hince sums up what remains as 'a tenacious survival . . . of the mediocre tradition of English choral music', with 'a dim reflection of Mendelssohn and, in the far distance, of Handel'.[30] Leon Caron, C. E. Horsley and G. W. Torrance are among the more interesting composers. Covell points out that Australia grew up too late to form a national musical tradition of its own, and did not have sufficient time or isolation before modern communications erased or blurred those differences and idiosyncracies which formerly helped to fashion national traditions elsewhere. Folk-song neither had enough time to develop nor gained sufficient currency 'to constitute a national melodic fund or savings bank on which any composer can draw at will in the knowledge that his source will be recognizable to his audience'.[31] Hence the search for a musical identity was to be difficult.

Watkin Tench recorded in his journal that on 4 June 1789 eleven convicts performed Farquhar's *The Recruiting Officer* 'in a mud hut, fitted for the occasion'. The theatre immediately went into decline and the long reign of low farce and melodrama began. The theatre and music-hall were immensely popular institutions in the nineteenth century, in the Australian colonies as in Britain and elsewhere. But they were often extremely disreputable, in the early years primarily a branch of the liquor industry. No lady or anyone respectable, or any Evangelical, would attend. In 1833 Sydney's Theatre Royal was built to hold 1,000, Hobart's still surviving Theatre Royal was built in 1834, Melbourne's built in the 50s held 4,000. From the early 40s, when George Coppin (1819-1906) began his half century's career as actor-entrepreneur, several professional companies were touring the colonies. The early gold-rush period saw the theatre's most riotous period when Lola Montez and her kind held sway.

But the gold rush migrants also demanded the very best and could pay for it. For the next twenty years many of the world's leading actors and actresses were attracted to Australia for short or long periods. G. V. Brooke came out to play Shakespeare in 1855 and spent most of the ten remaining years of his life in Australia. Gyles Turner, the historian, looked back about 1910 to the late 50s as by far the best period in colonial theatre. Charles and Ellen Kean, Barry Sullivan and others were attracted in the early 60s. The serious theatre became respectable, so much so that Governors could attend. But the wowsers were not reconciled and agreed with the Reverend Dr Adam Cairns's denunciation in 1856:

> The public acting of men and women; the vivid portraying of the warmest and the wildest passions; the progress and development of amorous intrigue; the impassioned look; the wanton gesture; the allusion and the equivoque; the sly hint and the significant inuendo; the witchery of female loveliness in distress or in repose; the nameless charm of youthful beauty dressed out with a voluptuous elegance; are all fitted, and are all powerful to stimulate the sensual affections, and to intoxicate the gazer as with a cup of sorcery. And well do the veterans in vice know the potency of this bewildering spell. Hither is the thoughtless maiden enticed. . . .[32]

From about 1870 Australian theatre was dominated by a small group of actor-entrepreneurs exploiting what was still a large market. The American, J. C. Williamson, founded his fortune on a melodrama, *Struck Oil*, captured the rights to Gilbert and Sullivan, and then developed the monopolistic 'Firm' in conjunction with Arthur Garner and George Musgrove.[33] In the 80s the Brough and Boucicault company was a first-rate professional group which mixed Sheridan and the contemporary Wilde and Pinero with less significant comedy. Alfred Dampier was a serious actor-producer who did his best to keep Shakespeare before the public, but found it necessary to present five nights of trash to support one worthwhile night. In 1881, D. E. Bandmann, an American actor, wrote:

the public in Melbourne is no longer what it used to be. In former years the people might very deservedly be denoted among the most intelligent, generous, and appreciative of civilized communities. . . . The city has become stupid, licentious, ungenerous, and for the most part indifferent to the higher aims and ideals of Art. In public taste and sentiment it has been systematically demoralized by managers, who, in their desire to please and attract, have made their entertainments too cheap. . . . The colonial generation of today prefers, at any time, a pipe, a mug of colonial ale, a dice-box, or a billiard-cue to the best drama in existence. . . . the two largest cities are dead to dramatic art and finer aesthetic sentiment.[34]

And yet in 1889 Melbourne could stage Ibsen's *Doll's House*, in the same year as London and five years before Paris.[35]

In a period so dramatically barren, when so few plays of quality were written in English between Sheridan and Shaw, nothing could be expected from colonies. The first play about Australia was actually written by a Frenchman, Citoyen Gamas, in 1792— *Les Emigrés aux Terres Australes* or *Le Dernier Chapitre d'une Grande Révolution,* imagining the fate of some of the French upper classes, if transported. The first and by no means the worst Australian play written (but not published) was 'The Bushrangers' by David Burn, a cultivated Tasmanian settler; it was actually first performed in Edinburgh in 1829 (and again in Sydney in 1971). A trickle of plays followed, growing in number in the 70s and 80s; hardly any can be taken seriously. They nearly all fall under three heads: melodrama, farce, and historical verse drama.

The titles of the melodramas indicate their nature well enough— *Foiled, Forged, Retribution* or *The Drunkard's Curse, All for Gold* (derived from *The Wandering Jew*), *Good for Evil.* The last two were written by a pastoralist, F. R. C. Hopkins, whose melodramas were performed in several countries. George Darrell's *The Sunny South, Back from the Grave, Transported for Life* and *The Squatter* were also successful. Most of these plays had Australian settings, though very often they were adaptations or plagiarizations of overseas successes. Like the novelists, the playwrights drew on the obvious dramatic elements in Australian history; convicts, bushrangers and miners provided the necessary violent ingredient of melodrama. Fairly successful adaptations were made of *Robbery Under Arms* and *His Natural Life.* Most of the farces and comedies were sheer burlesque and pantomime, but *Jemmy*

Green in Australia written in the 40s by the convict, James
Tucker, had some quality. It is a pity that the manuscript of
'Class', a political comedy by Grosvenor Bunster, which was performed in Melbourne in 1878, has not survived; its subject was
the comedy of class prejudice, and it was probably based on
the contemporary English play, *Caste*. A rare example of satire was
The Happy Land, partly written by Marcus Clarke, which pilloried the Berry government of Victoria in the late 70s, and was
censored because it was opposed to 'good manners, decorum, and
the public peace'.

Most of the Australians who tried and failed to write serious
plays in the nineteenth century adopted the verse-drama form,
following the tradition of Dryden, Coleridge, Byron and Shelley.
The models regarded as most appropriate were, of course, Shakespeare and the historical dramas of the classical eighteenth century.
In England hundreds of such plays were published much more
often than produced. Hence in Australia, listed in Ferguson's
Bibliography of Australia are dozens of published and unper-
formed dramas like *Tarquin the Proud, Salathiel* or *The Jewish
Chieftain, Raymond, Lord of Milan, Francesca Vasari, The Were-
wolf* (set in Henry IV's France), and *Quentin Massys* (written by
Alfred Deakin in his 'teens about the Flemish artist). Charles
Harpur's *The Bushrangers*, written in Shakespearian style, was
probably the most interesting of them all.[36]

From the 40s all Australia's migrant architects were products of
the battle of the styles, largely between classical and Gothic re-
vivalists, fought out in England in the early part of the century.[37]
J. M. Freeland has noted that a truce with regard to public buildings seems to have been reached in Australia: broadly, that courthouses and other government buildings should be in classical
style, and that churches and usually schools and universities should
be in early English Gothic—for example, the many, lamentably
surviving, Birmingham-redbrick-Gothic state schools built in Melbourne after the 1872 Education Act. Freeland suggests that this
habit or formula was largely brought about by Mortimer Lewis,
Colonial Architect of New South Wales from the mid-30s. Certainly, little of native origin can be discerned in nineteenth
century public buildings, except perhaps for the frequent cast-
iron-verandahed large hotels and the distinctive local style of
Melbourne's bluestone and Adelaide's sandstone. Melbourne is
the outstanding case where revivals came crowding in on each

other as eclectic architects and builders dipped into history as the whim took them.[38] Perhaps no architect has left a greater mark on any city than Joseph Reed, who worked in Melbourne from the 50s to the 90s and designed the Public Library, the Town Hall, the Wesley, Scots and Independent churches, the Exhibition building, Ormond College and the old Wilson Hall, ten banks and many other buildings in any and every style. Robin Boyd writes:

> The aims were to absorb the rules of the masters, to discriminate, to borrow gracefully. He was not tempted by individualism or interested in curious cults of romanticism which affected others of the late Victorian era. One may search his various buildings fruitlessly for the characteristic touches which distinguish some architects' work and cut through stylism in any age. He was wonderfully irrelevant and proudly inconsistent. [His] work remains to mock the modern critic, because it has a generosity and a scale which are proportionately beyond the capacity of today's enterprise.[39]

The second major figure was Edmund Blacket, who dominated ecclesiastical building in New South Wales for forty years. 'Essentially an archaeological Gothicist', he is most noted for the Great Hall at Sydney University, but much of his finest work was in small churches. The third distinguished architect was William Wardell, who was responsible for the Catholic cathedrals of both Melbourne and Sydney; a leading English art historian was once heard to remark that St Patrick's is possibly the finest example of the Gothic revival anywhere in the world. It has been pointed out that Wardell, as a colonial, had the great opportunity to build cathedrals, whereas his friend Pugin, the leading figure of the Gothic revival, was confined in England to parish churches.[40]

Loud-mouthed Melbourne, flushed with golden wealth, built a remarkable set of public buildings; obsession with size, reflecting the colony's status, did not always spoil the effect. Parliament House was the grandest in the Empire outside Westminster and the Catholic cathedral the largest in the Southern Hemisphere. Government House was larger than the Viceroy of India's or the Lord Lieutenant of Dublin's and its ballroom was larger than Buckingham Palace's. Then in the boom 80s, the business section was largely rebuilt in weird variations on Venetian Gothic, Greek, Roman, Moorish and Turkish styles. Perhaps the chief aesthetic triumph of the period was Wardell's E.S. & A. Bank.

The most distinctive form of private housing came to be the pastoral homesteads—not the baronial halls which sometimes disfigured the bush, but the natural, unpretentious, roomy, sprawling, leafy-verandahed extensions of fairly simple farm-houses. The plain verandahed box of Georgian derivation—two or three rooms deep, passage down the middle and long high front windows— remained standard over wide levels of urban society. The eventual compromise between Georgian and Italianate broadly favoured the latter. As early as the 40s Georgian symmetry was occasionally broken, when the first Gothic cottages pushed out one front room into bow windows to make an L-shaped front, reducing the verandah to half the front but sometimes extending it around one side. Terraces dropped out of fashion, as the working classes came to insist on detached houses with gardens, however modest. The most distinctive local characteristic of domestic housing and some public buildings was the wide use of ornamental cast iron, which spread fast from the 50s. At first the iron was imported from England, but very soon it was almost entirely locally produced; the patented designs often included native animals, birds and plants—a curious early example of Australian patriotism. Nowhere else in the world was cast iron used so extensively; New Orleans is on a comparatively minor scale.[41]

Rural housing became standardized into a national type. Tin and timber, normally in the simple verandahed box: timber frame, weatherboard, galvanized iron roof—materials easily transported for long distances by dray, whereas brick and stone were often out of the question. According to Freeland, the balloon frame of widely spaced light timber was introduced by American migrants of the 50s. It was modified in various ways, especially to combat the sun, and its constructional evolution was very Australian. When galvanized iron became cheaper in the 50s, it quickly came to predominate for roofing, and was widely used for walls as well, until machine-cutting and dressing of weatherboards developed. At first it was placed on top of the wood shingles which were left for insulation, but came to be a ubiquitous panacea—durable, cheap, and efficient in preserving rainwater, however ugly. The chief regional variation, which came close to an indigenous style, developed in Queensland and northern New South Wales. The timber frame was left exposed and the one set of boarding served both externally and internally, roofs became steeper, and the houses were lifted on stumps or stilts, both for ventilation and to combat white ants.[42]

Until late in the century the major contributions to scientific knowledge continued to be made by government officers or private scholars rather than by university men. Some of these scientists could still have the joy and satisfaction of almost alone blocking in huge areas of knowledge. Ferdinand Mueller was appointed Victorian government botanist in 1853 and in the next three years made three trips on horseback lasting several months; he was the first to explore botanically the Alps and High Plains and was probably the first to climb Mt Bogong and Mt Hotham. On his first trip, after travelling 1,500 miles, he added 936 plants to his list of Victorian flora. (Regrettably, he used to distribute blackberry seeds to struggling settlers.) Mueller's ambition to which his distinction fully entitled him was to compile the definitive *Flora Australiensis*. However, the authorities at Kew Gardens decided against him, on the reasonable grounds that the work had to be done in England by someone with access to major existing collections and libraries. Nevertheless, he eventually made a massive contribution to Bentham's *Flora Australiensis* (1863-78).[43] A. W. Howitt, who had brought in the bodies of Burke and Wills, became magistrate and mining warden of east Gippsland for twenty-five years, based in Omeo and Bairnsdale. He mapped much of the area but also, reading in the saddle on the thousands of miles he rode annually, he made himself a distinguished scientist. Working together with Lorimer Fison on the Gippsland tribes, he became the first major Australian anthropologist, and also made an imimportant contribution to geology and a useful one to botany.[44] Mueller and Howitt were unusually able men: so was A. R. C. Selwyn, Victorian government geologist from 1852 to 1869 before moving on to make a great contribution to Canadian geology. In South Australia, Tenison Woods, a Catholic priest, was a remarkable amateur geologist. Basic institutions were slowly established. Following the foundation of the scientific museum in Sydney in 1836, Melbourne followed in 1854, Brisbane in 1855 and Adelaide in 1856. Local Royal Societies were founded in Melbourne (with a forerunner from 1854) in 1859, Sydney in 1866, Adelaide in 1880 and Brisbane in 1884. Museums of Applied Science opened in Melbourne in 1870, Sydney in 1880 and Adelaide in 1893. The Australasian Association for the Advancement of Science held its first congress in 1888.

A further scattering of names must serve to indicate the achievements of intellect in the colonial period. One of the quite outstanding (and usually overlooked) literary contributions of the nineteenth century was John West's *History of Tasmania* (1852).

49

William Westgarth's pedestrian but wise series of books on Victoria and Australia are notable for their insight into colonial society. James Bonwick, pedagogue extraordinary and amateur scholar, wrote many useful books and, through his transcription of records, helped to lay the basis for historical scholarship in Australia. G. W. Rusden's histories of Australia and New Zealand (both 1883), though extremely Tory-prejudiced and cantankerous, were major achievements. In sheer distinction of scholarship, Charles Badham of the University of Sydney, who was an eminent world classical scholar, was almost unrivalled. His one competitor is probably Charles Pearson, schoolmaster, historian and Victorian minister of Education, who was both a brilliant colonizer of modern ideas in Australia and a highly original political thinker who anticipated much of the twentieth century welfare state; his *National Life and Character* (1893), warning of the rise of Asia, made a profound international impact.[45] W. E. Hearn and David Syme were both economists of minor international repute.[46] The statisticians, W. H. Archer, H. H. Hayter and Timothy Coghlan, in turn were highly original in world terms in their scope and techniques. As rare examples of technological innovators, we must mention Louis Brennan, inventor in the 70s of the dirigible torpedo, who made a model of a helicopter in 1883; Lawrence Hargrave, whose experiments of the 80s and 90s have established him as a major figure in the pre-history of aviation; and A. U. Alcock, electrical experimenter of the 80s, who eventually laid down the principle of the hovercraft. Passing mention should also be made of the many innovators in agricultural machinery in the 70s and 80s, such as John Buncle, Hugh Lennon, James Morrow and H. V. McKay. Finally—although their work extended to the 90s and later, they are so much distinguished products of 'Marvellous Melbourne'—the Sutherland family: William, research physicist, who established 'Sutherland's constant' and ranged widely in his sixty-nine papers;[47] Alexander, educationist, historian, literary critic, whose *The Origin and Growth of the Moral Instinct* (1898) is a landmark in the history of sociology; Jane, almost a major painter; and George, inventor and journalist and father of Margaret Sutherland, the composer.

Only three of the twenty-seven men mentioned in the last two paragraphs were native-born. Yet the privileged few were being well trained; nowhere in the world could Australia's two most famous 'native sons', Edmund Barton and Alfred Deakin, have had much better educations—the one at Fort St, Sydney and with Badham at the University, the other with Dr J. E. Bromby at

Melbourne C. of E. Grammar School and with Hearn and Pearson at the University. Melbourne University was well in advance of Sydney, having schools of Law, Medicine and Engineering from the 60s, whereas Sydney branched out into Medicine, Engineering and Science only in the 80s, when its students increased from fewer than 100 to more than 500. One of the great achievements of the age was G. B. Halford's foundation of the Melbourne medical school; Anderson Stuart followed in Sydney, and Australia's medical training was established on the highest world standards. Melbourne had a marvellous generation of students in the 70s which included the giants of the early Commonwealth, H. B. Higgins, Isaac Isaacs, John Quick and Deakin, also the great philosopher, Samuel Alexander, and Richard Hodgson, the investigator of psychical phenomena. The universities made a significant advance in the later 80s when a new generation of young men—all migrants—began teaching: the scientists, Edgeworth David, Orme Masson, Baldwin Spencer, T. R. Lyle, and David Bragg; and the humanists, Mungo MacCallum, T. G. Tucker and Francis Anderson. Meanwhile, many of the best of the native-born, such as Alexander and Gilbert Murray, the classicist, had left permanently for overseas.

THE GROWTH OF CULTURE IN COLONIES

4

The cultural achievement of the first century was meagre indeed. But, after all, how much more could reasonably have been expected from a population of only two or three million people, separated into six communities with little contact with each other? Such a simple explanation takes us far, but is nothing like adequate.

All beginnings are difficult, remarked Goethe, and this certainly applies to the arts in new countries. Australia seemingly inherited the whole glorious tradition of English literature, for example; but it was a kind of negative asset, tied-up capital which could not be productively used. Culture is a highly perishable growth which, transplanted, cannot bloom as before. Once the geographical break was made, in creative terms the tradition was broken or became very tenuous. Simply from observing what happened, it is obvious that a fresh start had to be made, and that the establishment and early growth of the new culture was painful indeed, that the history of culture in Australia must mainly be seen as growth from the very beginning. Henry James once observed of the United States:

> The flower of art blooms only where the soil is deep, . . . it takes a great deal of history to produce a little literature, . . . it needs a complex social machinery to set a writer in motion. . . . it takes such an accumulation of history and custom, such a complexity of manners and types, to form a fund of suggestion for a novelist.[1]

After all, there was remarkably little writing, painting or music of high quality (but there was a great architecture) during the American colonies' first two centuries.

In the mid- to late nineteenth century men interested in the arts who hoped to see great creative works produced in Australia were usually very pessimistic. One exception was the journalist, Frederick Sinnett, who in the *Journal of Australasia* in 1856 inquired into the feasibility of writing Australian novels, into the suitability of Australian life and scenery for the novelist's purposes. He began by examining the general belief that it was simply not possible to produce literature in Australia, in the absence of a local tradition. It was undeniably argued that Australia was a new country, with no associations in most of the colonies of more than a score of years, that there were no archeological accessories, no storied windows casting a dim religious light, no ruins for ivy to creep over, no spring panels or subterranean passages in historic buildings, no antiquity. There had been no genius, like Shakespeare, to break the dam and let loose the flood. Despite Dickens, it was widely assumed that great novels were not created from the foreground of experience, that they had to be set in the distant past like Scott's. Nonsense, said Sinnett, all the emotions which made for great novels—love, hate, avarice, etc.—were present in Australia.

> We have here 'the same organs, dimensions, senses', as the good folks in Europe. 'If you tickle us, do we not laugh? If you prick us, do we not bleed?' Human nature being the same, the true requisites of the novelist are to be found in one place as well as in another. Australia offers fresh scenery, fresh costumes, and fresh machinery, new as to its details—great advantages to those that know how to use them—and, for the rest, presents a field neither better nor worse than most others, in which people love, and hate, and hope, and fear, and strive, and are disappointed, and succeed, and plot, and scheme, and work out their destinies, and obey the good and evil impulses of their infinitely various natures.

Admittedly, the fresh scene was a problem, it was a different kind of romance; but what a great unworked quarry it was! 'The recorders are tuneless only because there is no one who knows how to play upon' the 'rude amorphous materials'. 'The fault is ours, if . . . we regard the whole scene as tame and prosaic, and able to furnish the materials for no books but ledgers.'[2] Though it did not often reach print, debate in these terms continued throughout the colonial period, with on the whole the pessimists holding sway and agreeing with Henry James that in the absence of history, tradition and a complex society a 'fund of suggestion' could grow only very slowly.

One favourite argument, deriving from de Tocqueville's *Democracy in America*, was that democratic societies promoted cultural mediocrity, that democracy abhorred distinction. New societies, compared to the old world, lacked hereditary standards and were unstable, there were no fixed social classes, all was in flux. 'There is no class, then, in America in which the taste for intellectual pleasure is transmitted with hereditary fortune and leisure and by which the labours of the intellect are held in honour.' Remembering how much of the world's great art and literature down to the nineteenth century had sprung from private patronage, we must recognise the absence of patrons in Australia apart from the rare exceptions like N. D. Stenhouse in Sydney. Americans, said de Tocqueville, were content with a 'middling standard' in 'manners, morals, knowledge and the arts'. But—and this applied to Australia, too—if the observer 'only singles out the learned, he will be astonished to find how rare they are; but if he counts the ignorant, the American people will appear to be the most enlightened in the world'. Democracy, however, meant the tyranny of the majority, the persecution of those with minority tastes, for example the decrying of those who valued the arts and intellect above all else. Democratic nations cultivated 'the arts which serve to render life easy in preference to those whose object is to adorn it'.[3] If these generalizations are applied to nineteenth century Australia, it should be noted that they do not take into account the fact that culture in colonies is not static, but a process of growth and development out of spiritual squalour gradually to something better. And de Tocqueville was mistaken about the potential cultural quality of American civilization.

Another feature commonly accepted was the overwhelmingly dominant materialist tone of colonial society and consequent contempt for the arts. Harpur remarked that 'During my whole manhood I have had to mingle daily amongst men . . . who have faith for nothing in God's glorious universe that is not, in their own vile phrase, "money's worth".'[4] Badham wrote in 1882:

> This country now presents what, to European eyes, are strange phenomena—(1) an enormous amount of wealth in the hands of men utterly illiterate; (2) the learned professions, including the church, with very little learning to divide amongst them; (3) the mercantile classes of all grades very much below the standard of their congeners in western Europe in literary and intellectual tastes.[5]

Francis Adams, a brilliant young disciple of Matthew Arnold, who spent eight years in Australia in the 80s, was appalled by the 'crude provincial hedonism' and the dominance of the philistine. Another astute observer of colonial life noted that honour and glory were bestowed on success in horse-racing and smartness in dress and manners: 'social approval is not secured by culture, but rather social disapproval'.[6] This is all very well—Melbourne and Sydney, we have noted, had highly sophisticated audiences for the arts; but it must be admitted that the tone of colonial society was set by *nouveau riche* boors. For the dominant reason for migration was material self-betterment. A colony was a fair field for the materialist struggle to get up and out of the ruck and on top, no holds being barred. Acquisitiveness is the mortal enemy of the life of intellect and creativity. A long time has to pass before a new society will recognize praiseworthy virtues other than hard work, manual skills, and the ability to cope and improvise. Colonists striving to establish themselves materially regard the thinker or the artist as a bludger and a drone, one of the superior people of the Old World from whom they are escaping.

There is little doubt that writers and artists felt themselves to be confronted by a viciously hostile society. Could it have been just chance or a succession of personal factors which led Gordon to shoot himself in the scrub at Brighton and Barcroft Boake to hang himself with his own stockwhip; or made Kendall, Lawson and Brennan hopeless alcoholics; or turned Price Warung to morphia? On the other hand, the painters seem to have been eminently well balanced. It is worth recalling Van Wyck Brooks on American writers:

> Have not defeat, disease, disappointment and early death characterized the lives of writers in all times and countries? The literary temperament is prone to the stresses and strains that have made 'the calamities of authors' everywhere a by-word; and yet the complaints of so many Americans can scarcely be ignored, nor can the evidence of so many American lives.[7]

The writer, anywhere, is usually alienated. Still, it must be said, at the very least, that the social climate for the artist in colonial Australia did not contribute to personal stability.

The educational basis of the community is obviously relevant. Historians tend to exaggerate the immediate effects of the Education Acts of the 70s (1880 in New South Wales). They certainly improved the situation greatly at the lowest level and encouraged many to go on educating themselves after leaving school at fourteen, but may have had little effect on higher cultural standards. For the Acts did not touch secondary, grammar-school education, which was very slow to develop. In quality and quantity there was to be precious little improvement in secondary education over three-quarters of a century. There were a few good schools like Melbourne Grammar and Scotch College, Melbourne, and Fort St High in Sydney, but until after the 1914-18 war secondary education was almost entirely confined to the tiny minority who could afford to pay for it. Despite its social progressiveness, Australia between 1875 and 1925 probably had no higher a proportion being educated to sixteen or eighteen than Scotland, England, the United States or most European countries. The growth of high schools is a mid- rather than an early twentieth century phenomenon. The assumption here is that a fair to good education is usually (by no means always) necessary for the aesthetic sense and creative talent to develop; the great majority of the best Australian writers and painters have had a goodish education or at least had parents who cared for culture. It may be that there could be no general breakthrough in cultural appreciation, until much higher general levels of education developed than prevailed in the nineteenth and early twentieth century.

Other than talent, the economics of the arts are all-important. Colonial society was on such a tiny scale that no writer and only a very few painters (most of whom were fashionable portraitists in periods of prosperity) could be professional, live by their work, or even buy time by potboiling to work seriously.[8] Kendall, with some help from friends and admirers, for a few years eked out a miserable existence just from writing. Even Henry Lawson, with all his 'success', made only £700 from writing in his first and best twelve years—less than half the equivalent of the basic wage! There was some reason for his self-pity: in 1899 he wrote,

> My advice to any young Australian writer whose talents have been recognized would be to go steerage, stow away, swim, and seek London, Yankeeland, or Timbuctoo—rather than stay in Australia till his genius turned to gall or beer. Or, failing this . . . to study elementary anatomy . . . and then shoot himself carefully.[9]

Miles Franklin got £24 all told from the several editions of *My Brilliant Career*. Boldrewood, Clarke, Ada Cambridge and 'Banjo' Paterson could earn no more than useful subsidiary income from their writing. The size of the local market was small enough, and was further reduced by the prejudice of so many of the migrant reading classes, whose interests were centred on 'home', against local writers. Australian novelists had largely to depend on the English market and to seek publication in England. The only important Australian publishers were, before 1890, George Robertson (1825-98) of Melbourne and, after 1890, George Robertson (1860-1933) of Angus & Robertson in Sydney.[10] There was almost no hope of distribution in England of books published in Australia and Australian publishers had so often lost money on local works that they would accept few manuscripts other than sure successes. Australian authors published in England had the slight advantage of the spicy appeal of the exotic; inevitably, however, they tended to tailor their work to what they imagined the English public would like—to the detriment of writing in Australia. For local income the writers were largely dependent on the weeklies, such as the *Australasian*, the *Town and Country Journal*, and then the *Bulletin*; the magazines, good though they often were, had to compete with the English quality journals and had small circulation, and apart from the *Australian Journal* were not often able to pay contributors. All operated on too small a scale to pay generously.

Size of market is all-important: writers in large countries with an established literary life have every advantage; Australian writers have been exposed to competition from all writing in English, and have lacked the natural protection by language which writers in countries of comparable size, like Holland and the Scandinavian countries, have had. Until very recent years it has been impossible for Australian writers, except at low levels, to live by writing; historically Australian writers have had to be amateurs or quarter-professionals. Consequently, the possibility of formation of coteries or groups of professional writers, who might stimulate and encourage each other and stand on each others' shoulders, has been limited. In Melbourne, briefly in the late 1860s, there was almost such a group; and the *Bulletin* in the 90s provided a productive focus, as did the Heidelberg painters. But in all the arts, talented youth felt a need to go abroad in the hope of becoming professional.

Above all, if creative culture was to develop, Australia had to begin to grow out of the stage of simple colonialism with all its attendant intimate, uneasy, deferential attitudes to 'home' and the smothering inherited culture. A writer must have an easy relationship with his country, see it as a fit subject for art, must know and understand people and place intimately in order both to make easy use of them as a context for broader issues and to make penetrating comment. Rosa Praed looked back sadly in old age:

had I been only simple and natural, had I only tried to describe what I knew, there was a rich virgin field waiting to be tilled under my very feet. I had the Australian bush with its glamour, its tragedy, its pathos and its humour; I had the romance of the pioneer upheavings and the social makings of a new-born colony—had I but known it, the whole stock-in-trade of the novelist. . . . Alas! when I think that in those early days of mine, it never struck me that my worthiest ambition might be to become a genuine Australian story teller! Then it was rather the fashion to despise native surroundings and the romance of the bush. We all wanted to be English. . . .[11]

To the extent that colonial writers and painters felt barriers between themselves and their subject-matter, were uneasy and uncertain of themselves as Australians, and found it difficult to form clear ideas about the nature of Australian life and of Australians, so their work was unsure. Perhaps it was necessary for the native-born to 'take over'. The Australian experience provides striking evidence for the difficulty of migrants fulfilling their artistic talents and for the importance of lifelong familiarity with native background in creative achievement; for there is hardly one major Australian creative artist, after Marcus Clarke and Buvelot, who is not a native Australian, if such child-migrants as Boldrewood, Tom Roberts and Hans Heysen are claimed as virtually native-born. The American experience seems to indicate that in a colonial situation a phase of national assertion is perhaps inevitable and positively desirable (provided it is only a phase). Fenimore Cooper wrote about English duchesses before he began exploiting backwoodsmen. In his preface to *The Spy*, which has been described as the first American novel of any consequence,[12] he wrote unhappily in terms reminiscent of those writers whom Sinnett was criticizing:

There is a scarcity of events [in American history] that drives an author from the undertaking in despair. [A murder] is much more interesting in a castle than in a cornfield. In short, all that glow which can be given to a tale through obscure legends, artificial distinctions, and images connected with association of ideas, is not attainable in this land of facts. Man is not the same creature here as in other countries.

Thus, Australia needed an Emerson to repeat: 'All art—yet to be created; all literature—yet to be written; all nature—new and undescribed. . . . Why should not Americans enjoy an original relation to the universe?'[13] An Australian Whitman was required to inject native life and vigour, a Poe to proclaim a cultural declaration of independence, and above all a Melville to write a masterpiece.

To grow out of colonialism, another half-century was still required. The *Bulletin* writers and the Heidelberg painters were about to make a start. But for Australia to acquire sophistication in the arts, as in other fields, a much more complex society had to develop. As R. M. Crawford says,

> Immaturity in the life of the spirit was only to be expected, then, so long as colonial society continued to be sheltered by British power from the challenges of the world at large, so long as it continued to be preoccupied with those tasks of pioneering which bred admiration of action rather than of reflection, and so long as it offered relatively meagre opportunities for a professional life in scholarship, literature, and the arts.[14]

In particular, Australia needed to grow in scale and diversity— from diversity comes disagreement, stimulus and excitement. And it also needed to move towards nationhood, in order to find the interpretative artists who would begin to state in aesthetic terms what it might mean to be an Australian.

5

The 80s were the springtime, adolescent period of Australian history. In these boom years, the utopian assumption of Australia's destiny as another United States, peopled by a chosen white race, superior to the Old World and free from its vices, held sway as never since. The native-born were taking over, and in Victoria the Australian Natives' Association was defining their responsibilities, the first of which was the formal creation of a nation by federation. The centennial celebrations provoked intense controversy over future nationhood and the ultimate relationship with Britain. The trade unions, reinforced by new organizations like the Shearers', braced themselves to launch a political party which would reform Australian man. Naive, confident optimism was reflected by writers and artists striving to express a new civilization. But in the 90s depression and class war shattered such illusions. As Brian Fitzpatrick wrote: 'What took place was like the ending of a childhood: the curtain's fall on wide-eyed expectation, the entrance instead of uncertainty, doubt and mistrust; "never glad confident morning again".'[1]

Founded in 1880, the Sydney *Bulletin* quickly became a great national weekly with, by 1890, an astonishing circulation of 80,000. It was rude, slangy, smart, happily vulgar, modern in journalistic style, and above all funny—especially its cartoons. It held an extraordinary combination of extreme attitudes: it was radical, republican, and despised the monarchy and the English ruling classes; it was viciously racist and anti-Semitic but also fought magnificently against the 'yellow dog' of sectarianism. Its particular strength was a blend of fervent idealism, down-to-earth commonsense and gaiety. It was a revelation to the young native-born especially; Randolph Bedford said he 'entered a new world' when he saw his first copy: 'It was Australia; whereas all the daily papers of Sydney were English provincials.'[2] J. F. Archibald, the presiding genius, saw his creation as an instrument to define and express the national being. The *Bulletin* certainly built up a group myth about Australians and their destiny; in seeking a 'usable past' it promoted a version of history which exposed the shame and horror of the English convict-transportation system and glorified the digger and Eureka. Its views were far too extreme to be widely accepted; it represented only one section of nationalism, a movement which took many forms, and it had little influence in the southern colonies.

But very clearly the *Bulletin* came to be aimed at and to speak for the men of the pastoral interior; it became the 'bushman's Bible'. It did not begin with this clear intention, although Archibald always had in mind, as his ideal reader, 'The Lone Hand— the very salt of the Australian people, the educated independent mining prospector';[3] the link was quickly forged in the early to mid-80s. The trend to up-country material may be argued to have begun with the publication of the ballad, 'Sam Holt', by 'Ironbark' (G. H. Gibson) on 26 March 1881. There followed a trickle, then a flood of paragraphs, yarns, tall stories, anecdotes, ballads and stories; the tap was turned on and stores of creativity were released, although it was to be some years before there were major literary results. The *Bulletin* not only became a forum for outbackery, but to a remarkable extent was written by its readers—and one of its virtues was that almost anyone could gain a hearing for almost any outlandish idea. In some respects the bushman has been unduly romanticized; nevertheless, outback pastoral society was a queerer phenomenon, perhaps, than even Russel Ward described in *The Australian Legend*. It included a strong leaven of well-educated and self-educated men who formed innumerable, perpetually changing debating societies round the campfires. By late in the century the bushmen as a class had developed a range of radical nationalist assumptions, were confident in their environment, knew they had something to say, and said it in the *Bulletin* which also said it for them. The extent to which the *Bulletin* moulded or reflected their views is an unanswerable problem.[4]

The *Bulletin* tapped the folk undercurrent which had been running strongly for half a century or more. For a genuine folk culture had begun to emerge in the pastoral interior, which had three main forms—the song, the narrative ballad for recitation and the yarn. Isolated men in small groups, many of whom were itinerant—drovers, shearers, bullockies, casual labourers—in the absence of any other, created their own entertainment. Sometimes one or more of them made their own song or ballad; sometimes they were picked up from newspapers and journals. In either case, they were passed on orally, were sometimes written down, circulated in varying versions and were polished as they went. One particular work-feature which encouraged the bush song was drovers' need to sing, or at least provide a reassuring drone, to their cattle at night. Songs had always been a vital part of the

culture of the unlettered; from the eighteenth century the broad-
side street ballad and song was perhaps the chief form of both
news and entertainment among the uneducated sections of the
convicts and poor migrants who settled early Australia. It was
natural to adapt these songs and make new ones in the old styles,
of which the Irish street ballad was the most influential. As Judith
Wright puts it,

> Songs were seized on, memorized, altered, parodied, sung in
> camps and riding round the cattle, at shearing sheds and on
> the track. They came to mirror the kind of life that their
> singers led; often hard and crude, almost always womanless,
> and because of this lack of normal balance, generally naive
> and sentimental under the tough hide induced by hardship
> and the remorseless conditions of the Australian outback.[5]

It cannot be claimed that many of the folk-ballads have true
literary quality; but, as Edgar Waters says, most of them have
vigour and the 'authentic, sweaty smell of a hard life' about them.
The pastoral folk culture had only a limited time to develop in
isolation before the impact of industrial society first diluted and
then eliminated it. The spread of settlement after the gold rushes
and improvement of communications exposed the bush increasingly to the metropolitan press and the popular songs of music-
hall and stage. More than anything else, the spread of the railway
broke down isolation—shearers in the 90s began to ride bicycles
from railheads and the area dependent on horses and bullocks
steadily dwindled. Henry Lawson, in nostalgic vein, wrote:

> Those golden days are vanished,
> And altered is the scene;
> The diggings are deserted,
> The camping-grounds are green;
> The flaunting flag of progress
> Is in the West unfurled,
> The mighty bush with iron rails
> Is tethered to the world.

The automobile rounded off the process. By the early to mid-
twentieth century, drovers usually sang the songs of Tin Pan Alley
or American country-music to their cattle.[6]

Despite the folk-ballad undercurrent—and it seems odd—few or
no literary ballads were published before the 60s. Gordon made

his contribution in the late 60s and had a few imitators, but the flood did not begin until the 80s with Gibson, John Farrell, Barcroft Boake and Paterson; the debt then to folk inspiration was very clear. Australian balladry was a sub-species of a very popular international fashion, and Australia was late in taking it up. One of Gordon's three ballads set in Australia, 'From the Wreck', was essentially an adaptation of Browning's 'How we Brought the Good News from Ghent to Aix'. The change in atmosphere, diction and values from Gordon to A. B. Paterson (1864-1941), whose first ballad appeared in the *Bulletin* in 1886, is very marked. As John Manifold has defined it, the Gordon-style ballad, at least as put out by his imitators, usually had a hero who was a high-born, public-school Englishman, had been in the Army, was an outstanding amateur rider, came to the colonies because of womantrouble, took an assumed name, punished the grog severely, died in the bush (his noble background then being revealed), and was buried in a bush grave and mourned by bronzed and bearded bushmen.[7] Paterson created the Man from Snowy River, Clancy and Saltbush Bill.

However modest his literary achievement, Paterson has been Australia's most popular poet; *The Man from Snowy River* sold 100,000 copies, his *Collected Verse* was printed for the twenty-sixth time in 1959. With his contemporary, Rudyard Kipling, and Robert Service of Canada, he is one of the three most popular balladists in English of modern times. He and Lawson, more than anyone else, set the notion of the bush and the bushman as the true and admirable Australia and Australian. He should not be dismissed as a poet; despite all the doggerel, there are subtle, interesting aspects; like other Australian balladists, he had Scottish ancestry and learned something from the border ballads. He transmuted the experience of a huge 'uncultured' audience into art. His great strength was his easy *rapport* with the bush audience of all classes. From a small pastoralist background, he studied law and became a journalist with spells back on the land. He was not really a radical or a political animal, but he detested what was happening to the pastoral industry—the takeovers by banks, companies, urban capital; there is a strong element in his work of nostalgic harking-back to the pure old days. And as H. M. Green says, his conception of the ideal station-owner was of a man who worked with his men on the run, paid high wages, and sympathized with unionism; who was generous to the passing swagman and just to the drover with his hungry mob'.[8] It's a pity Joe Furphy never met him. It can even be argued that in 'Waltzing Matilda'

Paterson brought together the traditions of convict 'treason songs' and 'jackeroo songs' (that is, those composed in the homestead). Like Rabbie Burns, he won the supreme achievement of being put into oral circulation by 'the folk' so that his poems were recited in numerous variants. And he repaid his debt to 'the folk' by his pioneer collection of *Old Bush Songs*.[9]

Continued by Will Ogilvie, 'John O'Brien' and others, the ballad remained vigorous for nearly half a century, and important as a minor art-form with a large popular audience. R. H. Croll's protest about the end of the century indicates how it dominated the popular idea of what Australian poetry was:

> Whalers, damper, swag and nose-bag, Johnny cakes and billy tea,
> Murrumburrah, Meremendicoowoke, Youlgarbudgeree,
> Cattle-duffers, bold bushrangers, diggers, drovers, bush race-courses,
> And on all the other pages, horses, horses, horses, horses.[10]

The *Bulletin* was interested in short-story writers, not novelists. In his strictly editorial capacity, Archibald insisted on brevity, boiling-down into a 'par'. Unlike its predecessors, the *Australian Journal* and *Sydney Mail*, which both encouraged local writers more than is generally known, the *Bulletin* did not serialize novels. Archibald sought and found stories in which the emphasis was on life, realism, 'grit not gush', topicality, everyday colloquial speech, getting Australia down on paper. Their rough vigour is in striking contrast to earlier colonial or Anglo-Australian writing. Lawson and others such as Edward Dyson, Ernest Favenc, E. J. Brady, Randolph Bedford, Albert Dorrington, Price Warung, Louis Becke and Dowell O'Reilly, though most of them came to live in Sydney, had usually grown up in the bush or spent long periods knocking around; they consciously felt themselves part of a new, different Australia.[11]

Henry Lawson (1867-1922) was incomparably the best of them. And yet in his day his large public and his tolerant publisher, George Robertson, regarded him as Lawson the Poet, although most of his verse was churned-out, sixpence-a-line doggerel. His stories were badly underrated by his contemporaries and usually judged to be no more than natural artless sketches. His contemporary reputation had almost nothing to do with his quality as a writer: he was the People's Poet, who articulated the egalitarian democratic protest-sentiment of the day when he wrote:

They lie, the men who tell us, for reasons of their own,
That want is here a stranger, and that misery's unknown.

Or:

But the curse of class distinctions from our shoulders shall be
      hurled,
An' the sense of Human Kinship revolutionise the world;
There'll be higher education for the toilin', starvin' clown,
An' the rich an' educated shall be educated down.

Many a man seized on his humanitarianism as a sort of 'reach-me-down Laborite secular religion'. But he was much more than that. His stories are very uneven, but in the best of them he is a highly finished artist and craftsman. He was a writer of high originality—precise, restrained, constantly understating—and almost the only Australian protest-writer whose art successfully carries his message. He was a preacher, of course, of how white men ought to behave to each other, of brotherly love, of mateship; yet fundamentally he was pessimistic, a radical who sensed the futility of radicalism and of Australian utopianism. Green remarks that 'it would be hard to find any writer of his calibre in whom so deep and romantic a love of his fellows is accompanied by so keen and humorous a perception of their inconsistencies and pettinesses, and, on the whole, by so conscientious a determination to show them just as they are.'[12] He was a master of sentiment, of command over laughter and tears, who escaped sentimentality again and again, except in some of his potboiling stuff, by an ironic twist. He was a master over a narrow sphere of writing and the first major Australian writer, worthy of comparison with Maupassant, Chekhov and Gorki, although in the rank behind them.[13]

In 1892 Lawson suggested to Paterson that they write in verse against each other in the *Bulletin*, as a means of increasing their incomes, expressing their different views of the Bush. For weeks they 'slambanged' away at each other, on the whole good-humouredly, to the great delight of the mass audience, several of whom added entertaining contributions. Many years later, Paterson recalled:

We were both looking for the same reef . . . ; but I had done
my prospecting on horseback with my meals cooked for me,
while Lawson had done his prospecting on foot and had had
to cook for himself. . . . I think that Lawson put his case better
than I did, but I had the better case, so that honours (or dis-
honours) were fairly equal.[14]

In fact, Lawson was putting a very serious case for realism against romanticism, to which Paterson would not or could not reply. Lawson was arguing that 'idealization of the bush falsified the "true" Australia, that the conventional diction of idealization was a barrier to accepting the outback as it was, and that the outback's real inhabitants could not be understood as long as the bushman of literary romance continued to be celebrated'.[15] The *Bulletin* school long remained ambiguous on the matter—the balladists tending to be romantically sentimental, the prose writers on the whole grimly realistic. But much, of course, depended on the Bush which was the subject—the gentle inland pastoral slopes or the harsh interior—and on the optimistic or pessimistic, hedonistic or stoic, values of the observer. Much of the balladry (and some of the later pastoral novels) were about Sydney or the Bush, identified with vice and virtue. Judith Wright has detected in the ballads a cult of the Bush representing the virtues of hard work, abstemiousness, monastic loneliness, chastity, purity, cleanliness, whereas the city or town stood for self-betrayal. The Bush almost came to act as a kind of conscience for Australians, as the city man came to yearn for an 'idealized vision', a 'lost Eden'.[16]

The greatest achievement by a *Bulletin* writer was Furphy's novel, *Such Is Life*. In a sense it is Australia's *Moby Dick,* for it was similarly neglected for thirty or forty years and discovered as a classic. 'Tom Collins' (Joseph Furphy, 1843-1912) was born at Yarra Glen, the son of poor Irish migrants, and worked as a miner and bullocky for many years, then in his brother's agricultural implement works at Shepparton. He laboured at this gloriously ambitious novel, which was completed by 1896 and published in truncated form in 1903, and almost achieved a masterpiece. 'It is a novel based on the theory of the novel,' remarks A. D. Hope; '. . . he is putting forward an entirely new theory of the relation of literature to life and announcing a revolution in the nature of prose fiction.'[17] It is a disquisition on free will, determinism and chance, about how things happen, the consequences of taking one course of action rather than another, about responsibility for actions. It is a determined attempt to state what really happens in life and attacks romancers like Kingsley, R. L. Stevenson and Kipling. It is also a descriptive analysis of Riverina society, of the new, very odd, democratic society which Furphy knew inside out. For example, there is his acute gallery of the five types of squatters. It is about the art of riding horses and the art of swapping them, the modes of spinning yarns and of telling whoppers, the varied crafts of the bushman and the formidable mnemonic power which they demand, the reticent loyalties to mate and dog, the eccentricities of bush-scholarship, the curiosities of bush-etiquette, and the firm pattern of bush-ethics.

All done by a master of irony, a child of Fielding and Sterne, soaked in Shakespeare, the Bible, and the *Encyclopaedia Britannica*. It was an extraordinary achievement for a self-educated man, dependent on the local Mechanics' Institute library and odd hours snatched at the Melbourne Public Library, in total isolation from other members of the craft, except for a lifeline to the *Bulletin* to which he contributed pars from 1889. It is the most Australian book of all. But the demands Furphy makes are too great, it is too intricate, it is full of the bog-philosophy of the self-educated man, the relentless intellectual purpose grinds many readers down. Amusing though it is, his anti-Englishness is shrill colonialism. Fundamentally, Furphy was a very angry man, who detested both the exploiting fat man and the 'deserving poor' for being exploited. He glorified the proletarian virtues:

> Without doubt, it is easier to attain gentlemanly deportment than axe-man's muscle; easier to critize an opera than to identify a beast seen casually twelve months before; easier to dress becomingly than to make a bee-line, straight as the sighting of a theodolite across strange country in foggy weather; easier to recognize the various costly vintages than to live contentedly on the smell of an oil rag.

That needed saying, but he was no philistine. *Such Is Life* is the most freakish achievement of colonial Australia.[18]

The man who published *Such Is Life* was A. G. Stephens (1865-1933), editor of the *Bulletin's* 'Red Page' from 1896 to 1906—the first important Australian literary critic. He was both stern and constructive in his criticism, and his greatest asset was his breadth of literary interests. He knew his world (especially French) literature, he introduced current trends and used them, he said, 'as a measuring rod to beat those indulging in antics around the parish pump'. But he was also an ardent patriot and a very knowledgeable barracker for the local team, knowing very well what some writers were contributing to Australians' understanding of themselves. He fused world and Australian literature as no-one else did for nearly half a century.[19]

No historian or critic has yet taken adequate notice of A. A. Phillips's bold claim about the *Bulletin* group:

> it was a strikingly original school of writing; indeed it might have been a revolutionary school, had it occurred to English writers to have learned from it—or even to have read it. For the first time for centuries, Anglo-Saxon writing had broken out of the cage of the middle-class attitude. Dickens, Hardy and Bret Harte had, it is true, written sympathetically and knowledgeably of the unpossessing; but they had written for a middle-class audience. They were the guides who conducted their middle-class audience on a Cook's Tour of the lower orders. But to Lawson and Furphy, it was the middle-classes who were the foreigners—and they the often jingoistic nationalists of the poor. They wrote of the people, for the people, and from the people. In that task almost their only predecessors later than Bunyan were Burns and Mark Twain—and neither had the full courage of his convictions.[20]

Certainly, no foreign parallels spring to mind; this does appear to be a unique case of writers of high quality from humble origins stating radical democratic attitudes to a fairly wide working-class audience. These were the early years of mass literacy anywhere, and in this regard Australia was among the world leaders. The case would be much stronger if there had been other writers of the quality of Lawson and Furphy, if the *Bulletin* writers as a whole had not come from such a wide variety of social backgrounds, and if one or two more had put forward as explicit a radical message. And if (with slight doubts about definition) we allow Lawson and Furphy to have been working-class intellectuals and writers, they had no immediate successors. Nevertheless, the case broadly stands: we have not yet recognised what a phenomenon this was, for 'poetry' to have been given to the people and for the people to have liked it.

But there wasn't enough real poetry or literature; and what 'the people' liked were the ballads. A strong popular school of writing continued well into the twentieth century but, reflecting the collapse of utopian idealism in the 90s, the writers had little of a serious nature to say. A tradition of democratic writing had been set, but it was not to renew itself, at one or two removes, for several decades. And the new writers of the early twentieth century were mediocre. One exception was (Stella) Miles Franklin (1879-1954), who at the age of sixteen wrote the promising squib, *My Brilliant Career* (1901). The major new figure was Steele Rudd (A. H. Davis, 1868-1935) who set out 'to tell faithfully all I knew of the life our family and neighbouring families had lived, and were then living on the land'.[21] *On Our Selection* was a serious and immensely popular work, but Rudd's talent for farce led him in later work to play to the gallery; Dad and Dave and the others became caricatures, were eventually further debased in radio, film and popular oral story, and became the butts of the superior city man. Throughout, the *Bulletin* school had made little impact on the inheritors of the values of English literature; for together with its vigour and life, it had a certain anti-intellectual aspect—a lack of respect for the craft of writing and of appreciation for high cultural values.[22] Unfortunately it tended to widen the gulf between the proponents of European culture and Australian writers, for the highly educated élite sheered away in distaste as Australian writing seemingly became identified with democracy, radicalism and, in the period of the Boer War, treason almost. Nevertheless, to adapt one of Arthur Phillips's images, whereas before the 90s there was no continuous stream of Australian literature, only isolated works like waterholes in a sandy creek-bed, after the *Bulletin* writers of the 90s there was at least a continuous trickle.[23]

If Australia needed a Whitman it almost gained him in the red-bearded seer and polymath and disciple of Whitman, Bernard O'Dowd (1866-1953). He was very much a product of late nineteenth century Melbourne, with all the moral earnestness of that city's intellectual tradition; but he was also an intellectualizer of the *Bulletin* ideology who reinforced the broad Lawson-Furphy outlook. Of Irish descent, he renounced Catholicism in his youth, worked his way on scholarships through the University of Melbourne, and spent most of his life as Supreme Court librarian and parliamentary draughtsman. He was a militant secularist when young and wrote the extraordinary *Lyceum Tutor* (a ritual handbook for secular Sunday schools); in the 90s and later he was engrossed in left-wing politics, was a founder and editor of *Tocsin*, and prominent in the Victorian Socialist Party. As Judith Wright puts his viewpoint:

> Australia, as the youngest of the continents and hence least trammelled by tradition, was to devote herself to the task

of creating the new society on purely rational lines. Human thought had now been freed from all traditional claims; the Darwinian theory had done away with the notion of divine sanctions and the old political tyrannies had been broken. At last it was open to man to create the just society.

Australia was 'the whole world's legatee': 'She is the scroll on which we are to write/Mythologies our own and epics new'. O'Dowd came to poetry late, in his thirties; in turning himself into a poet, he may have had some notion that he could fulfil Australia's need for a modern mythmaker. The long, portentous and didactic poem, *The Bush* (1912), was his most famous, and contained nearly all his prophecies, hopes and idealism for men to live freely and in brotherhood. The Bush symbolized his idealism: 'Faithful to dreams your spirit is creating,/Till Great Australia, born of you appears'.

Modern critics treat O'Dowd harshly. While some agree that his passion carries him far and that a true poet lurks behind his stilted language, it is commonly said that he did not learn to distinguish poetry from oratory, that his verses limp along arthritically, and that his learning is far too obtrusive. But to quote Green in his favour, he was 'a new voice . . . a strong and individual voice, often dry and monotonous, but swelling at times in passages of real beauty and power'. Brian Elliott reasonably claims him as the forerunner in using the landscape metaphysically and mystically, not just descriptively and in imagery. And he and Brennan were the first poets of serious ideas.

But O'Dowd was probably much more important as a cultural influence than as a poet. He was by no means a simple, cocksure nationalist but—in this sense a post-90s man—full of doubt about the future. Perhaps his most influential statement was *Poetry Militant*, a lecture given in 1909. Poetry for poetry's sake should be postponed to the millenium; contemporary poets were merely making crazy quilts out of pretty words. The poet's tasks were, while remaining a poet, to work usefully for the progress of the species, to make the findings of science and philosophy digestible, to help men win the battle of life, to chart the day and make it habitable, to unveil frauds, to imbue the masses with high ideals, to awaken them to a sense of the wrongs they endured or inflicted, to answer for them the real questions of the age, to promote wise rebellion and stimulate reconstruction. The true subjects of poetry were politics, religion, sex, science and social reform. 'And at no [place] was the need for the Permeator poet, the projector of ideals, the Poet Militant greater than in . . . this virgin and unhandicapped land of social experiments, embryonic democracy, and the Coming Race, Australia!' Katharine Susannah Prichard left the lecture 'too exalted and exhilarated to speak',[24] and other young Melbourne writers were also deeply impressed by the high demands of their calling.[25]

The Heidelberg painters of the late 1880s achieved a remarkable breakthrough in quality, style and range of painting.[26] The return from Europe in 1885 of Tom Roberts, bringing new theories and techniques, is usually seen as the vital precipitative event. Much of the painters' inspiration and what they had to say was clearly a reflection and product of the ferment of nationalist idealism of the day. It needs to be added that a school or movement was only possible because of a considerable growth in the number of serious practising painters, in Melbourne especially, over the previous decade. Many of them were migrants from Britain and the Continent, attracted by opportunities in the flourishing illustrated press, which for many years to come gave much greater monetary reward than painting. Julian Ashton (1851-1942), for example, was brought to Melbourne by Syme of the *Age* in 1878, but in 1883 moved to Sydney where he became a father figure of art for more than half a century. Ashton had immediately advised young Frederick McCubbin to give up academic history painting in the studio and to get out and paint the life around him. In Sydney Ashton, and others such as the French-trained A. J. Daplyn who had migrated in 1881, sketched in the weekends around the harbour, on the ocean beaches and up the Hawkesbury River. Ashton claimed that in 1882 he was the first to complete a painting in the open. In Melbourne, the Scots, John Ford Paterson and John Mather, also continued Buvelot's *plein-air* tradition by sketching in the Healesville district, along the eastern shores of Port Phillip Bay and in the Heidelberg area, sometimes in the company of young students. Most of these painters were influenced by the French Barbizon school and the English water-colourists and, as Bernard Smith puts it, 'continued to analyse the true values of colour as seen through an envelope of atmosphere. In consequence they came, despite the lowness of the tones in which they customarily painted, to a more faithful depiction of the colours of the Australian landscape than any of the painters before them.'[27]

The four major figures of the Heidelberg school, the founders of an Australian school of painting, were young radicals in revolt; in 1888 Tom Roberts and Frederick McCubbin were in their early thirties and Arthur Streeton and Charles Conder were just twenty. All of them were highly interesting individually, and had great zest for life and infectious enthusiasm which make this episode in Australian history so attractive. Tom Roberts (1856-1931) had migrated in 1869 from England with his widowed mother, became a photographer's assistant, attended classes at the Artisans' School of Design at Collingwood, then evening classes at the National Gallery, and saved enough to sail for England in 1881 to study at the Royal Academy school. When he returned in 1885, he was the best-trained artist of his generation, as his immediate paintings, *Coming South* and *Bourke Street* show—and he was in total revolt from the prevailing local aesthetic assumptions and had the persuasiveness of a great teacher. Roberts struck up again with his old mate, Frederick McCubbin (1855-1917), who managed a small family bakery and studied at the Gallery school until in 1886 he was appointed drawing master, a position he held for the rest of his life. These two and others used to walk out ten miles or more in the weekends to paint, to Templestowe, Eltham, Diamond Creek and elsewhere and back; then they made camp for a few weeks a mile north of Box Hill and really got to work. Roberts wrote of it in retrospect:

> Happy Box Hill—the barked roof of the old people, Houstens—the land sylvan as it ever was—tea-tree along the creek—young blue gums on the flat bit alongside, and on the rise, our tent. The evenings after work—the chops perfect from a fire of gum-twigs—the 'good night' of the jackies, as the soft darkness fell—then talks around the fire, the 'Prof' [McCubbin] philosophic—we forgot everything, but the peace of it.[28]

Then the summer camp at Mentone in 1886-87, where one day there was a momentous meeting: they saw a lad 'standing out on the wet rocks, painting there, and I saw that his work was full of light and air. We asked him to join us. . . .'[29] It was the nineteen-year-old Arthur Streeton (1867-1943), a lithographer's apprentice born in Geelong. Roberts visited Sydney late in 1887 or early in 1888 and met Charles Conder (1868-1909) who had arrived from England in 1884 and was working as a surveyor and lithographer. He persuaded Conder to come to Melbourne and for the next two summers the artists set up camp in an old weatherboard house at Eaglemont.

They formed a true school, teaching and learning from each other, their painting techniques and views of the world interacting. Roberts opened the door—Streeton strode through it (Clive Turnbull has remarked).[30] We may be sure that Streeton gained his blue-gold vision of Australia by looking from Eaglemont up the Yarra valley to the Warburton-Healesville range, and there began working out the problems of light and heat and space and blue distance. (Blue-gold was his vision; according to Hans Heysen, amber and lilac were the characteristic colours.) The group issued its challenge in the famous 9 x 5 Impressions exhibition of August 1889—148 paintings mostly on cigar-box lids, by Roberts, Streeton and Conder, plus a few by McCubbin, C. Douglas Richardson and two other painters. The public tended to think the works were unfinished sketches, and James Smith, the senior critic, was scathing:

> Of the 180 exhibits catalogued on this occasion four-fifths are a pain to the eye. Some of them look like faded pictures seen through several mediums of thick gauze; others suggest that a paint-pot has been accidentally upset over a panel nine inches by five; others resemble the first essays of a small boy who has just been apprenticed to a house painter; whilst not a few are as depressing as the incoherent images which float through the mind of a dyspeptic dreamer. . . .[31]

The group broke up from 1890 and went their various ways, but the memories of arcadian youth remained strong all their lives.

The degree to which the Heidelberg painters were actually Impressionists remains a matter for argument; and the question of how they became Impressionists to the extent they were is complex, for there is such a complicated interplay of direct and indirect overseas and local influences. For a start, it may safely be said that the background to Impressionism was the growing emphasis in nineteenth century painting on experiment in naturalistic portrayal of landscape, the emphasis of Constable, Corot and others on natural vision and homely familiar scenes, the found and not the invented subject; in the mid-nineteenth century Courbet and Millet strengthened the realist approach.

Roberts returned in 1885 full of the *plein-air* gospel—paint in the open and 'go to nature without any immodesty';[32] and he also brought the doctrine of the flat brush instead of the round. Roberts here was clearly influenced by Bastien-Lepage, a realist who at the time was popular in English student circles. He was certainly also influenced by Whistler; Heidelberg painters came to use a palette very like his, moreover Whistler's London exhibition of 1884 was largely of 9 x 5s. Rather too much, perhaps, has been made of Roberts's chance meeting in 1883 with two Spanish painters from Paris who were working in the Impressionist manner; for it is likely that he had several such contacts. It is still frequently held that Roberts had had no direct contact with the work of Monet, Sisley, Pissarro or Renoir, but they had exhibited in London in 1882 and 1883 and Roberts spent some weeks in Paris in 1884. Alan McCulloch goes so far as to claim that *Bourke Street* could only have been painted by someone who had seen a Monet. Roberts's overseas correspondence, after he returned, included discussions of the Impressionists. One particular local influence was the Italian painter, Girolamo Nerli, who certainly told Conder much about Impressionism; Daplyn, Conder's teacher, was also fresh from France. The most extraordinary thing about the precocious Conder, however, was that somehow he came under Whistler's distant influence, down to the Japanese touches.

So far as they went, their statement of intentions were purely Impressionistic. The slogan on the 1889 catalogue was 'When you draw, form is the important thing; but in painting the first thing to look for is the general impression of colour.' The catalogue-note ran:

> An effect is only momentary: so an impressionist tries to find his place. Two half-hours are never alike, and he who tries to paint a sunset on two successive evenings must be more or less painting from memory. So, in these works, it has been the object of the artists to render faithfully, and thus obtain first records of effects widely differing, and often of very fleeting character.

Much of the argument about whether they were really Impressionists comes down to a matter of definition. Robert Hughes gives several technical reasons why they were not: they had no theory of colour, they accepted the abrupt distinction between form and colour which Monet and his fellows rejected, they did not use the divided palette which was indispensable to Impressionist technique. Bernard Smith asserts that only the narrowest definition of Impressionism, confining the term to the Monet circle, can exclude them. Ursula Hoff makes perhaps the most useful statement:

> Though Roberts and Streeton never used the 'rainbow palette' of true Impressionism nor resorted to the broken texture of brushwork in the period under discussion, they regarded themselves as Impressionists and adopted the high tonal key, the pure colours, the direct manner of painting and the study of momentary effects advocated by the French Impressionists.[33]

The Australians living in France—John Russell and Phillips Fox—became the Australian French Impressionists. All this is a little beside the point. For while it would have been fascinating to have had a pure branch of French Impressionism in Australia, the Heidelberg painters were not trying to copy, but to adapt. As Bernard Smith says, 'It was an original attempt to apply impressionist principles to a different set of visual and social conditions.'[34] It was the culmination of a century of colonial attempts to master the visual landscape.

The 9 x 5 exhibition was a statement of rebellion by young painters declaring themselves part of an international modernist movement. From then on, the emphasis of their thinking became national. They were helped by the liberating element in Impressionism which insisted that one's *own* impression of nature was the guide. In tune with the times, Roberts, Streeton and McCubbin were developing the tremendous aspiration to grasp the country and set down a vision of as much of it as they could. (But not the sophisticated Conder, who was a dandy, an aesthete, a great womanizer, essentially a visitor to Australia and anyway incapable of national idealism, who became a close friend of Oscar Wilde and frittered away his talent on fan-painting.) Streeton was innocent, romantic, a wide-eyed optimist in his youth—Julian Ashton said of him that when he wasn't painting, he was spouting Keats and Shelley[35]—but he did have a vision of the immense and elemental in Australian scenery and a yearning to symbolize the country as a whole. The idea of the 'Sunny South' was developing. In 1891 'Smike' was writing to 'Bulldog' Roberts:

No, I'm not a bit tired of Australia. . . . I want to stay *here*, but not in Melb. If I can raise this coin I intend to go straight inland (away from all polite society), and stay there 2 or 3 years and create some things entirely new, and try and translate some of the great hidden poetry that I know is here. . . .

(And later)

I picture in my head the Murray and all the wonder and glory at its source up toward Kosciusko . . ., and the great gold plains, and all the beautiful inland Australia, and I love the thought of walking into all this and trying to expand and express it in my way. I fancy large canvases all glowing and moving in the happy light and others bright decorative and chalky and expressive of the hot trying winds and the slow immense summer. It is IMMENSE. . . . But somehow it's all out of reach. . . . I love Australia (and yet have seen so little). . . .[36]

In 1891 when he was painting *Fire's On*—symbolic of the opening-up of the country by railways—Streeton was captured by the dignity of labour and the praiseworthiness of elemental toil. But this was passing and untypical: people were only incidental in his art.

Roberts and McCubbin were very different, being intellectuals with a deeply felt national consciousness. Roberts advised his friends to leave the suburban bush and paint the national life of Australia, and himself produced a great series of historical paintings. Beginning with *Coming South*, a study in the hopes and fears of migrants, he followed with his two shearing studies, then *The Breakaway*, *Bailed Up*, the 'Big Picture' (the opening of the first Commonwealth Parliament) and others. The dignity of labour was one of his inspirations, in line with Millet's and van Gogh's noble peasants:

being in the bush and feeling the delight and fascination of the great pastoral life and work I have tried to express it. If I had been a poet . . . I should have described the scattered flocks on the sunlit plains and gum-covered ranges, the coming of spring, the gradual massing of the sheep towards that one centre, the woolshed . . . the shouts of the men, the galloping of horses and the barking of dogs as the thousands

are driven, half-seen, through the hot dust to the yards . . .
but being circumscribed by my art it was only possible . . .
to give expression to one portion of this . . . it seemed that
[in the woolshed] I had the best expression of my subject, a
subject noble enough and worthy enough if I could express
the meaning and spirit of strong masculine labour . . . and
the great human interest of the whole scene. . . .[37]

Roberts is a classic transmitter of the urban idealization of the
outback, who helped considerably (in Russel Ward's terms) to
bring about the apotheosis of the nomad tribe. He makes an
interesting parallel to the *Bulletin* writers, especially in his concentration on realism and truth to nature. Lawson comes to mind
here (and Roberts was a great craftsman too), but there are
likenesses to Paterson in the element in Roberts of myth-making,
of harking back to the past, of idealizing pastoral life and the
good old days. (Paterson was a frequent visitor to Roberts's Sydney
studio in the 90s.) Roberts knew Archibald well and was friendly
with many of the rising Labour men, especially Dr Maloney; but
he was broad in his sympathies, democratic rather than radical in
outlook. Roberts's shearers are depicted with infinite care and
attention to detail, but not without elements of ennoblement
and idealization; it is remarkable that there is no hint in his
pastoral paintings of the terrible current conflict in the industry
between labour and capital. There is a little truth in the claim
that he was a city man returning to the rural past with much
less close knowledge of the outback than the *Bulletin* writers
had; nevertheless, bushrangers were of the very recent past,
breakaways of stock still occurred, and Roberts spent much time
outback in the 90s.

McCubbin was slower to adopt Impressionist techniques, but
was probably more inspired than the others by the need to
establish a national school of painting. In 1886 he began a long
series of social history paintings with *The Lost Child,* based on
that all too frequent incident of frontier life which Kingsley and
Clarke had already used in literature and which Lawson and
Furphy were also to adopt. It was followed by *Down on his Luck,*
Bush Burial, On the Wallaby Track and, eventually, the extraordinary tryptych, *The Pioneer.* McCubbin is the painter of life
and death, of the hardships of the pioneer—'their individual
resourcefulness, the loneliness and sadness of their life, the
unostentatious heroism of their achievement'.[38] This is another

case of an urban-based glorification of the frontiersman, by one who possibly never travelled further inland than Mt Macedon. There is an element of bathos in these works, a link with Lawson in his use of sentiment and in the note of melancholy which had more in common with earlier painters than with the joyful Roberts and Streeton.

The range and variety of these painters deserves special note. McCubbin developed out of his genre and historical painting; especially after his one overseas trip in 1907, he was much influenced by the work of Turner and in the last decade of his life became very much an experimental Impressionist. Streeton, Roberts and Conder were not just landscapists (though Streeton became little more than that); they painted many beach and river scenes and, naturally in view of their background, many urban scenes, having a special interest in the lights and reflections of wet city streets. Roberts was 'equally accomplished as landscapist, portraitist and painter of "history pieces" ';[39] he was frequently irked by his role as society portrait-painter but high fees enabled him to buy time to follow his major interests. Conder was closely akin to the early Streeton, but in the last year before he left Australia forever in 1890, he was deeply involved in aestheticism and symbolism.[40] The prolific Walter Withers (1854-1914), whose reputation is steadily growing, had a wide range of subject-matter and diverse European sources of inspiration.[41]

The great contribution of the Heidelberg painters was, as Bernard Smith says, 'to produce, for the first time, a naturalistic interpretation of the Australian sunlit landscape'. They brought a 'new sense of optimism, joy, and love of the sun' in contrast to the 'conviction that Australian nature was monotonous and melancholy', and made a major statement on behalf of the school of hope and freedom against the school of exile.[42] Streeton's bold pastoral landscapes and the history-painting of Roberts and McCubbin (despite their very different approaches) reflected the new interest in the Australian past, celebrated the achievement of a century, and in the values they affirmed were akin to epic- and myth-makers of all ages. Other painters, such as G. W. Lambert, J. F. Paterson and Frank Mahony, joined them in glorifying outback life. But by the late 90s this phase was virtually ended; the mood had changed, the national outlook was no longer so optimistic or cocksure, the 'dream-time' was over. Moreover, the Heidelberg painters had won very little public approval. Their Impressionism was too revolutionary for many to be able to recognize the Australia presented to them; even the history-paintings do not seem to have been widely appreciated. A small group of patrons supported them warmly, but neither Roberts's *Bourke Street* nor Streeton's *Golden Summer* were sold when first exhibited at modest prices. The Melbourne Gallery bought its first Streeton in 1896, its first McCubbin in 1900, its first Roberts in 1920, and its first Conder in 1932! The Sydney Gallery's record was much better. Roberts, at least, had made a good income, but in the depressed 90s the market dried up almost entirely and the sale of any painting was good reason for celebration. The small conservative public interested in art at this stage sheered away in distaste from painting reflecting Australian nationalism, however moderately. Some were disturbed by Roberts's depiction of common shearers and stockmen, and implored him to seek more worthy subjects. The Heidelberg school began to be accepted as a national movement only after another twenty to thirty years. Streeton then became a national institution, but his reputation was based on his later inferior paintings rather than the glorious work of his youth. Nearly three-quarters of a century had to pass before the superior achievement, at least in range and significance, of Roberts was widely recognized.

There was no musical composition of any consequence which reflected the springtime spirit of the 80s and 90s. Lorna Stirling has remarked that the history of European culture demonstrates that music, by its nature, is a slow starter. It long remained the laggard among the Australian arts, as late as the 1940s 'rather more of a phantom than a fact'.[43] The search for a musical identity—as Roger Covell puts its, the 'desire to find means of musical expression that are both personal and international at the same time as they are unmistakably and in the best sense, provincial'[44]—was to prove extremely difficult. Most composers probably hoped to find an Australian idiom; for while music is a universal language, 'there must always surely be room in it for dialect, for distinguishing tone and inflection, for a general style of expression that points to the country of its origin'.[45] But hardly any succeeded in finding a way.

There is, however, the remarkable case of Percy Grainger (1882-1961), who perhaps is best considered at this stage. In recent years he has come to be accepted as a major figure in twentieth century music, but on the face of it he seems barely relevant. Born in Melbourne, he left Australia at the age of thirteen and after many years in Europe as a pianist and collector of folk music, settled in the United States in 1914 and is generally known as an American composer—widely known for arrangements of folk-tunes and for potboiling pieces like *Country Gardens* but also as a major, modern, highly original composer. But Grainger was a quite fanatical Australian patriot, who persisted in regarding himself as an Australian composer making an Australian contribution to music, and believed that in his most ambitious works he expressed identifiable Australian attitudes. One of his first works was *A Song of Autumn*, written at the age of seventeen, which was a setting of words by Adam Lindsay Gordon. His *Marching Song of Democracy* (1916) was dedicated to Walt Whitman (whom, like O'Dowd, he worshipped) and the preface explicitly stated an Australian relevance: he had

> felt a keen longing to play my part in the creation of music that should reflect the easy-going, happy-go-lucky, yet robust hopefulness and the undisciplined individualistic energy of the athletic out-of-door Anglo-Saxon newer nations. . . . An athletic out-of-door spirit must . . . be understood to be behind the piece from start to finish.

The note attached to his *Colonial Song* (composed between 1911 and 1914) runs in part:

> in this piece . . . I have wished to express my personal feelings about my own country (Australia) and people, and also to voice a certain kind of emotion that seems to me not untypical of native-born Colonials in general.
>
> Perhaps it is not unnatural that people living more or less lonelily in vast virgin countries and struggling against natural and climatic hardships . . . should run largely to that patiently yearning, inactive sentimental wistfulness that we find so touchingly expressed in much American art; for instance in Mark Twain's *Huckleberry Finn*, and in Stephen C. Foster's adorable songs. . . . I have also noticed curious, almost Italian-like, musical tendencies in brass band performances and ways of singing in Australia (such as a preference

for richness and intensity of tone and soulful breadth of phrasing over more subtly and sensitively varied delicacies of expression) which are also reflected here.

Grainger believed *Colonial Song* was 'Australia's first attempt to express itself nationally—however clumsily and unsatisfyingly'. Roger Covell (whose account of Grainger I have been following) believes that

> it succeeds completely in what it sets out to do: it expresses an aspect of the Australian (and not only Australian) musical consciousness of its period. . . . That Australia will have to wait until it has achieved something like musical maturity before it can contemplate *Colonial Song* without embarrassment is as much a criticism of Australia as it is of the piece.

When Grainger first returned to Australia in 1903,

> I had a feeling that most of my music (based chiefly on Bach) was too involved, unclear and monotonous to appeal to Australian ears as they then were. So I resolved to change over to a clearer, simpler, more transparent style, based on Handel or Haydn—for I have never had any ambitions to be anything but an Australian composer. So I consciously wrote in a clarified and simplified style, in the interests of suiting Australian ears, and out of this came *Molly on the Shore* etc.

In old age in the 1950s he tried to account for the differences between European conceptions of musical form and his own:

> I realize that the small fields, or broken-up geography, of such countries as Italy, Austria, Germany and England make for small conceptions of form and the wish for constant contrast. It is only natural that English and German composers should have what I would consider a 'bijou' conception of musical form, while an Australian should have a continental conception (and *such* a continent, so grandly monotonous, uneventful and unbroken-up).

And even later, he remarked that Australia, 'a leader in social experimentation, should also lead in musical go-ahead-ness'.

Grainger linked his background even to the forward-looking aspects of his work. He placed the origin of his interest in 'Free Music' to boating on Albert Park Lake at the age of six and his fascination with the sounds and movements of water lapping against the boat. Late in life, says Covell, he had 'intensely practical schemes for "elastic scoring", which allowed performances of his works by almost any conceivable combination of voices and instruments and which formed part of a democratic ideal—an Australian ideal, he would have said—in which every performer is able to feel he has something important to contribute to the whole.' On his tour of Australasia in 1933-5, he introduced a vast range of non-European music to bewildered audiences and encouraged Australian musicians to acquaint themselves with the music of Asia and the south Pacific. In the 1930s he established a museum of his musical effects at the University of Melbourne which, after thirty years' neglect, is now being used and appreciated. It may be that this man had genius—and a genius largely inspired by the virtues and potentialities of Australian civilization: a sobering thought.[46]

As a footnote we must mention Henry Tate, a minor composer and naive nationalist theorist about the possibilities of Australian music—yet critics agree he had something interesting to say. Tate was a friend of Bernard O'Dowd and others of the Melbourne group of intellectuals who developed the *Bulletin*'s cultural nationalist approach. O'Dowd wrote a patriotic Introduction to Tate's *Australian Musical Possibilities* (1924):

> Those of us whose faith it is that Australia is the matrix of a richer humanity and a kindlier as well as more enlightened civilisation than the present, here or elsewhere, will welcome Henry Tate's little volume as a new witness to that faith. . . .
>
> Already there have been scouts and forerunners—a few newspapers, many poems, *Such is Life*, those who . . . frame the politic ground-plan itself, from Lang and Vern through Higinbotham, Lilley and Lane to Higgins and others of to-day, and so on in many branches, not forgetting the obscure devotion of bird-lover, flower-gatherer, moth-collector, and totem-interpreter. All have their parts in the team-work that shall at last, if we are worthy the destiny, drag the New Jerusalem from apocalyptic dreams to a shining fulfilment in Australia. . . .

Whether you are musical or not, you cannot hear him discoursing on his favourite topic of the development of an Australian music, 'racy of the soil', and yet throbbing in unison with the great music of all the world, without feeling that Australia has a great part to play in the future of the world, that that part will be a beneficent and not a malevolent or parasitic one, and that towards the shaping of the soul that will become the real Australia a music of our own will not be the least potent of the creative wands.

Tate's main proposals, says Covell, 'related to the sounds of the bush, the natural noises of rustling bark and wind-stirred eucalypts and, in particular, to the distinctive calls of bush birds'[47]—the butcher-bird, mopoke, grey thrush, magpie and pallid cuckoo—some of them fairly to be claimed as the equals of the lark and nightingale in musical eloquence and beauty and as a possible inspiration for what in the past elsewhere has resulted in much notable music. Tate was also long before his time in realising the urgency of studying Aboriginal music. Covell notes the contrast between Grainger reaching towards an Australian music via social attitudes and Tate via the adaptation of natural sounds.

1886 is one of the crucial dates in Australian architectural history; for it was then that the Marseilles tile began to be imported in quantity.[48] Sydney and Melbourne especially were carried away. It is odd that this should have been France's greatest influence on Australia. The orange tiles were cheap, cool, waterproof and lasting; and—it was widely believed—nicely matched the newly predominant red brick walls. Wunderlich's alone imported 75 million tiles before 1914. The uniform tyranny of red brick and orange tile, stretching for countless mile on suburban mile—'Wotta lotta terracotta'—was to last for half a century and in its standardized uniformity to symbolize Australia of its period.

Partly inspired by the variety of coloured brickwork and plaster ornament which had developed during the boom 80s, a frantic search for new domestic styles culminated in the triumph by the mid-90s of the 'Queen Anne' style which dominated down to the first war. It was characterized by red brick, painted timbers and emphasis on roof-shape; madly broken-up gables and spires

displayed the new tiles to the greatest effect. Bernard Smith has
called for closer study of the phenomenon:

> The historical sources, of course, as in the case of all
> deep-rooted and vigorous styles, are many: a congeries of
> local materials and techniques, Gothic asymmetry and
> picturesqueness, the survival and transformation of the
> veranda, structural polychromy, the ideas of Pugin, Ruskin
> and Morris at work in the minds of men like Blacket,
> Wardell, Barnet, Kemp, Hunt and Sulman. Out of it all
> there emerged a house which is not quite like anything else
> in the world. . . . [It] has little in common with the English
> domestic brick architecture of the first decade of the eight-
> eenth century, and much which distinguishes it from Nes-
> field, Stevenson and Shaw's revival of it during the 1870s. . . .
> The style in question is an Australian style if ever there was
> one, and deserves its own name. My own nomination would
> be Federation style. For it was born within the context of a
> discussion about the nature of an Australian style which
> parallels the political discussion that led to the foundation
> of the Commonwealth. [It is a style] with characteristics as
> marked and definable as any domestic style within the
> tradition of western architecture. Like the Australian accent
> this style has been discussed for too long in terms of its
> derivatives. But to call it Queen Anne tells us as little about
> it as to call our accent cockney. Perhaps we have not grasped
> its originality because it has so often offended our archi-
> tectural tastes.[49]

Or, as Robin Boyd remarked, when some architects deplored the
lack of an Australian style, they were really saying there was no
existing Australian style of which they could approve.[50]

From the 80s leading architects frequently discussed the problems of developing an Australian style of architecture. In 1887,
for example, John Sulman advised seeking it

> not in Gothic, a stone style developed under the misty skies
> of northern Europe, nor in Queen Anne, a red brick style
> full of quaint conceit and petty details; but rather in the
> broad, simple treatment of Italy. . . . It will have to be
> developed, however, with a difference. We are of the English
> race, and love light and air; hence window spacing must be

larger. . . . The first step in advance must be the recognition of the verandah as a portion of the whole design, and indeed, when properly treated, as its leading feature.[51]

The usual assumption, reasonably enough, was that an Australian style would necessarily have to be largely an adaptation of, or a series of variations on, some foreign style. Keenest discussion of a possible Australian style broadly coincided with or followed shortly after the late-century period of national aspiration; and the most fruitful period of limited application was probably in the 1900-1914 period. We need to distinguish the rare aesthetic achievements of nationally-minded innovating architects, from the mass of popular construction by builders and from the normal run of minority architect-designed housing which had few aesthetic claims after the 1830s. (How should we, by the way, relate the Queen Anne or Federation style to the spirit of the period?) Superficial decoration was frequently of Australian inspiration—cast-iron often had national motifs; Queen Anne roofs frequently featured not only 'great bunches of leaves and flowers, winged dragons and other mythological beasts' but also 'gable panels and apex pieces in the form of waratahs, gum nuts and gum leaves, lyrebirds, kangaroos and kookaburras';[52] looping and swirling *art nouveau* decoration, when it came in, sometimes included Australian flora and fauna. Two major Australian building innovations, which had world-wide impact, were the cavity wall and brick veneer. And, above all, the pattern of Australian domestic living had been firmly set as a quest for a fifty-foot frontage and a backyard, a quest for privacy partly inherited from early Victorian England with its property-owning ethos and made possible by cheap land and high wages. The aesthetic (but not the social) effects were calamitous, and architecture and town-planning did not benefit.

There is only occasional slender evidence to indicate that architects were sometimes succeeding in translating their theorizing about a national style into practical achievement in domestic housing; there is almost nothing which could be interpreted as Australian about public buildings of the period. Architects do not frequently put their precise purposes on record; it is always difficult to establish or distinguish any theoretical 'national' approach from an original, innovatory use of a particular environment. Nevertheless, it happens that much of the most original and distinguished work of the period after

the turn of the century was by architects who were most concerned with the theoretical possibility of a national style. Almost
the only extreme nationalist statement on architecture on record
was by the exceptionally eccentric and inventive native-born
H. Desbrowe Annear:

> the isolation of Australia, geographically and climatically,
> will help. The importation of ideas from other countries
> cannot help us; they must be our own, born of our own
> necessities, our own climates and our own methods of
> pursuing health and happiness.[53]

He was the 'first pure Functionalist' in Australia no doubt; but
at Heidelberg shortly after 1900 he built a house on the open
plan, with careful geometric relationship to surrounding trees,
with a glass-walled sun-balcony and retractable windows with
sliding fly-screens.[54] It is not entirely fanciful to suggest that he
was well aware of the national painting associations of the area.
In 1918 he designed a house in Toorak—a white, roughcast,
entirely unornamented cube. Robin Boyd writes:

> The big allotment was a controlled wilderness of gumtrees
> not greatly appreciated by the neighbours in this conserva-
> tive retreat. It was a good building trying to be sensibly
> Australian, and it was one of the world's early pioneers of
> rational architecture. The gum trees went in the nineteen-
> thirties; the building itself went while I was writing [*The
> Australian Ugliness*].[55]

In Brisbane R. S. Dods made a sustained attempt to answer local
climatic peculiarities, while under the general influence of
American Colonial style; his exaggerated verandahs, louvred
windows and schemes of ventilation were highly original in their
time.[56] Robert S. Haddon was outstanding in the *art nouveau*
idiom, but his teaching manual, *Australian Architecture* (1908),
stressed the need to relate domestic building to Australian life.
He pointed to the 'great beauty of cast shadows' and the importance of the sun in relation to ornament, and believed that
atmosphere, sky and light should dictate forms of architecture.[57]
In 1902 Walter Butler was the first to state the principle of solar
planning, advocating northern exposures and eaves of widths
calculated to provide only summer shade.[58] But remarkably, the

sun was generally shunned in domestic housing until the 1930s; this must be almost the most extreme example of Australian tardiness in acclimatization. Just before the 1914-18 war Hardy Wilson began to campaign for appreciation of old colonial architecture as a possible basis for an indigenous tradition. But despite considerable originality, awareness of Australian peculiarity, and resistance to blind acceptance of foreign fashion in this generation, the innovators' efforts were quite inadequate to establish an autonomous tradition. The outstanding innovator came to be the American, Walter Burley Griffin (1876-1937), a product of Frank Lloyd Wright and the Chicago School. Having in 1912 won (with his wife) the competition for the design of Canberra, he arrived in 1913; but the bureaucracy finally beat him, in 1921 he dissociated himself from the planning of Canberra, and the city's final version was only a pale reflection of his plan. Griffin's work in Melbourne and Sydney in the 20s and 30s, such as Newman College, the Castlecrag estate and many small houses revealed him as by far the most original architect of the time, who sought always to build as closely as possible to Nature and who was masterly in the handling of space.[59]

The publication in 1898 of two dictionaries—E. E. Morris's *Austral English* and Joshua Lake's Australasian supplement to *Webster's International Dictionary*—was recognition of the degree to which both standard new word-usages and colloquial speech had developed. Several minor attempts to list slang vocabulary preceded and followed the two dictionaries. The *Bulletin*, by including so much reportage by its readers, had brought the colloquial into print. The growth of new words was mainly a response to a need not only to describe novel flora and fauna but different activities and functions in a new society. Vocabulary was borrowed or adapted, rather than invented, from British regional dialects and slang and from the United States and other new countries. New meanings were given to words like bush, paddock, gully, creek, station, fossick, mullock. Surprisingly few words, like barrack and larrikin, were entirely new or taken from Aboriginal usage. Some English words tended to drop out —like meadow, woods, copse, spinney, glen, inn, village. Innumerable new colloquial expressions developed, whose antiquity is impossible to measure (such as over the fence, going crook, on the outer, get stuck into, rough as guts), and a tendency to adopt truncated terms (super [phosphate], poddy) and familiar diminutives (bullocky, cocky, wharfie). Slang and the colloquial naturally developed most among the working-class and the services during the two major wars. Australian English has been a dialect of English with peculiarities of vocabulary, idiom, syntax and pronunciation. Australian literary English has developed a few words of its own, but if any consistent new idiom or syntax has been adopted it has not yet been recognized.

An Australian accent developed very quickly among the native-born; as early as the 1830s youth was being criticized for its dreadful 'snuffle'. But continued waves of migration and the influence of parents on children delayed the natural process. Barton and Deakin, for example, are believed to have been indistinguishable in accent from educated southern Englishmen. Modern scholars scorn as nonsense the stereotyped view of the Australian that 'he is supposed to speak Cockney, to speak through his nose, to speak through an immobile slit in his face, not making use of his lips, to speak in a dull monotone, to have no rhythm in his speech, flattening vowels and ignoring most consonants'.[60] They sometimes attribute disapproval of the accent mainly to the propaganda of elocutionists trying to impose a neutral artificial manner of speech. They similarly brush off, perhaps too readily, any contention that climate, physiology or national psychology are relevant. Most of them begin their study from the 'mixing bowl' assumption, that the accent derives chiefly from an amalgamation of the dozens of British dialects brought to Australia. The urban working-class from south-east England and the Irish are properly held to be the chief influences. In conditions of great population mobility with considerable intercolonial migration, a generalizing and levelling process very quickly produced remarkable uniformity of accent from one end of the continent to the other. Three styles of speech are held to have developed: a small minority Educated or Cultivated Australian, a majority General Australian (which is fairly 'broad') and a large minority Broad Australian. The limited degree of originality and variation of language and accent from the British model is perhaps symptomatic of a general Australian cultural tendency.

The nationalist surge of the 80s and 90s proved to have been a false start. Depression, drought, class war and military adventuring in South Africa ushered in the twentieth century. The achievement of federation, against the tide, brought little revival of national aspiration. In fact the period 1900-1940 marks a perpetuation of colonial dependence and a curious hesitation in development towards nationhood. For Australia was captured by jingo-imperialism and British racism; evangelical imperialism almost fulfilled the function of organized religion. Rudyard Kipling was perhaps the most important intellectual influence on two generations of native Australians; they at least displayed all his hatred of liberal intellectualism. The most notable Australian contribution to the imperial cause was possibly the Reverend W. H. Fitchett's *Deeds that Won the Empire*. When Britain, under increasing threat from rival powers, called on the colonies for support, there was an overwhelming sentimental response. Australia's exposed geographical position, the need to safeguard the White Australia policy and the growing potential threat from Japan provided strong arguments to support emotion. In the earlier twentieth century Australia's foreign policy, so far as possible, was not to have a foreign policy but to follow Britain; and Australia lagged well behind the other Dominions in accepting each advance towards equal status in the British Commonwealth.

Most Australians early in the century would have given a hesitant answer, either way, if asked whether their prime loyalty was to Australia or the Empire. The King's head and the Australian coat-of-arms on coins, and saluting of either the Union Jack or the Australian flag in state schools symbolized the double loyalty. The more conservative of the middle classes resisted further development towards nationhood; the more radical, like Deakin and Hughes, promoted Australian ambitions towards equal, responsible nationality within the Empire. The more militant of the working class and many Irish Catholics, among whom nationalist feeling had been latent but potentially strong, flared up under the stress of the events of 1916-17. After initial overall enthusiastic rallying to the flag, the war ultimately divided the country bitterly. National consciousness was greatly heightened, if only because most Australians firmly believed Australia actually became a nation at Gallipoli, and 300,000 soldiers in England and France became so aware of their national distinctiveness. The Protestant middle classes, especially, developed their sense of Australianness; a new form of right-wing nationalism (of which the *Bulletin* was a close reflection largely captured the digger tradition which had derived much from the bush ethos. The returned soldier-Country Party-farmer, who was very Australian in social attitudes and manners and yet a conservative imperialist, was an extreme example of the new confusion. For in the face of Labor-Irish Catholic-anti-conscription dissent, the Protestant conservatives thumped the imperial drum and deplored political manifestations of Australianism (such as the appointment of a native-born governor-general) even more strongly than before. Imperialist indoctrination in the schools and through the press—'the mingling of war and religion and Empire' which Graham McInnes remembered[1]—was never stronger than in the inter-war period. There was little for the older brand of nationalism to feed on. The main Australian dream had been of a society in which none would be poor and all would live in at least modest comfort, in a community free from the evils of the Old World. The twentieth century saw no improvement and possibly a decline in the standard of living, constant unemployment, little further development of the welfare state despite Australia's early reputation as the world's social laboratory, and international war and depression. The idealistic impulse from the Bush had died away, while industrialization and urbanization proceeded.

It is difficult to discern any coherent cultural development or much achievement in the first third of the century, while the population grew from $3\frac{3}{4}$ million to $6\frac{1}{2}$ million. It was a curiously disappointing period of delayed development, false starts and unfulfilled talents. Only in literature, especially poetry, were there signs of marked advance. A large proportion of the many talented young naturally sought their fortune at the heart of Empire. Few of the migrants attracted to Australia, unlike those of the mid-nineteenth century, were capable of helping to raise cultural standards. It may be that the first couple of native-born generations from the state school systems were no better educated than their migrant parents and grandparents. The educated middle class, with few exceptions, was content to import culture like other consumer goods and had minimum contact with any living creative culture. There were immense advantages in the sense of being involved, however remotely, as part of a great metropolitan culture; but one of the tragedies of being colonial is the customary fawning on the metropolis and automatic disbelief in and neglect of local endeavour. The political rulers were now philistine businessmen, farmers and trade union officials—no longer like Henry Parkes, a determined versifier, or Alfred Deakin, a playwright and literary critic, or Samuel Griffith, a translator of Dante. Australian taste in the arts was now utterly conservative and backward—the product, it seemed, of growing isolation and a wider time-lag of ideas than in the nineteenth century. However, in the 1930s and 40s, the drought was at last to break.

If Australian painting was provincial, isolated and backward in world terms during the first third of the century, it was largely because most of the best painters spent so long overseas. Conder left permanently in 1890. Roberts was away from 1903 to 1923, Streeton from 1898 to 1924 (apart from two short trips home), George Lambert from 1900 to 1921, Phillips Fox from 1901 to 1915, Max Meldrum from 1899 to 1911, and George Bell from 1904 to 1919. Two of the very best, John Russell (who helped Matisse on his way and was a close friend of Van Gogh) and Rupert Bunny, spent just on forty and fifty years respectively overseas before returning to spend their old age, with little recognition, in their native-land.[2]

They had to go. The depression of the 90s ruined the small local market. They had been taught by migrant artists who urged them to go to the founts, Paris and London, and train further in the great schools. Much more important, they simply had to see the work of the masters. They had the chance of a much better career overseas and their natural ambition was to test themselves in world competition—for what did an Australian reputation matter? But there were great dangers: it might be argued that Roberts and Streeton lost their cultural roots and did not paint nearly as well overseas. Both went through long black periods when trying to establish themselves in England and found it difficult to adapt to the European landscape; both ultimately won through to minor positions in the English art-world. Roberts was sixty-seven when he returned and though he

91

continued painting with integrity he never found his former touch. Streeton came back in his mid-fifties and mechanically ground out landscapes without a semblance of his youthful inspiration. Lambert and Meldrum profited more by their experience, but none of these painters either gained fame or substantially built on their promise. Bernard Smith sums up:

> The history of modern European art can be written, apart perhaps from a passing reference to Conder, without mentioning the men who created the Australian school of painting. Nor are they forgotten only in Europe. Their failure was most fully realized in their own country. If the Edwardian excursion brought little or nothing to European art neither did it bring back much of lasting value to Australia. . . . In refusing to be satisfied with the provincial and second-rate standards prevailing in Australia around 1900 their instincts were soundly based and their years abroad bravely asserted the fact that the world of art, at its best, is always an international community. Perhaps their failure lay in the motives which caused them to leave the country. Perhaps the European venture ceased too quickly from being part of a lifelong process of self-discovery and became, for most of them, a step on the road to success and public acclaim. In the end many of them did achieve success of a sort in the years after the First World War, but only by clinging to the image of a world that was quickly passing.[3]

Meanwhile, McCubbin, Withers and Julian Ashton held the fort. The main formal influence early in the century was imposed by Bernard Hall, who was in charge of the Melbourne Gallery school for forty years from 1895. He was there too long and probably produced more good painters in his first ten than in his last thirty years, for his teaching became rigidly orthodox. He must be forgiven much, however, for his purchase as early as 1905, of a Pissarro. Through the munificence of the wholesale druggist, Alfred Felton, Melbourne could now begin to build its great collection, although reactionary trustees again and again were to miss marvellous opportunities.[4]

It is illuminating to observe that few young artists of the 90s were attracted by the Heidelberg approach. To keep up with the latest overseas fashion was the natural aim, *art nouveau* was all the rage, the Bush was peopled with classic mythic figures by

Sydney Long and others, but perhaps the most stylish examples were the cartoons of D. H. Souter. Blamire Young was another leading influence. And out of Melbourne at the turn of the century came the charismatic Norman Lindsay (1879-1969)—the last man in Australia likely to be attracted by any nationalistic approach to art; the main influences on him were the Greek and Roman classics, Rubens and Nietzsche. In 1900 he moved permanently to Sydney to a job on the *Bulletin*. Lindsay excelled as a pen-and-ink man and etcher, and came to painting relatively late. His general cultural influence was profound and he is best considered seriously in a literary context. For the moment we shall note what the art historians have to say about him. Bernard Smith is very respectful to 'a magnificent illustrator', 'the most talented, imaginative and prolific pen draughtsman in the country':

> During the first two decades of the century Norman Lindsay became a liberating force of considerable power in Australian culture. Far more than any of his contemporaries, he helped to widen the range and deepen the curiosities and interests of Australian artists and writers. From the beginning he opposed nationalism and brought a most salutary breadth of interest in the masterpieces of European literature, art and music, to the local scene. His own art became a lifelong protest, . . . against the strict code of Christian morality. . . . he acquired a profound belief in the overwhelming importance of the artist's role in society as a creator aligned against the forces of a Philistine establishment habituated to hypocrisy, wowserism and corruption. The conception of the dedicated artist alienated from society was not familiar to Edwardian Australia; and the spectacle of its enactment in real life created . . . a series of crises with officialdom. . . .[5]

Robert Hughes, on the other hand, has issued a scathing indictment:

> Lindsay has some claim to be the most forceful personality the arts in Australia have ever seen. His energy was immense, and he scattered it across a wide field: painting, drawing, watercolour, etching; art criticism, polemics, philosophy; illustration and political cartooning; novels, occasional bursts of poetry, and writing for children. He even made

model ships and cast-concrete fauns. It seemed that wherever the Australian Renaissance was heading, a real *uomo universale* was leading it there.

Never was more fuss attached to a sprint up a blind alley.... He believed, basically, in an élite of vision: the great artist was a superman, subject to no external compulsions, spurned by the society around him but, by sheer dynamism, bending its hostile will to his own. His actions revealed Life-Force, whose main impulse and ingredient was Sex....

... But to the honest Australian burghers, this whooping adolescent was Satan incarnate. They reviled him as a pornographer, a perverter of the young and a diabolist....

... Lindsay's melon-breasted, ham-thighed Playmates are wholesome and dated. Their eroticism is depersonalized and cow-like; ... they smirk and pout and wiggle their elephantine buttocks but never become human; they are no more than the furniture of an escapist, a provincial rococo daydream. Lindsay lived in a pantomime world of cavaliers, troubadours, Greek gods, courtiers, imps, panthers and magi; his art was a costume party.

... Lindsay is the star example of a problem which is peculiar to isolated cultures like Australia's. He had no sense of history whatever but he disliked and distrusted the present. Therefore he tried to flee backwards into an illusory past whose true nature he could not and would not comprehend. He suffered, to an appalling degree, from provincialism in time as well as in space....

... Lindsay's art was a tradition-substitute [which] satisfied the widespread desire for a past, *any* past that could dispel the terrors of provincialism.[6]

The argument will long continue.

The other main source of influence was Max Meldrum (1875-1955), a Scottish migrant and a fine painter, but another whose theories of art could win such wide acceptance—he had hundreds of practising followers—only in an isolated provincial society. Lionel Lindsay called him 'the mad Mullah'; he was 'the Calvin of the middle period of Australian painting'.[7] Velasquez was his idol, but his leading belief was that art was impersonal and essentially concerned with the objective depiction of appearance, and that the artist's aim should be an exact illusion; painting was a pure science of optical analysis or photometry, everything is seen as a set of patches. Lloyd Rees, who for a time was under his influence, describes how in the early 20s in Sydney the book, *Max Meldrum: his art and views*, was read and re-read again and again—in so isolated a world it had so much authority.[8] Meldrumism became a cult; he required total conformism from his followers, none of whom approached the master in quality. Part of his strength was in being a social rebel, a pacifist throughout the first world war.

The chief development of the Heidelberg vision was through Hans Heysen (1877-1968), a South Australian of German parentage with headquarters in a largely German district of the Mt Lofty Range. He, more than anyone, made the gumtree the symbol of Australian art and led generations of Australians to see it as he saw it; it is not his fault that a host of imitators debased his vision. His drawing was excellent, his relation of figures to landscape followed the European masters, his scale was ample and heroic; but he was perhaps lacking in imagination and had almost nothing to say in social or intellectual terms. He adjusted the Streeton approach, writes Hughes, 'for deflection into an academic system'.[9] But he also moved on beyond the Flinders Ranges to pioneer painting in the desert and the Centre; through Rex Battarbee, his influence was passed to Albert Namatjira and other Aboriginal painters. The other typical landscape painters of the period were J. J. Hilder, the water-colourist, and Elioth Gruner. Both, with their lyrical approaches, were subtle students of light. In the 30s Norman Lindsay named Gruner as the greatest landscape-painter in the world.

When he found that the value of his early paintings was rising dramatically, Streeton returned home twice before the War to exhibit. Substantial private collecting and patronage of artists date from the decade before 1914. By the 20s the Heidelberg school and its successors were enthusiastically accepted by the art public and most of the critics as a great national expression in painting. The national element was played up and distorted and used as an argument for isolation from world artistic trends. The paintings of the later Streeton, Heysen and their myriad followers, of gumtrees, of sunny pastoral landscapes with winding rivers, green pastures and mountain backgrounds, or of Sydney Harbour—comfortable, pretty depictions of the landscape at its tamest, friendliest and most domesticated—suited

95

the new conservative patriotism of the post-Anzac era. They also fitted in well with an upper-class version of Australian history which was developing as the Victorian centenary (1934) and the New South Wales sesquicentenary (1938) approached. The old families were beginning to glorify their ancestors; worship of the pioneers 'who made us what we are', who began the triumphant story of enterprise and progress, who created a great new Dominion of the British Empire, was well under way. A conservative mythology of the past, which provided clichés for premiers and shire presidents, was being created (but Australian history after 1850 was rather too disturbing to be accommodated). So doctors, dentists and businessmen-collectors vied in bidding for the works of the masters who painted such noble landscapes.

Bernard Smith has some excellent passages on the creation of the reactionary art establishment of the 20s and 30s:

> Returning to Australia one by one after the Armistice the expatriates found to their surprise and joy a flushed economy and a receptive public awaiting them. For most, expatriation had meant years of struggle and disappointment, tempered by limited academic success. But the war brought them, often as official artists, in contact with the Commonwealth Government and they were welcomed back as artists who had achieved some measure of success in Europe and knew, in all things artistic, what was what. They became critics, connoisseurs, gallery directors, and advisers to the Government on art matters. Longstaff and Streeton received knighthoods. . . . Australian society still had little knowledge or understanding of the life of the artist and scant respect for his integrity. But it was now rich enough to corrupt; and it did corrupt as it yearned for culture. The expatriates became the aesthetic mentors of this economically flushed but artistically naive society, for they had earned by the fact of their expatriation the right to know.
>
> But the irony of it was that they did not know. They rejected Cézanne, and what sprang from Cézanne, almost to a man. . . .
>
> Ironically, too, the erstwhile exiles, their wander years over, became champions of the Australian tradition. The expatriates became patriots. But the new nationalism of the 'twenties and 'thirties differed markedly from the nationalism of the 'eighties and 'nineties. Then, nationalism had been closely linked with revolt and innovation. . . . But now nationalism

allied itself with reaction. The achievements of the Heidelberg School, fostered by the ageing Streeton and his ageing
friends, became a national legend. They alone had discovered
how to paint the Australian landscape. Before them came the
primitives who saw with English eyes and after them came
the decadents who saw with French eyes. . . .

. . . Let us keep Australian art healthy and sane, they said,
and not allow the madness going on in Europe to sap the
vitality of the true Australian art which we began.

The air was heavy with the arrogance and respectability of
old men. . . .[10]

J. S. MacDonald, director in turn of the N.S.W. and Victorian
Galleries from 1926 to 1940, was the most extreme Streeton-
worshipper, though untypical in his racist chauvinism. In 1931 he
wrote of Streeton's paintings:

They point to the way in which life should be lived in Australia, with the maximum of flocks and the minimum of factories. . . . If we so choose we can yet be the elect of the world,
the last of the pastoralists, the thoroughbred Aryans in all
their nobility. . . .

. . . it is the national chord that Streeton has struck that
will be of value to us. . . . For we are not only a nation but a
race, and both occupy a particular territory and spring from
a specific soil. The racial expression of others will not be ours,
nor the methods of interpreting their own country and folk.
We will be mainly contented only with our own imagery expressed in our own independent-minded sons, and of these, in
landscape, Streeton is the protagonist.[11]

Melbourne tended to be far more reactionary than Sydney in
the inter-war period. Sydney's greater tolerance was in part due to
the influence of Sydney Ure Smith, long-time president of the
Society of Artists, and of George Lambert, a flamboyant character
and a very good painter, especially as portraitist and war-artist,
who on his return in 1921 knew enough to be tolerant, saw himself as the champion of youth and was the leading spirit in the
Contemporary Group in Sydney from 1926. Ure Smith's quarterly
Art in Australia (1916-42), with its lavish colour reproductions,
was an important educative influence and medium of publicity
for Australian art. A few 'modern' painters had been working
since the period around the 1914-18 war, but were a tiny minority,

almost unknown to the public. Australian painting and public taste were to be extraordinarily backward and cut off from world trends until the mid-30s.

Literary development in the first two decades of the twentieth century was anything but spectacular, but there is some ground for Kenneth Slessor's belief that poetry in Australia began consistent growth in this period;[12] however, apart from Furphy and Henry Handel Richardson, no important prose-writers appeared. Nearly all the major writers of the period (O'Dowd is an exception) wrote as though the *Bulletin* had never existed. Indeed the leading 'serious' *Bulletin* poets at the turn of the century—Victor Daley and Roderic Quinn, who were pillars of Sydney Bohemia—wrote almost without local inspiration and are most interesting, perhaps, as pale reflections of the contemporary Irish Celtic renaissance. Nearly all their 'serious' successors in the *Bulletin* continued to work in conventional outdated styles. A. A. Phillips has detected a counter-revolution against the mob of balladists:

> The Australian poets of the 1900s turned their backs squarely on their local predecessors; they felt the insufficiency of Australian writing by contrast with the work of the great English poets, so that it seemed natural to plunge back into the English tradition, and to ignore the Australian. . . . Exasperation with the truculence of the colonial revolt, and the rawness of its poetic expression, dominated their attitude.[13]

It is true that the inherited and the indigenous streams remained unblended, but Phillips implies a deliberation which Brennan, McCrae and Neilson perhaps did not have. Certainly, they worried hardly at all, as Harpur and Kendall had done, about the dilemma of being an Australian poet.

Christopher Brennan (1870-1932) was to be the only major writer for decades to come who was a product of pure European culture and the academic world. Born in Sydney, the son of an Irish brewer, he was intended for the priesthood, but took a first-class in philosophy at the University of Sydney and went to Germany on a scholarship. He returned, eventually became a lecturer at the University in French and German literature and at the age of fifty associate-professor in German, then was dismissed in 1925. (That was not entirely a black-and-white matter: he had broken up as a man, and there was some small excuse for making inadequate allowance for genius.) He was unquestionably an intellectual giant, in descent from the classical Greek poets and from Milton, influenced by Tennyson and Yeats and above all by the French symbolists, especially Mallarmé. His best work was completed shortly after 1900; *Poems 1913* has most of it, including 'The Wanderer'. He spoke through symbols drawn from the whole history of Western man; his work 'is the first and best emergence in Australian poetry of the depth and the universality of man's struggle with himself and his destiny'.[14] He was hardly a popular poet; his audience was limited to a few hundreds in his time. As a colonial, he was almost unknown overseas; but an article in *Meanjin Quarterly* in 1971 by a famous Italian scholar reveres him as one of the two leading theorists of symbolism (the other being a Russian).[15] His was a contribution to international literature, largely irrelevant to Australian literature in the sense that local predecessors had no influence on him and he could have little influence on successors. He was alienated from Australian life of his time and from British imperialism for he was an Irish nationalist. Nevertheless, his poetry is not entirely dissociated in imagery from his Sydney and national environment. His was the most weighty intellectual and artistic statement yet to have been made by an Australian.

Hugh McCrae (1876-1958) was another poet whose work was divorced from his locale and whose imagery was almost entirely alien. Grandson of the diarist, Georgiana McCrae, and son of George Gordon, poet and dramatist, he came very much under Norman Lindsay's influence; indeed his verse is largely a superior version of Lindsay's art. *Satyrs and Sunlight* (1910) was his first and best volume—novel and exciting in its time. McCrae was a singer—joyful, sensuous, vital, vivid. His subjects were drawn from the pagan world, mythology, the Middle Ages and romantic adventure—satyrs, pirates, knights, highwaymen. In Judith Wright's view, 'Rhyming for rhyming's sake, phrase-making out of pure joy or love, broke through the nineteenth century conventions. . . . we have a poet, sometimes of extraordinary beauty and joy, sometimes of incorrigible carelessness and airiness, sometimes of brilliantly decorative imagery. . . .'[16] But McCrae did not develop, he was intellectually shallow, and had little relationship with the world. He was a superb letter-writer and pen-and-ink illustrator of his letters.[17]

Another pure singer was John Shaw Neilson (1872-1942) who

had the most unlikely background for a poet. A Wimmera selec-
tor's son with little formal education, he worked as a labourer for
most of his life, and in middle age his sight became too poor for
him to read. He owed much to the advice and literary promotion
of A. G. Stephens from 1905. A. R. Chisholm considers it 'one of
the miracles of poetry that a simple Australian bushman . . .
should often achieve, without knowing it, some of the effects
which French Symbolists achieved by years of patient thought
and by the elaboration of an extremely subtle technique.'[18] His
freshness, clarity and (highly worked) simplicity are remarkable.
He was, above all, a visionary and was relatively unconcerned with
his surroundings, though occasionally he wrote angrily about
social injustice. His reputation is growing.

'Furnley Maurice' (Frank Wilmot, 1881-1942) is not usually included among the major Australian poets, but is interesting for the
intellectual content of his work, and his experimentalism and
modernity. The son of a socialist craftsman, he grew up in Melbourne imbued with national idealism and was much influenced
in his early years by O'Dowd; he spent most of his life as a book-
seller and ultimately became manager of Melbourne University
Press. His 'To God, from the Warring Nations' (1916) is a noble
statement of the agony of mankind, of a different order from
Brennan's anti-Hun 'Chant of Doom'. 'Echoes' (1918) lamented
Australia's confused and indecisive outlook and the harmful effect
of foreign ideologies—'Speak in a voice of your own. . . . Must
your young soul be flooded with foreign despairs?' His later
Melbourne Odes (1934) reflected the depression mood. Wilmot
followed Yeats and the Irish movement closely, and was writing
and lecturing on the early Georgians, Pound (in 1917) and Eliot
as early as anyone in the country. He was concerned to extend the
range of poetry to everyday things and to reflect everyday speech-
patterns and experimented with the techniques of American realistic poets, which may partly explain the rough unfinished aspects
of his work.[19]

No major novelist was to be recognised for a quarter of a
century after publication of *Such is Life*. Two minor figures who
made a new departure were Edward Dyson and Louis Stone.
Dyson, who was well known as a balladist and short-story-writer,
produced *Fact'ry 'Ands* in 1906. As he said in his introduction, his
characters were 'a choice selection from a large circle of acquaint-
ances earning honourable if humble subsistence in jam, pickle,
lollie and biscuit factories, in tobacco factories, box factories, shirt
factories, rope works and paper mills. . . . they are true types of a

pronounced Australian class not previously exploited for the purposes of the maker of modern fiction.' The novel was humorous in purpose—perhaps patronizing—but was also a serious attempt to catch idiom and accent. Stone was more successful in observing the larrikin type in his *Jonah* (1911), a study of a Sydney 'push'.[20] This vivid novel has never quite caught on, but some critics insist it is a minor classic. Another novelist, about whom critics violently disagree, is William Hay, author of several melodramatic historical novels set in the convict period; most refuse to take him seriously.

At last we may turn to a recognized novelist of world stature in Henry Handel (Ethel F.) Richardson (1870-1946). It is an appalling fact that after Marcus Clarke she is the first intellectual or formally well educated writer (ruling out Furphy) to write a very good novel. And she is only doubtfully Australian, for she left the country permanently, apart from one brief return visit, at the age of seventeen. She had a miserable childhood; her father, the model for 'Richard Mahony', died when she was nine after years of mental decline while struggling as a doctor. Her mother became postmistress at Maldon and the girl boarded at the Presbyterian Ladies' College, then went to Leipzig to study music, and met and married J. G. Robertson who became professor of German Literature at the University of London. *Maurice Guest*, about musical life in Leipzig, love and sexual jealousy, was published in 1908 and *The Getting of Wisdom*, which was based on her schooldays, in 1910. The three volumes of *The Fortunes of Richard Mahony* appeared in 1917, 1925 and 1929. She was almost totally unknown in Australia until the storm of applause in England for the third volume of the trilogy belatedly roused interest; in an *Argus* popular poll in 1927 for the top Australian novelist, she received one vote against 393 for Marcus Clarke. She had taken some pains to conceal her identity and sex from the English public; but many people in Melbourne knew her to have been the author of *The Getting of Wisdom*. It remains almost incredible that after four novels there should have been so little interest or curiosity about who the author was. The Mahony trilogy is a great tragic drama, a study of a misfit and a failure who was at home nowhere, the best of the novels on the theme of Anglo-Australianism. Her strengths are her psychological penetration, awareness of moral problems and insight into human vulnerability; her main weaknesses, stylistic clumsiness and unevenness. Nearly all she wrote was based on her experience in childhood and youth and on meticulous historical research. Tolstoy, Flaubert and Scandinavian writers were her main guides. She owed nothing to Australian literature, but was not an English writer for she owed almost nothing to experience in England or to English writers. She was a mixed Australian and European or international writer, who wrote mostly about Australia, who regarded herself as almost entirely shaped in Australia, and who made one of the first major Australian contributions, not to English literature but to writing in English.[21]

One comparatively healthy aspect of the period was the existence of several periodicals with a literary emphasis. The best of them came from Sydney—the *Lone Hand* (1907-21), A. G. Stephens' *Bookfellow* (1899-1925, intermittently), and the *Triad* (1915-27)—in addition to the *Bulletin* and its Red Page. *Steele Rudd's Magazine* (Brisbane, 1904-26), the *Booklover* (Melbourne, 1899-1921) and *Birth* (Melbourne, 1916-22) also deserve mention. Their decline and demise in the 20s is evidence of the sour, anti-cultural tone of that miserable decade.

In 1922 D. H. Lawrence visited Australia for three months. After a brief stay in Western Australia, he lived at Thirroul on the New South Wales south coast, was entirely unnoticed by the press, and met no writers except Molly Skinner; he partly rewrote her *The Boy in the Bush* which was published under joint-authorship. In six weeks, while at Thirroul, he wrote almost all of *Kangaroo*—surely the quickest and most spontaneous of all the visitors' books. His purple descriptions of the landscape are the most vivid in writing in Australia, and his statement of the man-against-the-land theme the most extreme. The land had a 'subtle, remote, formless beauty', he was struck by the 'curious sombreness', the 'sense of oldness' of this 'weird, unawakened country'. But it was terrifying, 'biding its time with a terrible ageless watchfulness'; real men, with limitless patience and perseverance were needed to fight this hostile and unlovable land. It was a brooding Bush; 'a dark country, a sad country, underneath—like an abyss'; 'a great fascination, but also a dismal grey terror, underneath'. And yet he saw only the coastal fringe. The passing comments on Australian life were, to say the least, provocative. 'The *vacancy* of this freedom is almost terrifying'; 'They treat the country more like a woman they pick up on the streets than a bride'; Australian democracy was stifling to the creative impulse. *Kangaroo*'s wild political content, acquired from intensive reading of the *Bulletin*, was not as remote from reality as is often assumed.[22] It is indeed a remarkable book: what might it have been if he had stayed longer and gained greater knowledge and insight!

Briefly there was a literary movement in Sydney in 1923-24

around the journal, *Vision*. It was based on Norman Lindsay and Hugh McCrae, both in their fifties, and carried through by Jack Lindsay (b. 1900), Norman's disciple-son, with peripheral help from the young Kenneth Slessor. They asserted—with glorious cheek—that another Renaissance might spread from Australia, for postwar Europe was entirely exhausted and disillusioned. But they rejected Australia entirely as subject-matter for inspiration. Greek mythology was the best source of imagery for Australian and all other poets,

> for the Greeks transmitted the whole mass of emotional imagery on which every poet has since built. . . . How then is the Greek to come to life in Australia? Not of course by merely writing hymns to the Olympians . . . , but by a profound response to life, by the expression of lyric gaiety, by a passionate sensuality, by the endless search for the image of beauty, the immortal body of desire that is Aphrodite. Thus we may found a genuine Australian literature. It is a short-sighted Nationalism that can be proud only of verse about shearers and horses, and measures the reality of a work by its local references.[23]

They were also especially fond of the sixteenth and eighteenth centuries as sources. Essentially this was a movement to reinforce the campaign Norman Lindsay had long been conducting against wowserism and provincialism, to reaffirm his Nietzschean art-values of Beauty, Life and Courage, and to glorify the kind of poetry Hugh McCrae had been writing. It was an escapist and reactionary movement, not so much because it derived from Beardsley and the *Yellow Book* period of the 90s, but because the Lindsays so detested contemporary trends—Eliot, D. H. Lawrence and the Sitwells in literature, van Gogh, Picasso, Matisse and Epstein in the arts; they approved of Rupert Brooke, Flecker and de la Mare. In being so reactionary, they tended to make Australia more out-of-touch and provincial. Two modern critics are very rude. Judith Wright remarks:

> the heavy emphasis on wenching and wining, the unconvincing roistering and unreal Bohemianism, make most of the verse influenced by *Vision* an obvious cardboard fake. McCrae could write this kind of verse because it so happened that McCrae was this kind of poet; as a prescription for other writers it was laughable. . . .

What was lacking in the *Vision* creed was any kind of understanding of what was actually happening in the development of European and Western art; and, worse still, any kind of human depth of relationship, either between man and man or man and woman. . . .

The 'mateship' ingredient in Australian tradition was always and necessarily one-sided; it left out of account the whole relationship with woman. The Lindsays replaced it with an equally one-sided exaggeration of the sexual relation, but still wholly from the male point of view. Woman in the *Vision* hierarchy, and also, alas, in McCrae's own poetry, is no more than the foil to the man's physical robustness. . . .[24]

Vincent Buckley describes the creed as vitalism, pagan vitalism with a larrikin touch. Vitalism is

the view which considers the primitive forces of life, amoral and irresistible, more important than the pattern of moral and aesthetic discriminations by which the adult human being lives. [It is] anti-tragic, anti-spiritual, and ultimately anti-human. [They] scorn intellect and values. . . . Nor is it a particularly passionate poetry. It is really a poetry of bravado; all cock-crow, and little loving.[25]

Vision ceased after four issues and an anthology, *Poetry in Australia*. Norman Lindsay, rather than the *Vision* movement, had a lasting influence. It is difficult to take Lindsay seriously as either artist or writer (except for *The Magic Pudding*!). And yet he is one of the dominant influences in Australian twentieth century cultural history. He did not regard his own novels as serious works, and there is little reason for anyone else to do so, although *Redheap* and *Saturdee* about childhood in Creswick have some small quality. Artistically and politically he was reactionary, and grossly offensive in his diatribes against Christianity, his anti-Semitism and the stridency of his wartime cartoons. Yet, however crudely, he proclaimed the supreme value of art and was a revolutionary leader against the philistines, wowsers and censors. For the young Douglas Stewart, *Redheap* 'proclaimed the freedom of sex, it stood for the wildness and the mutinousness of youth . . . ; it was our Unholy Writ; it was a banned book and it was our banner of freedom'.[26] Lindsay had been a pagan materialist and Nietzschean individualist before 1917, but he was ultimately horrified by the war and became something like a neo-Platonist and, for a time, a spiritualist. *Creative Effort* (1924) was the turgid manifesto of his revised doctrine. Vincent Buckley condemns it as a 'mélange of the incoherent half-truth and the adolescent fantasy', but 'mixed up with all the prophetic nonsense, there are a couple of important emphases: the emphasis on individual vision as the informing power of any art, and the emphasis on gaiety as a quality of great art'.[27] There was probably more to Lindsay than this: in conversation rather than through his book, he may have provided for his young admirers an intellectual structure which included at least some of the key concepts of traditional European thought.[28] Above all, as a man with a remarkable charisma, and like all the Lindsays of extraordinary verbal fluency and persuasiveness, he inspired confidence and assurance. When returning a manuscript to a young writer, he displayed his gift of combining enthusiasm with acute criticism. Three of the very best Australian poets— R. D. FitzGerald, Kenneth Slessor and Douglas Stewart—revered him, and though they all grew away from him remained admiring friends. Lindsayan gusto and joy remains central to FitzGerald's poetry. Slessor, who found him a 'perpetual powerhouse of stimulation and suggestion',[29] may have held to his intellectual structure more than is commonly believed. Stewart has asserted that 'it is beyond question that the majority of Australian writers—and especially the poets—have accepted him . . . as the fountainhead of Australian culture in our time.'[30] A ridiculous statement (though made in the 40s)—a myopic provincial Sydney statement!—but Lindsay was the sort of man who inspired such homage.[31]

Jack Lindsay went to England in 1926, and assisted Jack Kirtley in founding the Fanfrolico Press to publish limited editions, mainly of classical works illustrated by Norman Lindsay. Governed by the Lindsayan ethic, it was 'a sort of anti-imperialist Australian counter invasion of British soil; an attack from the "Australian Renaissance" aimed at proving the bankruptcy and dearth and corruption of British culture'.[32] In 1928 Jack Lindsay, with P. R. Stephensen, also proclaimed the *Vision* creed through the *London Aphrodite* of which six issues were printed. Almost half the contributions were by expatriate Australians, such as W. J. Turner, poet and music critic of the *New Statesman*, but contributions were attracted from Liam O'Flaherty, the Powys brothers, Aldous Huxley and Sacheverell Sitwell; Eliot was one of the chief targets for abuse. Eric Partridge was another contemporary of Jack Lindsay and Stephensen at the University of Queensland who took up fine publishing in England and crusaded there for literary emancipation. Jack Lindsay ultimately became an interesting Marxist, has written several dozen books and has been a novelist, biographer, classicist, translator, general man of letters and critic of Australian literature, and has never returned to his homeland.

Around 1900 the theatre in Europe was breaking out if its near-moribund condition for a century or more as little other than a medium of popular entertainment. Ibsen's social problem-dramas, Shaw's moral passion and Stanislavski's productions of Chekhov and Gorki were leading influences. In Ireland W. B. Yeats, J. M. Synge and Lady Gregory launched their great movement for a native drama in the Abbey Theatre. The repertory theatre was born—that is a theatre based on the author, not the actor or actor-manager, as driving-spirit, devoted to the drama rather than popular success. In the United States by about 1920 Eugene O'Neill and others were developing at last a national school of drama. In Australia throughout the twentieth century, serious theatre—both the importation and production of quality plays and new plays and performance of Australian plays—was to depend almost entirely on the repertory movement—usually amateur, sometimes semi-professional, rarely fully professional—and not on the commercial theatre.

J. C. Williamson's had early in the century reached a near-monopolistic position. The five Tait brothers were, however, widening their operations and when Williamson died in 1913 and was succeeded by George Tallis a merger was eventually made in 1920 with J. & N. Tait. 'The Firm's' record in serious theatre was mediocre throughout. They believed in 'giving Australia the best', and indeed constantly imported the popular best. Gilbert and Sullivan and musical comedy were the profitable staple; *Chu Chin Chow, The Girl Friend, Show Boat, The Desert Song,* and *White Horse Inn* and *Maid of the Mountains* starring 'Our Glad', Gladys Moncrieff, were some of the famous shows. Nearly all the 'straight' plays were popular overseas successes. Rare examples of classical theatre were the seasons by Allan Wilkie's and Oscar Asche's Shakespearian companies in the early 20s, Gregan McMahon's performances in the 30s of Ibsen, Pirandello and Shaw, and a production of *The Cherry Orchard* by the Dolia Ribush Players—all largely local companies. In 1932 Sybil Thorndike and Lewis Casson arrived to present the *Medea, Ghosts, Saint Joan* and *Macbeth*. These classics, writes the Taits' biographer, were 'widely regarded as box office poison, but with such celebrities the season was highly successful'. Williamson once stated his guiding belief: 'People go to the theatre as a distraction, to relax after the toil of the day and temporarily forget their troubles. They do not go to be instructed, to be puzzled or bored. . . .' Nevin Tait wrote:

> We cannot overlook the fact that the Australian public is really not so keen on the higher drama. But when all is said and done, attractions of a high-class nature are few and far between and if, for example, Shakespeare was presented too frequently he would lose a lot of his appeal and so would other high forms of drama.
>
> We have to look upon J.C.W. business as one looks at a General Store . . . we have to appeal to all sides of the public with our productions and I think the Australian public will always want its musical comedies and the lighter plays, and so on—with, of course, occasional 'prestige' presentations.[33]

Vaudeville apart, almost the only Australian 'plays' ever presented had sure popular appeal, such as adaptations of *On Our Selection* and *The Sentimental Bloke*. No responsibility to help create an indigenous drama was acknowledged. However Robert Helpmann's tribute should be noted:

> When I reached London [in 1932] I had already seen most of the great stars of drama, musical comedy, opera and ballet, all of whom had visited Australia for the Taits—and when they imported a 'star', you could be sure it was a star! Not only that, the Tait brothers created their own stars—great stars, such as Gladys Moncrieff, Josie Melville, Gus Bluett, Madge Elliott and Cyril Ritchard, to mention only a few, and presented them in productions of a standard equal to anything seen in London or New York today.
>
> . . . these standards created a vast Australian theatre public. A Gladys Moncrieff first night, for instance, reached a pitch of hysteria I have seen equalled only by a ballet first night at Covent Garden, with queues of people waiting sometimes two to three days for seats in the gallery. . . .
>
> The Taits were men who not only knew theatre, but loved it, lived it, and understood it. Hard men, clever men; men who made it their business to know their public and whose lives were spent in providing that public with productions of the highest quality.[34]

And, as we shall see, the case for the Taits providing the best and raising popular standards is stronger in music, opera and ballet than in theatre proper.

In 1907 Alfred Buchanan was writing:

> the country is not kind to its own theatrical children. The actor, like the prophet, has to look for his honours abroad. His fellow-countrymen find a difficulty in recognizing him, or at least in approving him, until he has broken in upon them from over-seas. . . . However tolerated or even admired he may have been, he is expected to seek the shades of a graceful retirement the moment that Brown, of Jones's English theatre, is announced. There is not an Australian-born actor or actress who could not testify to this fact; many of them resent it, but others have come to accept it as a matter of course. . . .
>
> If the actor of purely local experience finds it hard to make a living, the task is quite beyond the capacity of the local dramatic author. . . . Where is the rising school of Australian dramatists? Where are even the faint beginnings of it? And where are the supporters of such a school? Echo answers to these questions. . . . If an audience . . . were to find itself confronted with Circular Quay and Darlinghurst, or with Collins Street and Toorak, or with the people inhabiting them, it would receive such a shock that it would not recover until it had got outside the theatre door—and possibly not then. It would feel at first amazed, and then insulted. The recognized understanding is, that nothing worth looking at in the theatrical sense, and nothing worthy of presentation to an enlightened public, can by any chance take place unless it takes place in England, or on the continent of Europe, or in America, or in Japan.[35]

In 1908 Leon Brodzky (Spenser Brodney) wrote in the *Lone Hand*:

> Many of us are almost in despair when we see how little relation the theatre in Australia has to the national life of the country. There is no Australian dramatist earning his livelihood by writing for the Australian stage. No one, for that matter, can name any Australian play that has ever had any pretension to being considered seriously as drama. . . . We must begin by making up our minds that nothing can be done through the business men who own and control our theatres.

Their business is to make money by importing plays. Often, too, they import the players and the scenery. . . . These theatre managers are not concerned with art, or national aspirations, or local talent, though, of course, they all pretend to be intensely patriotic. Let us ignore them.

Brodzky had seen *Riders to the Sea* and other plays at the Abbey and had talked to Yeats and Synge:

When they set out in Ireland to establish a national theatre, they were faced with exactly the same seemingly hopeless struggle. The theatres all belonged to business men who imported theatrical entertainments from London for the amusement of the Irish people. But a little band of writers and players gathered together, determined to put Irish life on the stage. . . . 'And that', said Yeats, 'is what you must do in Australia'. Therefore, the first rule of the Australian playwright of this new and yet unfounded school is—No imitation of Shoreditch melodrama or Parisian farce, no rehash of cloak and sword plays, no aping Pinero or Jones or Bernard Shaw. . . . Allowing of course for many differences, we may safely say that Australia and Ireland have this much in common—that in both countries there is a distinct national sentiment which is not English and which is even opposed to some English ideas.[36]

Brodzky's call was premature, but may not have been unrelated to the promising development of the repertory movement. Brodzky had himself founded in 1904 an Australian Theatre Society (later the Playgoers' Club) which had frequent readings. In 1908 the still surviving Adelaide Repertory Theatre was formed; they began by playing Shaw and Yeats, and in future years frequently produced Australian plays. In 1909 and later in Melbourne William Moore organised occasional Australian Drama Nights.

The leading figure for thirty years in the repertory movement was Gregan McMahon (1874-1941), an Arts graduate of the University of Sydney and a fine character-actor, who in June 1911 launched an amateur repertory company at his own risk. With strong support from R. R. Garran, Archibald Strong and others, a Melbourne Repertory Theatre Club of subscribers, which retained a membership of at least 400, was formed to finance him. McMahon regularly produced Shaw's and Galsworthy's plays, as soon as possible after the first London productions; his friendship with Shaw brought about his world premiere of *The Millionairess* in 1936. McMahon was keen to use Australian plays, if he could find them; in 1911 four short Australian plays on a single bill for two nights attracted overflow audiences and Louis Esson's *Dead Timber* was well received. In the first six years of his company in Melbourne, McMahon performed thirteen Australian plays (although mostly one-act plays) out of a total of about seventy. He was a fine director and organizer with a gift for finding money-spinning potboilers to eke out resources. He closed down in Melbourne in 1917, re-formed in Sydney with the Taits' help in the early 20s, and in 1929 returned to Melbourne for another decade, but in this period refused to produce Australian plays. Coral Browne, who left Australia in 1934, was his most famous product.[37]

Louis Esson (1879-1943) devoted most of his later life to crusading for a national theatre. His story is also interesting because he was so influenced by Yeats; this is perhaps a unique example (other than Lawrence's) of a major modern European writer directly influencing Australia. Esson grew up in Melbourne in artistic circles, became a literary journalist, and by 1910 had written several plays of which some had been performed. He went overseas briefly about 1911 and visited the Abbey Theatre. 'You ought to have plenty of material for drama in Australia,' Synge said to him. 'All those outback stations with shepherds going mad in lonely huts.'[38] Almost the first thing Yeats said was, 'Keep within your own borders. The Greeks kept within their own borders and they were the greatest artists the world has ever known.' At the time Esson was disgusted with Australia:

> Australia was too young a country—it had no culture—there were no castles or abbeys, no folk-songs—there was no Bloomsbury or Montmartre or Latin Quarter of Paris, with its exciting Bohemian life—no one was interested in art or literature—it was crude, materialistic, Philistine; but Yeats was an extraordinarily eloquent speaker and in my inner soul I felt that he was right. To my objection that we had no traditions, he made the reply that it was no disadvantage that we had no conventionally romantic past to draw on, and that it should be our aim to conquer the outlying provinces and bring them within the kingdom of Art. . . .
>
> What he reckoned we required was a national theatre, like the Abbey. . . . Begin by little one-act plays in prose; verse

afterwards, if you are a poet, and long plays when you can construct. Write country comedies, added Yeats. Such comedies build up a country. . . .[39]

Esson was excited, but too pessimistic to take action when he returned home. He went to the United States in 1916 and saw something of the Washington Square Players, but not the more significant Provincetown Players. In 1919 he and Vance Palmer convinced each other that they must attempt to found a national theatre. In 1920 Esson visited Yeats at Oxford and wrote excitedly to Palmer to tell him how kindly and constructively Yeats had criticized his plays, and also:

> Plays on really national themes, he said, . . . help to *build a nation* in the spiritual sense; while the other type of play, so-called intellectual drama, abstract and cosmopolitan—Galsworthy, Bennett, etc. . . . will 'shatter a nation'. That is what our scholars fail to realise. Their arguments look good on the surface, rather difficult to meet sometimes, though they are quite unsound. We are on the side of life, and they ('they' means too many people in Melbourne) are on the side of death and desolation. . . .
>
> He thought we ought to get the theatre going, no matter how small. A good 50 enthusiasts are better than 500 indifferents. . . .
>
> Yeats said they had to kill the pompous literary humbugs for a start. Their idiom was objected to as not being English; they retorted by showing that the professors couldn't write at all. It is really the same battle; it always is.
>
> I wish I could give you the faintest suggestion of his intellectual power. . . .[40]

Esson returned in 1921 and began planning with Palmer and Stewart Macky, a medico who had been running an amateur theatrical company. In their view the commercial theatre was parasitic with no connection with the life of the country. The repertory movement was little better, producing higher types of plays in a more amateurish way, but again with grotesque lack of contact with the life around them; one producer had even refused an Australian play because he had no actor who could play the part of a swagman. The answer, they believed, was half a dozen dramatists working in their own theatre.

The Pioneer Players performed one night a week for several months in both 1922 and 1923. The plays were by Esson, Palmer and Macky—Macky's was about convicts and many in the audience found the subject quite improper—and programmes of one-act plays followed. In 1923 new plays simply were not forthcoming and they had to eke out the season with one-acters. The venture, which was revived briefly in 1926, was at most a half-success. The main weakness, probably, was in the actors, who were amateurs or former professionals, not young enough or dedicated enough, not working towards a professional career. The movement was badly organized and lacked publicity. Nobody other than the three leaders wrote a good full-length play. The plays on the whole were of fair quality, but too much of a type—in fact of *Bulletin* descent. Subject-matter included Eureka, convicts, a conflict between squatters, a prospector striking it rich, Indian hawkers, drovers; one was set on a Gippsland selection, another in the Northern Territory, another was about criminals in the Melbourne slums. H. G. Kippax has some interesting reflections on the clash between 'apathetic London-oriented city audiences' and 'an artistically unconvincing, naturalistic bush drama'. The Melbourne bourgeois theatre-going public—bankers, woolbuyers, wheat-traders, importers, exporters, retailers

> scorned a nationalistic culture derived from the bush and its legend [and] was in no mood for either the old melodramas, with their reminders of convicts and bushrangers and an unsavoury past, or for the new bush realism. The only bush plays which succeeded . . . were *On Our Selection* and its successors, travesties of outback life.[41]

Moreover, the Abbey Theatre approach was inherently unsuited to epic outback themes; the Australian playwrights on the whole succeeded only in illustrating and not dramatizing the outback:

> All drama derives from conflict: the Australian realist drama had to project an antagonist which was not human—the country and its climate. Realistic drama makes much of scene: but what stage could hold the Australian bush and plains? In the event, playwrights avoided the problem. They mirrored the hardness of the land in the hardness of characters dominated by the land; they peopled their plays with men who were brutes or virtuous boobies and with women who were drab Griseldas or neurotics. They dramatized the

violence of the land by substituting human violence. . . . Yet their Irish models had no difficulty in evoking a countryside. They did it by the use of language. The Australian realists rejected language and its resources.[42]

Esson himself was a playwright of considerable potential. His plays are mostly tragedies; and the one-act plays are better than the full length. *The Drovers* is almost unanimously highly praised; H. M. Green says of it:

> The full tragedy of the situation is drawn out, but it is not so much stated as implied: nothing is overdrawn, no word is wasted and every word is in its place; the play is like a little etching executed with power. It is a classic in more senses than one: it is constructed on classic lines and there is a classic feeling about it; it is a classic of Australian outback life and in Australian literature. But more particularly it is a classic of the Australian nineties.[43]

The Time Is Not Yet Ripe, an early political comedy after Shaw, has also lasted well. But what chance did Esson have of realising his talent? As his wife reasonably remarked, 'To try to be a dramatist, at a time when there was no theatre, no national consciousness which demanded the expression of its own life and problems on the stage, no tradition, was indeed a formidable task.'[44]

Briefly, in the early 30s, Carrie Tennant's Community Playhouse in Sydney was conducted as an authors' theatre. The theatrical situation remained essentially the same until the 50s: a popular commercial theatre with no serious Australian content, and repertory companies struggling to keep true theatre alive and to present an occasional Australian play—notably Doris Fitton (whom McMahon trained) in the Independent Theatre in Sydney. Barbara Sisley's Brisbane Repertory Theatre Society was founded in 1925 and was followed in 1936 by Rhoda Felgate's Twelfth Night Theatre and the Brisbane Arts Theatre; all three survive still. Olive Wilton's annual productions led to the foundation of the Hobart Repertory in 1927. Allan Wilkie's Shakespearian company from 1920 played 1200 performances before going under in 1926; J. Beresford Fowler formed another Shakespearian company, and the Russian migrant, Dolia Ribush, was a stimulating influence in his few Melbourne productions of the late 30s and early 40s.[45] The visiting actor, Seymour Hicks, remarked in 1925:

The country is probably chock full of talent but . . . the Australian proper doesn't get a chance. The managers here seem afraid to encourage their own people. They prefer to pay expensive fares and inflated salaries to, in most cases, very second-rate English and American artistes.[46]

Another visitor, Arnold Haskell, similarly noticed in 1940 that 'The theatre as a serious art is almost exclusively in the hands of the various amateur repertory societies', of which there were about 300; some of them reached an 'extraordinarily high standard'.

There is a fierce determination, especially in university circles, that the theatre shall live. . . .
There is a fortune and honour awaiting the man who can [form] a truly Australian theatre. It will need courage and skilful propaganda. . . . But it can be done; the talent and the audience exist. . . . Once again apathy and the great national inferiority complex are working havoc with something essentially healthy though neglected.

With regard to films, he was amazed by a country which was content to 'import entertainment by the mile in tin cans and to export nothing'.[47]

At the more popular cultural level, in some forms of the arts which did not demand much sophistication, many Australians were achieving self-expression and enjoying the shock of self-recognition. In contrast, down to say 1930, the 'high' cultural achievement of writers and painters was modest, and in drama and musical composition it was negligible; while the audiences attracted had been very small.

The audience for popular writing remained strong. The old balladists captured another generation and new practitioners kept the form alive. 'John O'Brien' (the Reverend Father P. J. Hartigan) became a major cultural figure among Irish-Australian Catholics; his *Around the Boree Log* (1921) reached its 27th edition in 1952. C. J. Dennis (1876-1938) was, however, the new popular phenomenon. His first volume, *Backblock Ballads* (1913) was standard balladry except for some emphasis on farmers and a group of verses about larrikins. But when he strung a new series of larrikin poems together in *The Songs of a Sentimental Bloke* (1915), the volume sold 67,000 copies in the first year. Dennis had a dexterous lyrical talent and the gift of humour, but he had little direct knowledge of the larrikin, attributed to him a dialect which was far from accurate, and sentimentalised him for mass appreciation. He also had a knack of expressing the new patriotism based on the exploits of the Digger. In his next volume the larrikin, Ginger Mick, is a hero at Gallipoli and is killed; then Digger Smith becomes a returned soldier settler. In the 20s Dennis was widely regarded as being the nation's poet laureate, and when he died the Prime Minister described him as 'the Robert Burns of Australia'.[48]

In the 20s several writers made a fair living by writing frankly low-level stuff pitched to the widest possible audience. The New South Wales Bookstall Company for many years succeeded as paperback publishers. The Australian Authors Publishing Company announced it was 'in business to make a market for the work of Australian writers [and would] give its patrons cheerful reading-books that tell that life is worthwhile'. Some of the popular novelists were J. H. M. Abbott (convict stories), Roy Bridges (early Tasmania, convicts and bushrangers), Dale Collins (sea-stories), Jack McLaren (adventure), F. J. Thwaites (Pacific Island romances), and J. M. Walsh and Arthur Upfield (detective). In the first quarter of the century Nat Gould's racing-stories were the most popular novels of all. Another established genre was children's novels; Mary Grant Bruce, Ethel M. Turner and others were highly popular. In the 30s a new school developed of popular writers on the outback and Australian history; Ion Idriess, Frank Clune, William Hatfield and others established a lasting vogue. Some of these works, worthy successors of Mrs Aeneas Gunn's *We of the Never Never* (1908) and C. E. W. Bean's *On the Wool Track* (1910), like Jack McLaren's *My Crowded Solitude* (1926) or Francis Ratcliffe's *Flying Fox and Drifting Sand* (1948), deserve serious attention as literature. The landscape writers built on the traditional folklore element. Flora Eldershaw has written of them:

> together they give a romantic vision of a world with which many men secretly or openly want to identify themselves, the unique Australian world that is the possession and kingdom of our imagination. . . . They are wonder books, bringing to the reader the marvels and curiosities of a very old country . . . ; the riddle of the dark races and their customs that are often vestiges of something forgotten long ago; the skills of the bushman born of sheer necessity, the folklore and magics that grow up in the void; old wives' tales on a grand and perturbing scale. Another aspect of their appeal is that they

usually have homeliness to recommend them, familiar incidents, oft-repeated family jokes. . . . They are about *us*, even if we are townsmen, knowing no more of Australia than the face of the city in which we live.[49]

The black-and-white cartoonist also had a huge popular audience, and in the period roughly 1890-1940 the 'Australian school' was internationally famous. Nicholas Chevalier and Tom Carrington had been the pioneers in Melbourne *Punch*. But the tradition of high quality drawing combined with irreverent and sardonic wit and the brief caption was established on the *Bulletin* in the 80s by Livingstone Hopkins ('Hop'), an American who remained for more than forty years, and Phil May, an English visitor. The *Bulletin* soon recruited many more—D. H. Souter, Frank Mahony, George Lambert, Alf Vincent and Norman Lindsay who, from his arrival in 1900, was given a full weekly page. Will Dyson (1879-1938) is commonly considered the greatest of them all; when in 1910 he began work on the *Daily Herald* in London where he stayed until 1925, he made a sensational impact by drawing his Worker as young and handsome instead of downtrodden, and Capital and Power as 'Fat', a bully. David Low (1891-1963), a New Zealander who worked on the *Bulletin* from 1911 to 1919, made his fame through the *Billy Book*, his drawings of W. M. Hughes, before going on to a remarkable English career. The foundation of *Smith's Weekly* in 1919 boosted the medium; *Smith's* appealed even more directly to the returned soldier and the workingman than did the *Bulletin*. The cartoonists and their attitudes provide perhaps the best evidence of the traditional values bound up in Russel Ward's 'Australian Legend' and of its modification over the years, and they also provide a storehouse of examples of *Bulletin* and digger-type attitudes. The inter-war period was probably the greatest period of the cartoonists for opportunity and realized talent. Some of the leading practitioners were Stan Cross, who perhaps had the broadest impact; Percy Leason with his 'Wiregrass' series; Jim Bancks, whose 'Ginger Meggs' with its 'You Can't Win' theme won world-wide syndication; and Alex Gurney with his 'Stiffy and Mo', 'Ben Bowyang' and 'Bluey and Curley' strips, the most popular of all. There were many other artists of talent, but however wry and laconic their statements, they had only limited opportunity to develop high sophistication because of the popular nature of the journals to which they were confined.[50]

In the vaudeville theatre, at 'The Tiv' and elsewhere, a series of comedians like 'Mo' (Roy Rene) and George Wallace developed a patter full of local idiom in sketches based on the local scene. In the great age of radio, roughly 1930 to 1960, the local soap-opera serial was highly popular and on the whole was preferred to imports. But possibly the outstanding case of popular appreciation was film; for until the mid-20s Australian cinema-goers used to enjoy a large minority of Australian productions among the films they saw. (This is a popular cultural form, if ever there was one, for before the 30s, hardly anyone regarded film as an art-form, and by the late 20s most of the urban population was 'going to the flicks' weekly.) Film arrived in Australia in August 1896, eight or nine months after the first screenings in London and Paris. An American magician named Hertz showed the first motion pictures in the Melbourne Opera House as part of a vaudeville show. Several shorts, amounting to twenty minutes, showed a London street-scene, a seascape, a race-meeting and a scene from a play. By November five shows were running, and in that month the first Australian film was made, appropriately of the Melbourne Cup, by a Frenchman, Sestier; it was mainly of the Governor and other notabilities parading, for the camera was too slow to catch the race itself. In 1896 Melbourne journalists, having seen their first films, were anticipating sound movies and television. The first important development, oddly, came from the Salvation Army for whom Joseph Perry made 50,000 feet by 1900, culminating in *Soldiers of the Cross* (mixed slides and films)—almost the first long film, almost the first religious film, almost the first propaganda film, made anywhere. For many years, as elsewhere, the emphasis was on newsreel and short documentary material. *The Story of the Kelly Gang* (1906), written, directed and largely acted by the Tait family, was sensationally popular. It was the first Australian film to run for more than an hour (100 minutes) and among the first long films made anywhere. It was followed by scores more in the following decade—*Robbery Under Arms* (1907), *Eureka Stockade* (1907), *His Natural Life* (1908) and others which often were adaptations of successful stage-plays.

In scale of production the industry was among the world's leaders. Australia produced long feature-films very early, the audience for this drama of the masses developed early and in very large numbers by world standards, and the photography was outstanding (and has remained so). The films were made by businessmen, as theatrical entrepreneurs out to make money; they would have been amazed to know they were making world cinema history. The films were shot in the open much more than was common elsewhere. Costs were so slight that the local market alone could

117

E

return a handsome profit. There was immense public appreciation, of outback melodrama especially. The outstanding film-maker was Raymond Longford, whose *Sentimental Bloke* (1919) was probably his finest achievement; thirty years later, Longford was a tally clerk on the wharves—the sort of thing which has happened to talented artists in Australia more frequently than is pleasant to recall.[51]

The turning-point came about 1923. By then American interests had captured distribution outlets and local production quickly declined; moreover, American films were more technically advanced and sophisticated. Before a royal commission of incompetent parliamentarians in 1927-8, the Australian representatives of the distributing companies and managers of their 'tied' houses asserted vehemently that Australian films were of poor quality and unpopular—in terms similar to 'arguments' used against 'Australian content' by commercial television interests forty years later. The commission dodged the issue of protection and almost killed the Australian film industry by only introducing a quota of films made in the Empire. The advent of 'sound' increased the difficulties of local enterprise but from 1932 to 1940 K. G. Hall and Cinesound made seventeen popular and profitable films. Hall was a 'showbiz' man, interested in entertainment not art. Slapstick and melodrama were his staple, but his films reflect many of the *Bulletin* values and some feeling for the bush came through —and they are sociologically fascinating, not least in the combination of sentimental Australian patriotism and imperial loyalty. Charles Chauvel, a stauncher Australian patriot, was the most interesting film-maker, but he could manage only three in the decade. His films were 'a mixture of junk and genius', it has been remarked.[52] In the following quarter-century, Australian films could be numbered on the fingers of three or four hands.

In all these areas, there is ample evidence that Australians wanted to see themselves portrayed, a demand which was largely lacking at the higher levels of cultural endeavour.

LITERATURE AND THE
NATIONAL PROBLEM

Until the 1914-18 war and after, we have already noted, writing of high quality had been rare, and serious writers were isolated from each other, lacked an audience, and hardly ever received informed criticism. In the mid- to late 20s, however, there was a remarkable breakthrough and in the following fifteen years a dozen interesting novelists appeared. Only two or three of them, perhaps, have claims to high distinction, but all were of considerable stature—especially in terms of what had gone before—and the collective achievement was impressive. In contrast, with the great exceptions of Kenneth Slessor and R. D. FitzGerald, no new poets stood out until the 40s. Critics would have to agree that relatively half a dozen times as many good novels were written between 1925 and 1940 as between 1900 and 1925. (My own rough count of worthwhile novels in the two periods is fifty-six to thirteen.) It was almost as though the Balfour definition of Dominion status at the Imperial conference of 1926 had given Australian novelists the green light. When two or three good novels appeared close on each other's heels, and the *Bulletin* in 1928 organised a novel-competition with generous prizes (which attracted 524 entries), 'it seemed to most writers as if a door had been suddenly opened'.[1]

Vance Palmer (1885-1959), the son of a teacher, was overall the most remarkable writer of his generation—overall, for his range was so wide: short-story writer, novelist, publicist, spokesman for the arts, critic, historian, broadcaster, minor poet and dramatist. He played a crucial inspirational role in his generation: 'We broke through the scrub,' wrote Flora Eldershaw, 'our first books under our arms, and there was Vance Palmer ahead of us.'[2] He was a professional, devoted to serious literature, and to this end always had to live very modestly; indeed his professionalism was for a long time only made possible by the earnings of his distinguished wife, Nettie, as a critic. The most civilized and least parochial of men, a man of letters of the broadest culture (who in his youth made an unsuccessful pilgrimage to visit Tolstoy), the spokesman for liberal humanism, he combined the role of intellectual and leading inheritor of the Lawson-Furphy tradition. His claims for distinction are mainly in his short stories, but he wrote a dozen novels of which *The Passage* (1930) and the *Golconda* trilogy (1948-59) are probably the best. The sheer range of his fiction—the outback, the saga of a mercantile family, the man-of-the-people-Labor-premier, fishermen, and much more—gives it claims to consideration as a whole Human Comedy. But despite general agreement on his craftsmanship, the ability of his character portrayal and the maturity of his social observation, it is often said that his work had a 'bias towards the negative', sheered away from intense feeling, lacked vitality. A. D. Hope for one, however, believes that critics frequently overlook his vision, the poetic basis of his realism.[3]

Katharine Susannah Prichard (1884-1969) was probably the only other serious professional writer of the period, in the sense that she devoted nearly all her working life to the craft. The daughter of a journalist, she was at first a teacher and then for many years a pioneer woman freelance journalist, before launching out on her thirteen novels. *Working Bullocks* (1926), set in the timber country of south-west Western Australia, is much more than the landmark it was in its time; it was followed by *Coonardoo*, the first important treatment of the Aborigine in fiction. Moreover, in 1927 she wrote the anti-racist play, *Brumby Innes*, which was not performed until 1972 when it was widely acclaimed. She claimed to be an apostle of Lawson's values and her first resolution, she said, was to see and know Australia; this element is always intrusive in her work, but on the other hand she was very widely-read and knew well what Freud and D. H. Lawrence had to say. She was always a novelist of social protest and in the 30s became a rather rigid communist. Her Western Australian goldfields trilogy, beginning with *The Roaring Nineties* (1946), is a treasury, a classic view (though only one interpretation) of the Australian working-class tradition.

Frank Dalby Davison (1893-1970), son of a printer who for many years edited the journal of the Australian Natives Association, was a highly independent and original man and embodied in his life and character most of 'the Australian tradition' without its narrowness. He was never a professional writer in the sense Palmer and Prichard were: he knocked about in the United States in his youth, was a soldier, a farmer for many years early and late in life, and a journalist. During the depression he hawked his first book from door to door. It is doubtful whether he is best known for his animal stories, *Man-Shy* (1933) and *Dusty* (1946), loved by children but so much more than children's stories; or for his superbly written paean of praise for the horses in the Light Horse in Palestine, *The Wells of Beersheba* (1933); or for the vast novel on the varieties of sexual experience on which he spent most of the last twenty-five years of his life, *The White Thorntree* (1968). But he should be best known for his short stories, largely about farming life, notably 'The Road to Yesterday', which rank high in the canon of Australian writing.[4]

Eleanor Dark (b. 1901), daughter of the writer Dowell O'Reilly, published eight novels between 1932 and 1948, but little since. From the start she showed herself to be well schooled in modern fiction technique; moreover, novels like *Prelude to Christopher*, *Return to Coolamai* and *Waterway* were in the mainstream of contemporary English fiction in their concern with the psychology of personal conflicts. Mrs Dark then switched to her famous trilogy beginning with *The Timeless Land* (1941), reconstructing the foundation years of New South Wales with historical accuracy and insight. During the war years, she interrupted the trilogy with *The Little Company*, among the first significant novels of ideas in Australian writing.

Xavier Herbert (b. 1901) has been a pharmacist, journalist, prospector, stockman, aviator and a dozen other things. His *Capricornia* (1938), set in the Northern Territory, teems with characters and action and is inspired by blazing indignation against the treatment of the Aborigine. It broke new ground in its combination of passion and wild comedy, together with elements of allegory. But it was also traditional in its treatment of Nature as brooding malign Fate. *Capricornia* has strong claims as the outstanding novel of this period—of any period, some critics would say. Herbert's other important novel is *Soldiers' Women* (1961).

Christina Stead (b. 1902) is perhaps a more distinguished novelist than any of the above, but she is an expatriate and little of her work is set in Australia. Daughter of a naturalist, she was a graduate of Sydney Teachers' College, and left for Europe at the age of twenty-five. Her first novel, *Seven Poor Men of Sydney*, was written between 1928 and 1932 but not published until 1934. It was a highly unusual departure from Australian writing of its time in that it rejected conventional plot; the poetic style showed immense promise. *For Love Alone* was her only other (partly) Australian novel. An admirer of her masterpiece, *The Man Who Loved Children*, and half a dozen other novels might reasonably assert that no other Australian-born novelist is clearly her superior.[5]

Remarkably little literature had sprung from experience of the
1914-18 war; potential novelists seemingly preferred to suppress
and try to forget rather than write it out of the system. One exception was Leonard Mann (b. 1895), whose admirable *Flesh in
Armour* appeared in 1932. Mann, who is also a poet of stature,
wrote several other novels which had a wide variety of settings.
His *Murder in Sydney* and *The Go-Getter* demonstrate, together
with works by Dark, Palmer, Stead and others, that novels of city
life were by no means as rare at this time as is often assumed. A
characteristic novel-form of the period, however, was the pastoral
pioneering saga, with fire, flood and drought inevitably part of
the background. Miles Franklin in *All that Swagger* (1936) produced perhaps the best of the genre. It celebrates the Monaro
and pastoral life in the saddle over several generations; the chival-
rous Danny Delacey is one of the memorable characters of Australian fiction. Under her closely guarded pseudonym, 'Brent of
Bin Bin', Franklin wrote another five pastoral novels.[6] In contrast,
Brian Penton in *Landtakers* and *Inheritors* put forward a brutal
interpretation of pastoral life in nineteenth century Queensland.
A major historical novel of a different type was a mercantile saga,
A House is Built (1929) by M. Barnard Eldershaw. The unusual
literary partnership of Flora Eldershaw (1897-1956) and Marjorie
Barnard (b. 1897) produced several more novels. *Tomorrow and
Tomorrow* (1947) is a fanciful tale of great interest, which moved
from the depression and war years to revolution, international
intervention, and on some 400 years. The social documentary
approach was developed by Kylie Tennant (b. 1912) in six graphic,
humane and highly entertaining novels, of which *Tiburon* was
the first, between 1935 and 1946.[7]

The remarkable growth in the late 20s and 30s of novelists of
at least the second rank and the development in range of subject-
matter and of style are very clear. Harry Heseltine has written
suggestively:

> In the perspective of history, the great achievement of the
> Australian novelists of Between-the-Wars will be seen to have
> converted the events and experiences of the previous hundred
> or so years into an image wherein the rest of the nation could
> find reflected its own identity. The writers of the nineties had
> been immediately and practically concerned with the con-
> ditions of Australian life; their visions were located, if any-
> where, in the future. The novelists of the twenties and thirties

were concerned to transmute that earlier practicality into an imaginative vision of the country's past and present.[8]

We might go further to argue that in a period when there were still few Australian historians and almost no political scientists or sociologists, and when newspaper comment was of an abysmal quality, these able novelists were almost alone in attempting to define, analyse and comment on the nature of Australian society. At the very least, the novels of the 30s, in the comparative absence of normal sources, provide valuable historical evidence for what Australia was like. That some novelists were too preoccupied with trying to make sense of Australia and fell too often into a documentary, to the detriment of a universal approach, is understandable; but the charge is often made too sweepingly, and intense preoccupation with the local scene was not necessarily incompatible with universalism. Moreover, Australian novelists of this period were part of a world-wide trend—the final triumph of realism over romance. In their generally radical approach and scepticism about the foundations of bourgeois society, they reinforced Australian literature's subversive trend. Yet, surprisingly, hardly any novels of social protest were produced during the depression; most of the 'depression novels' were written many years later.

Another feature of the period was the prominence of women-novelists; however unconventional one's taste or ranking, it would be almost impossible to deny that most of the best novelists were women. Richardson, Dark, Stead, Prichard, Barnard Eldershaw, Tennant and Franklin were backed by a strong second rank, which included Helen Simpson, Jean Campbell, Henrietta Drake-Brockman and Mary Mitchell; and they were soon to be further reinforced by Dymphna Cusack, Ruth Park and Eve Langley. Some of them had the income-security of marriage, but the great majority were 'career-women'. Moreover, unlike female novelists historically, most of them were distinguished by their breadth, social involvement and far-reaching militancy. Regrettably, the trend did not continue beyond the 40s.

In retrospect the 30s appear almost bereft of new poetic talent but for Kenneth Slessor, in full flower, and the developing R. D. FitzGerald. Slessor (1907-71), a Sydney journalist but 'an incipient eighteenth century gentleman', above all was remarkable for the precision and delicacy of his language and diction. 'The verbal dandy appeared first: the poet followed after,' remarks Chris Wallace-Crabbe.[9] Another critic, Vivian Smith, neatly sums up

his achievement: 'Slessor stands at the head of most major developments in modern Australian verse: its thematic preoccupations
with time, memory and history; its humanizing of the landscape
or use of it symbolically to embody states of mind; its sardonic
use of humour to question and puncture illusions.'[10] The sea was
his main subject, as in 'Five Bells' and 'Five Visions of Captain
Cook'. He was the first Australian modern of the post-Eliot period
(though Tennyson was probably his chief inspiration); he was
also the first poet (except, perhaps, Neilson and Wilmot) to use
Australian background and imagery with complete naturalness
and ease. He was silent after 1945—some say from despair and
frustration, but perhaps rather because he knew he had said all
he had to say.

Mary Gilmore (1865-1962), although she began writing before
1900 and published perhaps her finest volume in her ninetieth
year, is best mentioned here in the context of the 30s, for in some
respects she was a bridge between Romantic and modern poetry
and she influenced many successors. To mention her basic religious
impulse, her preoccupation with passionate love, and her nostalgic
concern with convicts, Aborigines, the men of Eureka and the stuff
of Australian history generally, indicates her breadth. Her
occasional great achievement was profundity of simplicity.[11]

Criticism in the 30s was weak, in the absence of substantial
literary journals. All About Books (Melbourne, 1928-38) and
Desiderata (Adelaide, 1929-39) included first-class reviewing by
critics such as Nettie Palmer, F. T. Macartney and Frank Wilmot.
In 1938 M. Barnard Eldershaw produced Essays in Australian
Fiction, which was followed by T. Inglis Moore's Six Australian
Poets (1942)—both of them milestones in their time. The best-
known 'literary man' of the day was certainly Walter Murdoch
(1874-1970), a famous essayist and popular educator who wrote
nearly all his work for newspapers. The most liberal of conservatives, he had the qualities of wit and common-sense but had little
to say on Australian literature.

At this stage some general aspects of cultural life in the inter-
war period and of the writer's relationship with society require
discussion. We must consider, first, the phenomenon of expatriation.

All young Australians need to 'see the world', to see the best the
world can offer; indeed they cannot know or judge Australia until
they do. Every year thousands of them sailed for Britain—many of

the best of them had no intention of returning for a long time. Alan Moorehead has defined the 'root instinct in the Australian mind' as 'a sense of isolation', and has written of growing up in the inter-war period:

> As far as possible the local environment was ignored; all things had to be a reflection of life in England. . . . Everything was imported. And because they believed that the imitation could never be as good as the original, they were afflicted always with a feeling of nostalgia, a yearning to go back to their lost homes on the other side of the world. . . .
>
> To go abroad—that was the thing. That was the way to make your name. To stay at home was to condemn yourself to nonentity. Success depended upon an imprimatur from London, and it did not matter whether you were a surgeon, a writer, a banker, or a politician; to be really someone in Australian eyes you first had to make your mark or win your degree on the other side of the world.[12]

Moorehead himself used to go down to Port Melbourne to look at the ships and dream of the day when he had saved the £500 he had set himself and could escape to the centre of the world. Writing in early middle age, he dated his life from the moment his ship steamed into Toulon harbour: 'I had come home. This was where I wanted to be.'[13] Graham McInnes similarly wrote that for his generation 'the real challenge, the real excitement, the real possibility of success, lay 12,000 miles away in England. "Home" in fact.'[14] 'The older I grew,' Philip Lindsay recalled, 'the more fierce became this lust to escape, this tormenting dream of England, of London, of Dickens's and Chaucer's country . . . . dreaming ever of England . . . . some day, I shall get there!' (His father, Norman, incidentally, though he paid Philip's fare, advised against going, for 'it would be a betrayal of my country to leave it just when it was growing up and needed the voice of the novelist to bring consciousness'.)[15] Martin Boyd, on his return from the 1914-18 war, was appalled by Australia's crudity—Melbourne was the 'most snobbish place on earth'—and beat a swift retreat. On the other hand, Vance Palmer originally went to England, on 'Steele Rudd's' advice, deliberately to learn the writer's craft in the tough London school of freelancing. (Even in those Edwardian days there were many other expatriate Australians. 'The name of Dingo Dell, given by Barbara Baynton to one of their meeting-places, seemed an apt one. It suggested people who were dripping with sentimentalities about the old-world background and yet could not resist cooeeing to one another across the Strand.')[16] Louis Esson was tormented by the conflict between conviction of the hopelessness of Australia and the duty to attempt to do something about it. In 1917 he was writing to Palmer, who was back in Australia:

> it seems that any artist or writer has to get out: there is no help for it. I advise you strongly to pack your trunks as soon as you can. . . . It isn't fair to yourself to get lost in Australia, overwhelmed by young lawyers, grocers, and tailors. Australia, after all, is the place for the duffer or the martyr.

And in 1921:

> There's no escape in Australia from useless drudgery. I don't want you to desert your post: I would like everybody to return to Australia. But at present you can do no more there than here. . . . I don't want you to leave, but I don't want you to ruin yourself by attempting what can not yet be done.[17]

Nellie Melba vehemently advised Ray Lindsay: 'Get out of this country. It's no good for any artist!'[18] Of all groups, talented journalists possibly fretted most; for they knew very well how restrictive and hidebound Australian newspapers were—almost without exception.

For the writer, economic reasons were paramount. It was not just that payment for a story or article in England was five or more times as much as in Australia. There was also the possibility of income from reviewing, broadcasting, reading for publishers and the other freelance work which normally makes up a large part of a serious writer's earnings and which simply did not exist in Australia. The only possibility of becoming a serious professional writer was by migrating. The list of expatriate Australian writers is long and impressive: the playwright, Haddon Chambers (the Terence Rattigan of the Edwardian period), Barbara Baynton, H. H. Richardson, Spenser Brodney, Frederic Manning, Helen Simpson, W. J. Turner, Chester Cobb, Godfrey Blunden, Bertram Higgins, Miles Franklin, Christina Stead, Catherine Duncan, Mary Fullerton, Dorothy Cottrell, Velia Ercole, Jack and Philip Lindsay, Martin Boyd, Eric Partridge, Alwyn Lee, Graham and Colin McInnes, Alan Moorehead, James Aldridge, Peter Porter and others. A. A. Phillips has remarked: 'Australian writing was robbed of a leaven of venturesome minds. Our literature of the last [fifty] years might look very different if there were added to it the books these writers might have produced in Australia and the influence upon others of their talk, their enthusiasms and their rebellions.'[19] (The unanswerable question, of course, is whether they wrote more or less, better or worse, after digging up their roots.) The same features apply more broadly. England had a notable minority of Australian vice-chancellors, professors, scientists, law lords, Harley St. specialists, actors, and singers and other musicians. About one-third of Australian Rhodes Scholars did not return home; the better part of one thousand Australian university graduates worked in Britain. For many of them Australia could not provide: scientists, like Florey, Cairns or Oliphant, or a historian like Hancock, lacking research facilities; a prehistorian like V. Gordon Childe or a philologist like H. W. Bailey; singers like Melba and innumerable other musicians; dancers like Robert Helpmann.

Many of them had no intention of remaining overseas. Jack Lindsay, for one, never 'decided' to stay in England but circumstances engulfed him. In many instances a good job and the knowledge that its equivalent in Australia was unlikely, a new circle of friends, possibly marriage to an English spouse, as well as the cultural pleasures of the metropolis, combined to postpone indefinitely serious consideration of returning home. Quite often the expatriate was too proud to return until he had succeeded. Relatively few, perhaps, in the end were caught between two worlds, happy in neither; even Martin Boyd, who is often held to be an example, spent only four years in half a century back in Australia. Some writers returned deliberately in the knowledge that they were losing their roots. Patrick White's is the classic case. He had been away from the age of seventeen to thirty-six. But 'all through the War in the Middle East there persisted a longing to return to the scenes of childhood, which is, after all, the purest well from which the creative artist draws'. After the war he deliberately, sentimentally, returned 'home, to the stimulus of time remembered'. What did he find?

> In all directions stretched the Great Australian Emptiness, in which the mind is the least of possessions, in which the rich man is the important man, in which the schoolmaster and the journalist rule what intellectual roost there is, in which beautiful youths and girls stare at life through blind blue eyes, in which human teeth fall like autumn leaves, the buttocks of cars grow hourly glassier, food means cake and steak,

muscles prevail, and the march of material ugliness does not raise a quiver from the average nerves.

Nevertheless he stayed and worked, partly because of the 'possibility that one may be helping to people a barely inhabited country with a race possessed of understanding'.[20] And he has surely justified to himself his decision to return. George Johnston also, who had been so torn by love and hate for Australia, returned after twenty years to find himself as a writer, was reconciled to a country he came to understand, and noted 'with wry amusement that it is, after all, only in Australia that he has been recognized and rewarded as a famous writer—even if only as a famous "Australian writer".'[21]

Imperial capitals tend to attract much of the cream of colonial talent, which is only partly replaced by cultural pro-consuls making their careers in the colonies (and usually perpetuating imperial values). Brash colonials are sometimes discontented with their cultural status. Three Australian examples are Vance Palmer and his circle, P. R. Stephensen, and the Jindyworobak movement.

Vance Palmer's heroic literary career was at least as much concerned with building cultural life in Australia as with making his own individual contribution. In 1916-17 (as David Walker has demonstrated) he made a sustained attempt to build a national cultural movement. In 1905, at the age of nineteen he had contributed to *Steele Rudd's Magazine* an article entitled 'An Australian National Art', which stated, fairly crudely, the basic attitudes he was to hold throughout his life.

> art must be the interpreter of life, and it is the business of the artist to create interest in the life about him. . . . at the present stage of our civilization we are content to read English books for the interpretation of our life. We, who have in our power the makings of a glorious nation with no sordid past, such as is the legacy of most countries, are content to imitate the customs of old degenerate nations, and to let our individuality be obscured by the detestable word 'colonial'. Under such conditions our art must suffer.
>
> . . . until the Australian writer can attune his ear to catch the various undertones of our national life, our art must be false and unenduring. There must be no seeing through English spectacles. Our art must be original. . . .
>
> What we need in our present development is not so much cultured writers as nationalists. We need men who will bind

us together in an indissoluble bond as Bjornson did Norway....

... we are a bush people—that is to say, that our national
life finds most perfect expression in the different types of the
west . . . the bush for the present must be the mainspring of
our national literature.[22]

Palmer spent most of the years between 1906 and 1920 overseas,
but was in Australia for the greater part of the 1914-18 war. He
knew only too well how miserable the cultural achievement had
been, that there was no alternative to patient honest assessment
and creative rebuilding. The problem was that while the European heritage was a guide and a spur to higher achievement, it
was also a paralyzing reminder of Australian insignificance: how
imaginatively to possess Europe, yet not be overwhelmed by it?
To remain obsequiously colonial was spiritual death; to be
nationalistically assertive at least allowed the possibility of innovating live freedom. Contemporary Ireland was a useful guide.
Literary and artistic works were required which would express
and define the character of the incipient Australian nation and
thereby develop national self-awareness. At the same time Australia must remain open, not just to English but to European,
especially French, culture.

During the 1916-17 anti-conscription campaigns, Palmer believed he saw a prospect of an emerging Australian culture tied
to a new vigorous nationalism based on the working class. He cam-
paigned energetically against conscription, and wrote widely for
the Labor press and in *Fellowship*, the journal edited by Frederick
Sinclaire. Palmer, Sinclaire, and most of his other associates, such
as Esson, Wilmot, O'Dowd, Esmond Higgins, Frederick Macartney
and Guido Baracchi, were socialists. Palmer adapted the guild
socialist outlook he had acquired in England to the formation in
1916 of the Australian Authors and Writers' Guild; he was also
prominent in the Melbourne Literary Club formed in 1916. In
1917 he arranged for a new edition of Furphy's *Such Is Life*, which
he regarded both as a central document in an emerging Australian
tradition and a very relevant tract for the times. In 1917, also, he
helped to found the Victorian Labor College, which was envisaged
as a kind of counter-cultural workingman's university. Palmer
totally rejected the conservative universities and in 1916 made a
classic statement of a view commonly held by creative artists in
Australia:

Whatever is vital and creative in the life of their own day they ignore or stifle. Therein lies their particular danger. They can bring the authority of their culture . . . against anything that is new or novel in ideas, art or social experiment. And so whenever they assert that culture is a storehouse, we have to insist that it is a growth.[23]

In 1918 Palmer volunteered for the A.I.F. and made his fourth trip overseas. On his return, he sadly realized that the new emerging national spirit was not breaking away from imperialism, and in 1921 in a rather bitter article, 'Australia's Transformation', he argued that Australia was now largely urban-dominated and that its spiritual origins in the Bush were being suppressed. The chief significance of his campaign is, perhaps, that no-one else, then and for many years to come, was capable of putting a case so coherently for an Australian culture.[24]

A far more flamboyant nationalist was P. R. Stephensen (1901-65), Rhodes Scholar for Queensland in 1924, who at Oxford was briefly a communist and the first translator into English (from French) of Lenin's *Imperialism*. Stephensen joined with Jack Lindsay in the Fanfrolico Press and the *London Aphrodite*, later founded the Mandrake Press, and was lampooned by Aldous Huxley in *Point Counter Point*.[25] He returned to Australia in 1932 and established the Endeavour Press which published several novels. In 1935 he edited the one and only issue of the *Australian Mercury* which included his first instalment of *The Foundations of Culture in Australia* (1936). It was a lively and intelligent essay, and allowing for some polemical exaggeration, far more rational than the later political writings by which he was so discredited. His immediate target was G. H. Cowling, an English professor of English literature at the University of Melbourne, who in an article in the *Age* had been pessimistic about the prospects of Australian literature. His grounds were remarkably similar to those Sinnett had attacked in 1856: the countryside was too thin and lacking in tradition; there were 'no ancient churches, castles, ruins—the memorials of generations departed' and hence there was no hope of a Scott or a Balzac or 'a poetry which reflects past glories'; 'Australian life is too lacking in tradition, and too confused, to make many first-class novels'; the prospects for biography and books on travel were slight. Confound his impertinence, said Stephensen; 'is this the kind of anti-Australian nonsense these professors are imported from England to teach to the teachers of our Australian youth?' This was the kind of thing Americans had had to put up with for generations; moreover, 'his attitude is precisely that of the Latinists who, perceiving Wycliffe and Chaucer writing books in the English vernacular, sniffed (no doubt) at the very idea of literature in English.' Stephensen agreed that Australia was a cultural backwater; the arts were 'stultified, smug, and puerile' and in no other country was 'literary genius so badly treated, so humiliated and crushed and despised and ignored'. 'In what, at present, can an Australian take pride? In our cricketers, merino sheep, soldiers, vast open spaces—and what then? Until we have a culture, a quiet strength of intellectual achievement, we have nothing except our soldiers to be proud of!' The expatriates had been

> driven out by the intolerable hegemony of the second-rate in positions of authority here. Flight was easier than fight . . . the shirkers, they have cleared out, funked their job. Let them return to their muttons! ('No blooming fear', I can hear some of them murmuring. . . .)

Stephensen's basic approach was that

> Art and literature are at first nationally created, but become internationally appreciated. . . . Each nation contributes ideas to the culture of every other nation. . . . every contribution to world-culture . . . must be instinct with the colour of its place of origin. . . . There is a universal concept of humanity and world-culture, but it does not destroy individuality, either of persons or places or nations. . . . cultures must remain local in creation and universal in appreciation.

There was no reason why borrowings should not be made; English and other cultures should fertilize and stimulate the indigenous Australian culture. But Australia's contribution to the world would be its definition of itself 'in literature, art, and all the civilized achievements'; it would differ from the British Isles 'to the precise extent that our environment differs from that of Britain'. Australian writers should concentrate on expressing the land, Lawrence's 'spirit of the place'; and Australian children should be instilled with 'Australian sentiment, indigenous culture, Australian national lore and tradition and respect'.[26]

There were indications in the later sections of *Foundations* that Nietzsche, anti-imperialism (perhaps derived from his Leninist days) and super-patriotism were leading him to an extreme position. His later career was tragic. He became a leader of the 'Australia First' movement, was interned during the war, and ended up as 'ghost' for Frank Clune and a general hack-writer.

The Jindyworobak movement, whose leading spirit was Rex Ingamells (1913-55), was centred on Adelaide. Ingamells was inspired by Lawrence's *Kangaroo* and by Stephensen, and in 1937 issued in the journal *Venture* a manifesto, 'Concerning Environmental Values', which became part of his *Conditional Culture* (1938). His main beliefs were as follows:

> 'Jindyworobak' is an Aboriginal word meaning 'to annex, to join'. . . . [The Jindyworobaks] are those individuals who are endeavouring to free Australian art from whatever alien influences trammel it. . . . an Australian culture depends on . . .
> 1. A clear recognition of environmental values.
> 2. The debunking of much nonsense.
> 3. An understanding of Australia's history and traditions, primaeval, colonial and modern.
>
> The most important of these is the first. Pseudo-Europeanism clogs the minds of most Australians, preventing a free appreciation of nature. Their speech and thought idioms are European; they have little direct thought-contact with nature. . . .
>
> A fundamental break . . . with the spirit of English culture, is the prerequisite for the development of an Australian culture. . . . it is not in these ties that we must as a people seek our individuality. Its quintessence must lie in the realization of whatever things are distinctive in our environment and their sublimation in art and idea, in culture. . . .
>
> Our traditions are twofold. Inextricably woven with the transplanted European culture are our experiences of the Australian environment. How far we and this environment have changed and reacted through contact, we owe to self-honesty to understand, and such an understanding can arise properly only through cultural expression. But to ensure imaginative truth our writers and painters must become hard-working students of Aboriginal culture, something initially far-removed from the engaging and controlling factors of modern European life.[27]

It is fair to say that, though Ingamells was extreme in calling for a complete break with European culture, his view was on the whole moderately stated. However, the movement was greeted with immense derision, almost entirely because of its Aboriginal emphasis. This was strange, admittedly, but today's generation is not inclined to agree that there is *nothing* to be gained from study of Aboriginal civilization. The Jindys, unlike the *Bulletin* writers, were city men discovering the primitive outback, following Lawrence's concept of the 'Australian Place Spirit as a kind of terrible deity waiting his time to destroy white civilization'. The most remarkable aspect of Ingamells and his friends, however, was how ignorant they were of what had already been achieved in Australian literature, of how their environmental values—the problems of depicting Australian landscape and society—had been so much written about by the previous two generations of Australian writers such as O'Dowd, Prichard, Wilmot and the Palmers. The movement lasted about ten years and did not produce any major writers, although the Aboriginal stress encouraged the notable verse of Roland Robinson, and other secondary poets like Ian Mudie and William Hart-Smith were closely associated. The close of Ian Mudie's poem, 'Underground', perfectly expresses the school's attitude:

> Deep flows the river,
> deep as our roots reach for it;
> feeding us, angry and striving
> against the blindness
> ship-fed seas bring us
> from colder waters.

Being so preoccupied with the surface features of the countryside, they unwittingly reflected the English Georgian poetry they so vehemently condemned; and they were retreating into isolation from a mad world. But they were part of a trend—the rise of interest in anthropology, the discovery of Aboriginal art, and John Antill's 'Corroboree' music. (Writers such as Prichard, Herbert and James Devaney had already been pioneers in their respectful approach to Aboriginal civilization.) The Jindys' dreamtime myth helped to provide a new source of romantic imagery and suggestion for poets. And in general they were more valuable, perhaps, than their ideology justified. For they provided a movement—and Australian writers desperately needed a movement in order to meet and communicate; the controversy they caused was immensely provocative; and their annual anthologies enabled publication by many good poets.[28]

The frenzy (which was not typical of writers) of Stephensen and the Jindys cannot be understood unless placed in context. The serious writer was alienated from the community and could not find an audience. In the inter-war period Australians were still almost entirely ignorant of and uninterested in their history, which a few pioneers were beginning to write. Almost no Australian history and no Australian literature were taught in secondary schools (though there was a little in primary schools). There were no publishing-houses of any importance except Angus & Robertson and Lothian, whose production was small. Only about one-third of the more important novels were published in Australia and few of them achieved anything like adequate distribution. The majority published in England dribbled out to Australia, received a minimum of publicity, and sold much better in England than in Australia. There were no major literary journals like *Meanjin* or *Southerly* to provide a forum for criticism or a sense of literary continuity; two or three semi-serious reviews in the newspapers, the *Bulletin* or periodicals with tiny circulations were the most which could be expected. Writers were almost entirely isolated from each other and lacked any sense of a literary tradition; that even the Palmers were not aware of Henry Handel Richardson for fifteen years after she published her first major novel, that Ingamells had barely heard of the Palmers and most other writers when he launched the Jindyworobak movement, that Slessor by 1945 had never read Brennan's 'The Wanderer', illustrate the lack of communication or feeling of community. Serious writing was almost an underground movement. Every Australian industry, except the arts of course, was protected or subsidized; in the great age of protection, governments did not for a moment consider literature for possible assistance. Painters were protected by the difficulty of importing pictures for sale, and anyway, as Esson remarked in 1926, were 'treated like millionaires' in comparison to writers: 'it is curious how they have impressed the public that their work is up to the world standard, which it isn't, while no literary person is regarded as any good at all.'[29]

The serious writer wrote above the level of the popular market sympathetic to Australian material, while at the same time it was almost eccentric for an educated Australian to read more than an occasional book by an Australian. Norman Bartlett remarked that 'those who are well-versed in English and European culture are usually contemptuous of Australian literature'.[30] R. C. Bald noted that the Australian reader cast over English literature 'a kind of spurious romance. . . . he looks askance at a novel in which the hero walks down the Block instead of Piccadilly, or catches the electric train to Malvern instead of taking the Underground to Hampstead.'[31] The young Manning Clark wrote in 1943: 'there is a rift in our society—the élite flee to the garret, to the polite drawing-room, to Europe, while the people ape the mate ideal, being bonzer sorts.'[32] Esson diagnosed the situation: 'A small country like Norway can keep a score of writers going. We are handicapped in being a province, and proud of it, with no soul of our own. Imperialism is no good for literature.'[33] Nettie Palmer defined as endemic the state of cultural philistinism which gloried in despising 'all signs of mental or artistic vigour' and took 'pride in knowing nothing of our past'. Her answer was that Australians should simply admit that they were part of mankind, rather than part of the British Empire.[34] Bernard Shaw once said:

> You Australasians are extraordinary, really. Every year, thousands of you . . . journey to see an inferior country which you persist in calling Home in spite of the fact that its people ignore you and are scarcely aware of your existence. I wish I could persuade you that THIS is your home, that these lands should be the centre of your art, your culture, your drama.[35]

Visiting Americans, who were naturally sympathetic, were shocked. Hartley Grattan deplored the 'spiritual absentees' who despised the local scene as a possible field for art: Australia 'suffers from a literary inferiority complex. Her readers feel safer with a third-rate English or American book than with a first-rate Australian book. They cannot believe that men they see and know can write good books.'[36] H. S. Canby often heard it said that 'We have a literature already which came with us, and can import more whenever we wish. Why bother with a literature of our own. . . ?'[37] As late as 1952, Bruce Sutherland found that a common reaction to hearing his subject of study was, 'What Australian literature?', and he realized that

> these people honestly regard their native land, Australia, as a cultural province of Great Britain . . . they look upon themselves as Australians geographically, but as Britons culturally; and in the land of their nativity they see nothing that will compare with the cultural greatness of the land of their ancestors.[38]

Booksellers, knowing prevailing attitudes, made little effort to display Australian books; librarians were accustomed to the remark, 'If it's Australian, I don't want it.'

The disease of cultural colonialism lingered long. In 1950 A. A. Phillips brilliantly redefined the Australian 'inferiority complex' as the Cultural Cringe.

> Above our writers—and other artists—looms the intimidating mass of Anglo-Saxon achievement. Such a situation almost inevitably produces the characteristic Australian Cultural Cringe—appearing either as the Cringe Direct, or as the Cringe Inverted, in the attitude of the Blatant Blatherskite, the God's-Own-country-and-I'm-a-better-man-than-you-are Australian Bore.
>
> The Cringe mainly appears in a tendency to make needless comparisons. . . .
>
> The Australian writer normally frames his communication for the Australian reader. He assumes certain mutual pre-knowledge, a responsiveness to certain symbols, even the ability to hear the cadence of a phrase in a certain way. Once the reader's mind begins to be nagged by the thought of how an Englishman might think about this, he loses the fine edge of his Australian responsiveness. . . .
>
> The Australian writer is affected by the Cringe, because it mists the responsiveness of his audience, and because its influence on the intellectual deprives him of a sympathetically critical audience. Nor can he entirely escape its direct impact. The core of the difficulty is the fact that, in the back of the Australian mind, there sits a minatory Englishman.

But the writer had almost conquered colonialism; the reader had not. The worst effect of the Cringe was its estrangement of Australian intellectuals, among whom there was a prominent type who was 'forever sidling up to the cultivated Englishman', insinuating he was not an ordinary crude Australian. He disdainfully separated himself from the community: 'It is his refusal to participate, the arch of his indifferent eyebrows, which exerts the chilling and stultifying influence.'[39]

The natural attitude of a civilized person to nationality is roughly that put by Mary Gilmore:

> I have grown past hate and bitterness,
> I see the world as one;
> Yet, though I can no longer hate,
> My son is still my son.

All men at God's round table sit,
And all men must be fed;
But this loaf in my hand,
This loaf is my son's bread.

That is, not nationalist but recognizing some claims of nationality; involved in mankind and part of the brotherhood of man but naturally, from greater familiarity and day-to-day involvement, feeling closer affection and responsibility for one's own. Who is my neighbour?, is a difficult enough question. But only contemporary Australians have been fortunate enough to have had to face no more than the comparatively simple problem of having to balance Australia against the world. For all previous generations had to juggle a third element—loyalties to Britain and the Empire.

The 30s saw an extreme polarity of attitudes between nationalist writers like Stephensen and the Jindys and the contemptuous importers of culture. They were extreme examples of the inverted and direct Cringe, of the bumptious and arrogant Australians and the servile and pathetic anti-Australians, of the small minorities of hardliners—anti-imperialists akin to the old *Bulletin* type and exclusive imperialists. Most Australians fell between these extremes and held the double loyalty to Australia and the Empire in varying degree. Yet there was a fundamental class basis to the nationalist-imperialist division; historically, the older form of Australian nationalism had been identified with the left. Hence down to the 30s, the products of private secondary schools and the universities—the educated class—were overwhelmingly imperialist and conservative in politics. It was rare and eccentric for an educated man or an intellectual to support the Labor Party before the 30s, as did for example, the young H. V. Evatt. The extreme imperialists constantly talked and dreamed of 'home', decried everything Australian, kept alive the tradition of exile, were babus. Before 1915 they believed Australian soldiers would never be disciplined enough to be useful as infantry, they debunked all Australian manufactures, they imported English bishops, headmasters and professors and under-rated local candidates. Unlike any other sizeable group in any other Anglo-Saxon community, they were ashamed of the local pronunciation of English. The Adelaide Club—the *Adelaide* Club!—did not serve Australian wines before 1945. The notion of a distinctive Australian literature or culture was almost the last thing to which these Anglo-centred Australians would be converted. To the true imperialist any Australian national developments were unpatriotic, that is anything detracting from a united Empire or offering a national alternative variation on the imperial model. They recoiled from Australian sentiment or imagery in literature, while worshipping the patriotism expressed by the great English poets and their saturation in English scenery. Moreover, Australian writing was strongly linked with democracy, nationalism and social protest. H. G. Kippax has remarked that, by and large, the theatre-going public 'regarded Australia as a vast paddock on the outskirts of the civilization of Europe'.[40] The educated reading public was not very different. In so far as novelists anatomized the distinctiveness of Australian society or poets used local imagery, they implied criticism of an English-dominated United Empire, of the all-time, unquestionable verities of English civilization, and of the glory and perfection of English literature.

Having stated the extreme positions so bluntly, one must recognize how untypical they are. In the inter-war period, the national, imperial and international loyalties of the educated middle classes as a whole were thoroughly tangled and inconsistent. All the conventional rhetoric—at Anzac and Armistice Day ceremonies, on school speech-nights, from the pulpit—was still staunchly imperial with an Australian gloss. The newspapers almost every day featured imperial news and views of the world, carefully filtered through Reuter's cable-service, rather than local. And yet Australian sentiment was growing. The 20s was a period of 'Australia Unlimited' boosting, when notions of the nation's destiny as a major power of 100 or 200 million people circulated again. Governments did not allow imperial sentiment to influence their bargaining for imperial preferences; industrialists like Essington Lewis were proudly Australian in their economic pioneering; the Anzac achievement had instilled a deep sense of Australianism. Many conservatives were more patriotic than they allowed themselves to appear, for they had to preserve a staunch imperial front against supposed subversive Catholic-Labor nationalism. They confusingly tended to think of themselves simultaneously as path-blazing Australians and second-rate Englishmen. In their leisure activities—at the beach, bushwalking, fishing, camping, playing cricket, football, golf and tennis—they were thoroughly at home. They even sometimes bought safe Australian works of art—a Heysen landscape or a Lionel Lindsay woodcut. That so few of them read or bought Australian novels may by now have been as much because of absence of anyone to recommend them as of prejudice. The important truth is that, in colonial situations, cultural emancipation lags well behind political and economic.

There is no doubt that many writers of the 30s saw their task as, not just to write good poems and novels, but to help to build a new national culture and literature, to give Australia a cultural expression, to reveal Australians to themselves. As Nettie Palmer put it, does a country 'that is merely an imitation of its predecessors, that discovers no new thoughts and forms, that contributes nothing to the meaning of the world', deserve to exist?[41] Leonard Mann has said of his generation of writers that they 'were conscious of the separate identity of the Australian people and they were not unaware that what they were largely about was to show their people to itself', more profoundly than their predecessors had been able to do.[42] Prichard stated her view in exactly the naive-sounding language most likely to rouse the ire of many academic critics:

> I have loved the work of Australian writers and poets giving vision and understanding to sights with which many of us were not familiar. [It was a generation of writers] who loved Australia and sought to make others care for the glorious potentialities of the country and people. . . . The specific contribution Australian writers can make to world literature is an Australian view of places, people, traditions and customs, manners and ideas, in all their variations. I am not suggesting this should be chauvinistic, or anything but a taken-for-granted effect of environment on creative prose and poetry. . . . Australian writers may absorb international culture without imperilling their quality as Australians, whereas to deny an Australian spirit to the body of our literature, would be to foist a macabre dummy on the Australian people.[43]

Many writers took pleasure in trying to catch the idiom of Australian speech and the cadences of Australian life, in the hope of giving readers the delighted shock of recognition. A large proportion of their novels, but only a proportion, were historical, or anatomized country towns, or were documentary-sociological in emphasis. They knew, as a recent English critic has said, that

> The Australian or Canadian or New Zealander wants to know what he is: to have his inbred national aspirations

expressed; to have deciphered for him the complexities of his society, which he can experience but may not understand; and to have the scene which has determined his vision described.[44]

(Or perhaps they knew, rather, that the Australian *should* want these things.) They knew they were helping to define national identity.

Their conservative critics, who ignored rather than argued with them, in fact began from broadly similar assumptions, although they usually lacked the writer's intense love-hate attitude to his country. Both sides agreed that Australia was a culturally thin society, with few traditions or roots—that it was 'the poorest rich country in the world', as Sir Hubert Wilkins, the Antarctic explorer, remarked in the late 20s.[45] The writers were saying essentially: we must make the best of what we have, build up a local regional culture, try to translate Australia into art. Their traditionalist opponents were saying: we must carry on the European tradition, reproduce the best of the Old World, keep as up to date as possible in importing the current best of European culture, in order to combat and improve the appalling isolationist, provincial Australian cultural standards. They criticized local writers, in some instances with justification, for their ignorance of international cultural trends, and chortled over such outlandish excesses as the Jindyworobaks. In their way they were helping to civilize Australia, but fundamentally this was the old clash between the intellectual and the creative artist; and the intellectual, because of his Anglo-centrism, was usually incapable of recognizing the modest but considerable measure of local artistic achievement. The clash faintly reflects the ancient theories in American cultural history of the 'carrier' and the 'lag'. As an American historian has put it, it was assumed that if the long overseas procession of writers and artists

> dipped deeply and often enough into the major European streams we might hope to witness their rise among us. . . . What we might hope eventually to possess was an extension of European culture. . . . With enough European schooling and a sufficiently large number of civilized contacts, it has been hoped that esthetically we might at last begin to develop. We had only to catch up with Europe, so to speak, by diligent study.

But, inevitably, American culture would lag behind Europe at a distance. In reply, the American artist tended to assert that American culture would grow from a 'fresh configuration', that 'a special native fibre' preceded 'the greater breadth'.[46]

Critics often accused the novelists of provincialism, localism, lack of a world-view, because of emphasis on the Australian element of their Australian subject-matter. In reply it was asserted that the national approach was one of the surest roads to universality, that most great writing was first of all local, provincial and national. Henry Handel Richardson looked for 'the development of a characteristically Australian literature. The future is full of hope if the young writers will only remember to seek Australian themes, and refuse to be scared into imitating the mannerisms of the old-world writers.'[47] Esson wrote in 1943:

> we have not yet achieved full nationhood; so our writers, as was the case with the Irish writers a generation ago at the beginning of their renaissance, still have to make some kind of apology for daring to do their natural work. . . . No one would accuse Balzac, Dickens or Tolstoy of being local or provincial, lacking in universal appeal, because their subject matter comprised characters and themes typical of their own country and period. As Havelock Ellis once put it, the paradox of literature is that only the writer who is first truly national can later become international.
>
> The position of the writer in relationship to his own country and to humanity in general has been stated clearly and justly by André Gide [who has] declared that no one was more specifically Spanish than Cervantes, more English than Shakespeare, more Russian than Gogol, more French than Rabelais or Voltaire, and at the same time more universal and more profoundly human. . . .[48]

Other writers called on Ibsen ('Culture is unthinkable apart from national life'), D. H. Lawrence and Yeats for support. Nobody was more provincial or obstinately English than Chaucer. No work was ever universal unless it was right in the particular. A national tone or accent was as desirable in literature as it was accepted to be in music and painting, in that it increased diversity. As Tom Roberts had said, '. . . by making art the perfect expression of one time and one place, it becomes art for all time and of all places'.[49] If Australian writers didn't use local colour, they either had to crib someone else's or be colourless. Why should not Australia have a genuine national literature like everyone else? Let the critics stay colonial in outlook, let them feel as inferior as they like!

The writers were essentially correct. So much of the greatest writing is local and provincial. Consider how Russian Dostoievsky is, how southern American Faulkner is, how west-country English Hardy is. (Moreover, however much we may admire them, Dostoievsky on the whole must mean more to Russians, and Faulkner to Americans (and Lawson to Australians) than to foreigners. For this reason there can never be a precise universal standard, language differences apart.) Nearly all great writers have acquired their peculiar colouring partly from their local history and environment. The search for one's past is one of the great themes of world literature. There is no conflict between universality and nationality. Secure and unselfconscious acceptance of nationality (which few Australian writers yet entirely had) is one of the prime conditions of universality.[50] Most of the Anglo-centred critics were incapable of accepting Australia as a natural field of art, or were really objecting on non-literary grounds to Australianism or radicalism. But some of the critics were not quite making the point the writers were answering. As eventually expressed by H. M. Green and A. D. Hope, the criticism was rather that

> the writing of a particular novel is too often regarded as though it had been a journalistic assignment: to write up, let us say, circus life [or the life] of opal miners, or of the dwellers in a city slum. . . . The writer's subject in such circumstances is not life itself or some particular aspect of life as such, but some kind of life that illustrates Australian types and scenes and occupations. . . .[51]

The criticism in short was 'obsession with the scene rather than with the individual, with what is typical rather than with what is distinctive, and with what is specifically Australian rather than what is specifically human'.[52]

The criticism is to the point. A few writers deliberately subordinated literary purposes and adopted a semi-documentary approach in order to describe country life to city folk, or to explain Australia to the world, or to tell Australians what Australia and other Australians were really like. But the criticism is usually overdone. It does often apply to Franklin, Prichard and Tennant; it does not apply to Herbert and Stead; it applies only rarely, if at all, to Palmer, Davison, Mann and Dark.

By the 50s many of the university critics, who by then almost monopolized the field, were launching a sustained counter-attack on literary 'nationalism'. (It is necessary to look ahead to the 50s, for only then did the 'anti-nationalist' arguments become articulate, although the passage of time was making them increasingly irrelevant.) Vincent Buckley, for example, wrote: 'We have tended to praise, push, boom the inferior article on "Australian" grounds, and so compromise the claims or depreciate the standing of the superior.'[53] We may accept this view in so far as it refers to the Jindys or well-meaning patriotic bodies like various Australian Literature and Henry Lawson societies or the Bread and Cheese Club or criticism like Miles Franklin's or Cyril Brown's *Writing for Australia*. Similarly A. D. Hope in 1956 was applauding the 'move out of the period of provincialism and parochial nationalism',[54] and in doing so was less than just to the 'nationalists' who had done so much to raise standards. But the attack on 'those who adhere to a nationalist view of Australian literature' was commonly mounted in sweeping terms, with lamentable lack of attempt at definition and in ignorance of the process of historical development.[55] The issue was frequently confused with legitimate objection to the attempt by some left-wing 'nationalists' to proclaim themselves as inheritors of *the* Australian tradition.

Part of the difficulty lies in the word 'nationalism' itself, which is as ambiguous as 'imperialism' and which historians have failed to elucidate in the Australian context. Moreover, intellectuals as a class, in a period of natural revulsion from the evils of nationalism on a world scale, have tended to brush off as chauvinistic any expression of affectionate patriotism and have been suspicious of any concern with development and expression of a national culture—even in a 'new' country like Australia. 'Dominion' nationalism—nationalism in countries like Australia and Canada—is not the same phenomenon as European nationalism, with all its overtones of hate and military aggression, or as colonial nationalism as in the cases of India, Africa or Vietnam. Australian nationalism is not just old-style *Bulletin* xenophobia, but is usually accepted by historians as being a far wider concept: the process of Australia becoming a nation, moving towards independence, emancipating herself from the mother country. The paradoxical fact is that most of the leading literary 'nationalists'—and especially the Palmers—were staunch internationalists; while most of their derogatory critics, in the days of cultural colonialism, were narrow imperialists. Similarly, one of the strongholds in the last generation of literary 'nationalism'—C. B. Christesen's *Mean-jin*—is distinguished for its international contributors on world literature. In their time the leading writers of the 30s, however aggrieved and alienated they felt themselves to be, on the whole made their case for a national literature with considerable dignity. Palmer knew example was the best teacher. Davison said of him (and the same might be said of Davison—could either of them conceivably be accused of parochialism!):

> Palmer got rid of our national inferiority complex by the difficult and simple-seeming method of dropping it. He just took Australia for granted—like Lawson and Furphy in their more grown-up moods. From the very beginning, Palmer wrote on the sensible assumption that Australians were human beings complete in all natural attributes, and that life here had a validity and interest equalling life elsewhere.[56]

It is easy to say there was no problem: Australian writers had no need to worry about their Australianness, they had only to accept it. On the contrary, the relaxed upright stance, as distinct from the cringe or the strut, demanded extraordinary sophistication.

In their admirable sustained attempt to establish a canon of Australian writers which can be fitted to a world canon, many modern critics have sternly attacked any notion of a 'double standard'. Australian writers, they say, must be judged strictly by international standards; it is a great disservice to make any good-for-the-local-boy comment; anything illuminating writers have to say about Australia must not be a literary criterion. Of course they are right. And of course they are wrong—and impertinent, in that they are governed by a narrow definition of their professional literary concern. In several senses a double standard is inescapable. One function of art is to interpret us to ourselves, as Judith Wright says 'to relate us to the country and the society in which we live'.[57] The writer makes a contribution to understanding our existence—both as human beings and on the meaning of life in Australia, here, now—which has little to do with literary quality. One has only to mention *Power without Glory* or *The One Day of the Year* to make the point. (The critics know this, but somehow cannot accept it.) The second major point is the special function of literature in new countries, which is to make articulate the emotions and imagination of citizens of societies struggling to define themselves; literature acts as a catalyst of universal, in-herited values and the values developed from new experience.

It may even be argued that the major interest and worth of literature in new countries does not lie in its aesthetic qualities. Geoffrey Dutton remarks: 'The novelist or poet who may mean a lot to Australians, and to Australian history, may well be a pigmy alongside a Fielding or a Wordsworth; to ignore this is chauvinism, but to be cowed by it is to adopt . . . the cultural cringe.'[58] A third, lesser point is that universal standards are very rough and ready. Fashions change; and there are innumerable writers of quality, who because they are remote, like Scandinavians or South Americans or Japanese, or have an extreme national orientation like Burns, are and must be internationally underrated. Furphy and Dennis are obvious Australian cases. Fourthly, concentration on the universal standard tends to neglect the particular value of writers contributing to their national literary tradition in an innovatory capacity and thereby having a greater influence than their purely literary merits might justify; Patrick White's particular influence on Australian writers, as distinct from on writers in general, cannot be disregarded. Lesser works (like *Pamela*) can be crucial in the growth of a literature. Much of the academic critics' timorousness has derived, not so much from a latter-day cringe, but from traditional concern with form rather than content, and from disapproval of the particular kinds of values many Australian writers have displayed. Few of them have yet found the broad historical approach which so many distinguished American critics display.

The number of close parallels and near-parallels between Australian and American literature deserve sustained exploration. It is suggestive enough simply to cite some of the main features and incidents of American literary history. The leading mid-nineteenth century writers were consciously creating a national literature, and felt an obligation to explain Americans to themselves. Their sense of the need for a national cultural outlook was opposed by the cosmopolitan intellectuals and academic critics who, broadly, until about 1914 disparaged all American writers and assumed that the United States was no more than a literary dependency of England. W. D. Howells advised his literary friends to write, and stick to writing, about the life they knew best. Thackeray advised his American friends to think better of their artists. While San Francisco was famous throughout the world because of Bret Harte, San Francisco ignored him. Henry James's Roderick Hudson remarked: 'It's a wretched business, this quarrel of ours with our own country, this everlasting impatience to get out of it.'[59] James was vilified, later, and brushed off by nationalist writers and critics for his betrayal. When Whitman and others made American poetry truculently American, it became much more interesting and gained immensely in force and individuality. American writers were obsessed with American uniqueness and the need to explain it to America and the world; and yet they could not leave the relationship with Europe alone. The American writer has been notorious for his loneliness and his sense of a lack of native tradition. The richness of American writing from the 80s on was largely unrecognized by critics for a generation or more. Howard Mumford Jones sums up the terms of debate about American literature at the beginning of the twentieth century:

> Was our literature directly conditioned by, and expressive of, democratic values? Were these primarily social and political, or were they intellectual and cultural? If they were the latter, did we not lack that stratified society without which, it was alleged, a cultured literature could not exist? . . . Was not our literature bound to be regional, parochial, even local and assuredly second-rate; or was it somehow to produce a mighty masterpiece to be known as the Great American Novel? Did we not lack craftsmanship? Scholarship? Genius? Was not the commercial spirit of the republic now, and always, the enemy of art? Was not the tyranny of women over literature reprehensible? And always the ancient theme emerged: we are a young country engaged in subduing a continent, dedicated to material prosperity, impatient of the finer things.[60]

The arguments went on in the twentieth century. Could there be, or should there be, an autonomous American literature? Was it not remarkable how few novels there were of ideas? In 1920 H. L. Mencken produced his version of the Cringe:

> The American social pusher keeps his eye on Mayfair; the American literatus dreams of recognition by the London weeklies; the American don is lifted to bliss by the imprimatur of Oxford or Cambridge; even the American statesman knows how to cringe to Downing Street.[61]

American expatriates flooded to Paris and London in the 20s. The reaction against nationalism, when it came, was violent. Alfred Kazin states as 'the greatest single fact about our modern

American writing—our writers' absorption in every last detail of their American world together with their deep and subtle alienation from it.'[62] All this about the literature which, many would agree, has been the greatest of the twentieth century.

Australian literature finally grew out of the colonial-national dilemma in the 50s and 60s. Writers and their public are no longer afflicted with inhibitions about the naturalness of the Australian setting. As James McAuley, in his time one of the most anti-nationalist of writers, put it in 1971:

> A lot of people in my generation used to think that the cultural basis was too thin, the soil too poor. It just doesn't worry me as much now. Part of the argument used to be the nationalists versus the internationalists, with the nationalists saying, 'With your cultural cringe to the glories of overseas cultures you're neglecting to develop what is truly here.' There's always been some truth in that. . . . It isn't just a matter of assimilating a world culture. It is also finding out how to really respect and love the things that are here.[63]

By common consent, the 20s are seen in retrospect as a scurvy period, when Australians seemed content to accept second-rateness, were deferentially imitative in most aspects of public and cultural life, and shut themselves off as best they could from the world and modern thought. Viscount Bryce had assessed the situation in 1921:

> it is material interests that hold the field of discussion, and they are discussed as if they affected only Australia, and Australia only in the present generation. Nobody looks back to the records of experience for guidance, nobody looks forward to conjecture the results of what is being attempted today. There is little sense of the immense complexity of the problems involved, little knowledge of what is now being tried elsewhere, little desire to acquire such knowledge.[1]

'Even as social experimentation and creative political experiment declined,' Gordon Greenwood has remarked, 'so in education, art and literature, there was often aridity . . . and a seeming lack of passionate purpose. . . .'[2] The depression and the mass suffering it entailed once again destroyed the illusion of the inevitability of material progress and induced fundamental questioning of the basis of capitalist society. At the same time it became clearer through the 30s that Australia could not escape involvement in the deepening crisis of European politics.

In this period many thoughtful Australians were shocked into basic reassessments. R. M. Crawford has argued impressively that there were

> clear signs of a new level of maturity and professional skill in Australian life in . . . the late 1930s. . . . the evidence crowds in on the historian as he looks for the signs of growing maturity that a corner was turned in Australian history at that time. Rarely indeed is one given the means of dating the coming of age of a new nation so precisely as they are given in this case.[3]

Crawford was judging mainly by the quality of public life, though he argued that developments in the arts strengthened his case. The possibility of a cultural coming-of-age in this period deserves close examination.

The examples of improvement in public life which Crawford uses—the Commonwealth Public Service, the Council for Scientific and Industrial Research and the universities—all in fact indicate preliminary advances in the 30s which in the 40s became major qualitative developments. Although some remarkable self-made men were thrown up by the public service, it had been blighted by rigid rules of seniority and preference to returned servicemen. A few university graduates were enlisted for general administrative careers in the 30s and recruitment was greatly accelerated during the war; never again, for example, would academic advisers of government loom as large as Professors L. F. Giblin and D. B. Copland had in the depression years, in the absence of expert Treasury advisers. When an External Affairs Department was at last created in 1935, it was officered by a strange assortment of capable gentlemen; but during the war years it recruited some of the brightest university students of that generation and young graduates already in the service. South Australia, also, by the 30s had developed a knack for selecting young teacher-graduates for senior public service positions.

Scientific research developed little before the 40s. University resources were negligible. Baldwin Spencer had been financed to make his central Australian expedition with F. J. Gillen in 1901 only after seventy-seven eminent Englishmen, led by J. G. Frazer, had petitioned the governments of Victoria and South Australia on the grounds that it was 'to Australia, more perhaps than to any other quarter of the globe, that anthropologists are now looking for the solution of certain problems of great moment in the early history of science and religion'.[4] A few brilliant men like Edgeworth David and Douglas Mawson, both of whom were Antarctic explorers and professors of geology, made impressive reputations. A. G. M. Michell's thrust-block system of power-transmission was one outstanding invention. The geographer, T. Griffith Taylor, was publicly pilloried again and again in the 20s for daring to assert that there were strict limits to Australia's population-carrying capacity. A rare example of aid by a Commonwealth government enabled the establishment in 1925-6 of a department of anthropology at the University of Sydney under Radcliffe Brown, who was succeeded by A. P. Elkin. In 1925 the Waite Agricultural Research Institute was founded in South

Australia by private benefaction. The Council for Scientific and Industrial Research, after twenty years of ducking and shoving, was established in 1926. Bills to found a Bureau of Agriculture had failed to pass Parliament in 1909 and 1913; during the 1914-18 war an Advisory Council of Science and Industry was formed, and an Institute of Science and Industry was established in 1920 but starved of funds; Professor David Orme Masson perhaps made the greatest contribution to C.S.I.R.'s eventual foundation under David Rivett (1885-1961), George Julius and A. E. V. Richardson.[5] Its early concerns were almost entirely pastoral and agricultural; control of prickly-pear cactus by introduction of the cactoblastis insect was the first famous success. In 1937 a new emphasis on industrial research was made possible, and the needs of war enabled major developments in pure as well as applied scientific research by both C.S.I.R. and the universities. The Commonwealth had made its first grant to universities for research in 1936. Medicine fulfilled its early promise of high standards. J. B. S. Haldane remarked in the 30s:

> My highbrow friends complain that the Dominions have produced little great art or literature. I answer that at least they have done something unique. Before the war the average expectation of life of a baby born in New Zealand was sixty years, in Australia fifty-seven years. . . . England also ran. . . . I am proud to belong to a Commonwealth which has won the first and second places in the great race against death.[6]

But before the 1939-45 war, Melbourne's Walter and Eliza Hall Institute, which nurtured F. M. Burnet, was the only full-time medical research centre; expenditure on medical research was less than one-fiftieth of today's quite inadequate amount.

Any overall judgment on the quality of education in the inter-war period is impossible, but an impression remains of un-adventurous uniformity in the State departments. Nevertheless, there were heroes like Frank Tate and Peter Board, directors respectively of the Victorian and New South Wales departments from 1902 to 1928 and from 1905 to 1922, who in their time were innovating reformers. The major development of the period was the growth in number of state secondary schools which enabled some of the most talented to continue education sometimes to university level. Whereas in 1900 there were only three state secondary schools in the whole continent, by 1938 one-quarter of the $15\frac{1}{2}$-$16\frac{1}{2}$ age group (of whom half were at state high and technical schools) were still at school. Carnegie money brought about the foundation of the Australian Council for Educational Research in 1930. The universities continued to operate on a pinchpenny basis; it was common for a professor to teach half a dozen courses with the help of one or two lamentably paid junior assistants. Research was a luxury, not reasonably to be expected. The universities made little contribution to the study of Australian society, partly also because the social sciences were so undeveloped and because of lack of interest. In the mid-40s the educationist, K. S. Cunningham, protested:

> In the last fifty years, hundreds if not thousands of capable young Australians have studied the language and culture of ancient Greece or Rome, but next to none have been trained to study and record the life of the Australian aboriginal whose ancient culture was passing away forever. Nothing could more dramatically illustrate the preoccupation with the past, the neglect of local material, and the lack of interest in sociological studies.[7]

One seeks in vain for any major research in Australian government, sociology or current affairs, other than in economics and history, from the universities in the inter-war period. The first university course in Australian history was taught at Stanford, California, in 1907-8; the first full course in Australia was introduced at Melbourne in 1927 but it did not become a standard annual course, there or anywhere else, until 1946. After the war most of the universities began to give sustained attention to the Asian and Pacific regions as well as Australia itself. The universities had shown several signs in the later 30s of improved general health: the scientists were beginning to develop graduate work; at both Sydney and Melbourne lively new appointees were challenging entrenched conservatism; and for the first time the strong apolitical academic tradition was being modified by a minority engaging in public debate on 'controversial' questions. The needs of war led the Commonwealth first to finance staff, buildings and students for scientific purposes; then it introduced scholarship schemes for returned servicemen and for the most able students, and in 1948 founded the Australian National University. The immediate postwar number of students more than doubled the prewar figure; growth in scale and relatively generous financing marked a new era for tertiary education.

A few notable contributions had been made to international letters. Mungo MacCallum's *Shakespeare's Roman Plays* long remained the chief authority; T. G. Tucker's edition of Shakespeare's sonnets was for many years the standard one; A. J. A. Waldock's books on Shakespeare, Milton and Sophocles were probably the finest all-round achievement in literary studies in Australia. Philosophy had been dominated by Christian Idealists such as William Mitchell of Adelaide, Francis Anderson of Sydney and W. R. Boyce Gibson of Melbourne; Mitchell's *The Structure and Growth of the Mind* (1907) was the one major work. The arrival at Sydney in 1927 of John Anderson to present a 'realist' view (together with revolutionary opinions on the state and religion) enlivened the scene; and the further contributions from the late 30s by followers of Wittgenstein produced vigorous controversy, but little publication, in the 40s. Australia had won some reputation as a 'nursery of philosophers'.[8]

It is extraordinary that, not forgetting G. W. Rusden, H. G. Turner and Timothy Coghlan, there had been such little interest in investigating the Australian past before the 20s. Unquestionably the outstanding historiographical achievement of the inter-war period was C. E. W. Bean's editing of and contributions to the twelve-volume *Official History of Australia during the War of 1914-18* (1921-42). Bean's originality of approach and rigorous standards won world-wide recognition from war historians; his was probably the finest war history ever. His viewpoint was more that of the man in the trench than of the High Command, and in his attempt to weld the digger outlook to the outback tradition he made a fascinating contribution to defining Australian identity. It must be granted that the few university teachers of history and research students also made a remarkable contribution to blocking in outlines of Australian history. Professors George Arnold Wood of Sydney and Ernest Scott of Melbourne (who wrote *ten* books) were migrant Englishmen whose major interests were the European exploration and discovery of the continent; their native-born successors tended to begin their Australian history with the Aborigines and the land itself. Some landmarks were Myra Willard's *White Australia Policy* (1923, the first publication by Melbourne University Press), S. H. Roberts's *The History of Australian Land Settlement* (1924) and *The Squatting Age* (1935), W. K. Hancock's brilliant *Australia* (1930), E. O. G. Shann's *An Economic History of Australia* (1930), and the Australian volume of the *Cambridge History of the British Empire* (1933). It may be that, having filtered down into the schools, these works provided some guide for the degree of self-recognition which Australians achieved in the 30s and war years. There was a lag in the early 30s but late in the decade major works appeared by Brian Fitzpatrick in economic history, H. V. Evatt and Eris O'Brien. In the 30s, moreover, scholars (most of them independent of the universities) were working on basic reference-works in the humanities: J. A. Ferguson (*A Bibliography of Australia*, 1941-69), E. Morris Miller (*Australian Literature*, 1940), H. M. Green (*A History of Australian Literature*, 1961), Percival Serle (*A Bibliography of Australasian Poetry and Verse*, 1925, and *Dictionary of Australian Biography*, 1949), and William Moore (*The Story of Australian Art*, 1934).[9]

The most serious weakness in Australian intellectual life, which was not to be remedied to any extent until the 60s, was the poverty of discussion of current affairs. The newspapers were almost uniformly blindly imperialistic and conservative, as much in cultural affairs as political. In politics, the Melbourne *Age* was the only one (apart from short-lived Labor papers) almost to qualify as an exception, and in cultural matters the Melbourne *Herald* also, perhaps. By courtesy of Reuter's, all the newspapers presented the world through partisan British imperial eyes from a European point of view, and simply did not provide the facts for objective judgement of innumerable issues. They submitted to the consistent policy of governments in the 20s and 30s of discouraging informed debate. The formation of a Sydney branch of the Institute of International Affairs and of the Institute of Pacific Relations in Melbourne, and their federation in 1932 with two other branches as the A.I.I.A., was an encouraging development. In 1932, also, the Australian Institute of Political Science was founded in Sydney. But the major reforming influence came to be the Australian Broadcasting Commission. For in addition to its contribution to appreciation of music and drama and its role as a civilizing agency of adult education, it broke away from the newspapers' control of its news-presentation in the 30s to develop from 1947 an independent news-service which imposed new standards of objectivity. There remained, however, the basic lack of quality periodicals, other than the *Australian Quarterly* from 1929 (and the *Australian National Review* from 1937 to 1939)—an entire lack, indeed, of intellectually acceptable weeklies. On the other hand, professional journals had stabilized themselves—the *Australasian Journal of Psychology and Philosophy* (1923), the *Economic Record* (1925), *Oceania* (1930) and *Historical Studies—Australia and New Zealand* (1940). Moreover, the two literary journals—*Southerly* and *Meanjin Papers*—were founded in 1939 and 1940.

In the 30s once again, stimulus for reform came to libraries. Nothing better illustrates, perhaps, the stagnation of intellectual life in the first third of the century than the decline of the State Library of Victoria from its nineteenth century grandeur. The Carnegie-sponsored Munn-Pitt report of 1935 was a scathing indictment of the condition of public libraries, which led to the promotion of a free library movement aiming at State subsidy of local government libraries; the New South Wales Library Act of 1939 led the way to reform.

Perhaps the most significant development of all in the 30s was the growth of a much more diverse intellectual and cultural class. Professional men and artists had been almost identified, socially and intellectually, with the mercantile class. The new diversity was created not so much by the products of new educational opportunity or by a natural growth in numbers but rather by the effects of the depression and an increasing consciousness of Australian isolationism. For the first time in Australian history, an intellectual-cultural class arose which was predominantly dissident. For in this generation large numbers of teachers, journalists, writers and artists and a few lawyers, doctors and engineers came to reject the conventional wisdom of their elders, and in the long run a deep gulf was to develop between governments and the intelligentsia.

In music the 30s brought a dramatic improvement in standards. There had probably been a steep decline in general musical proficiency from the late nineteenth century; there was certainly a sharp falling-off in the proportion who developed musical capabilities as part of their general education. The major choral societies, which often had amateur orchestras attached to them, remained the chief driving-force, but the choral tradition was in decline. The main objective, for which many stalwart campaigners fought in vain for decades, was the establishment of professional symphony orchestras. Following the failure of the attempt to create a permanent Victorian orchestra after the Exhibition triumph of 1888, Professor Marshall Hall gathered a mainly amateur orchestra with some part-time professionals. Alberto Zelman (junior) founded the amateur Melbourne Symphony Orchestra in 1906 and the Melbourne String Quartet in 1905. Similar efforts were made in all the States, but standards were inevitably poor.

The best orchestra was probably the Sydney Symphony Orchestra between 1919 and 1922 when it was subsidized by the State government and was under the Belgian, Henri Verbruggen; when he left, the orchestra was disbanded as too costly. In the late 20s the Melbourne and Conservatorium orchestras amalgamated to good effect.[10]

Throughout this period, however, Australia had been internationally famous for the quality of its singers; this must be admitted to be the country's greatest cultural contribution of the early twentieth century. Nellie Melba (Mitchell) (1861-1931) had led the way. Daughter of a Richmond builder and contractor and trained in Melbourne by the Italian, Cecchi, she left in 1886 to become the world's greatest soprano of her generation at least, the world's most famous Australian, and the forerunner of dozens of Australians who have since sung the leads at Covent Garden. Some of those who followed her were Ada Crossley and, in the inter-war period, Florence Austral, John Brownlee, Browning Mummery, Harold Williams, Majorie Lawrence and Joan Hammond. No-one has satisfactorily explained why Australia has produced so many great singers. Many musicians are convinced that climate has much to do with it. Alleged Australian speech-habits are unlikely to be relevant. Roger Covell seriously believes that Australia's sporting prowess is relevant; for opera has 'elements of sheer display and brazen dexterity' and gives the 'same kind of opportunity for the instant exhibition of prowess' as many sports![11] However, any explanation must start from the strength of the choral tradition among nineteenth century migrants, especially the many north-country Englishmen, Germans, Cornish and Welsh; must note the strength of the eisteddfod movement in the Ballarat district and the long-term importance of the South Street competitions there; and give attention to the quality of teaching over several generations.

The one important figure in composition in the earlier twentieth century (other than Grainger) was Alfred Hill (1870-1960), who studied at Leipzig with Henry Handel Richardson in the late 1880s and was still producing in the 1950s. According to Covell, Hill's music was firmly in the idiom of nineteenth century romanticism of a rather conservative kind; although he was never a professional composer, his was a life of unremitting creative activity—12 symphonies, at least 6 concertos, 7 operas, 17 string quartets, and nearly 50 miscellaneous orchestral pieces. Covell sees parallels with both Hugh McCrae and Henry Kendall—like McCrae in his 'charm, euphony, nostalgic delicacy', like Kendall in that 'he was more at home with finding an equivalent in music for the cool, wet greenness of the Australian coastal valleys than with grappling with the immense, raw vistas of the inland'. His *Australia* symphony of 1951 was, however, a serious attempt to express the whole country, its life and its people, including the Aborigines, just as he had previously used Maori inspiration.[12]

From its foundation in 1932 the Australian Broadcasting Commission had immense influence in developing musical standards and audiences. Amalgamated Wireless (Australasia) had made the first experimental broadcasts in 1921; the first stations to broadcast regularly were 2SB (later 2BL) in 1923 and 3AR and 3LO in 1924. The Taits and J. C. Williamson Ltd. owned 3LO and made frequent direct broadcasts of concerts, opera and vaudeville. In 1928 the Commonwealth government announced its intention of taking over the 'A' class stations; meanwhile the Taits had amalgamated 3AR and 3LO, and then in 1929 formed the Australian Broadcasting Company with exclusive rights to operate all 'A' class stations in Australia.[13] By 1932 when the A. B. Commission replaced the A. B. Company, the latter had developed full-time groups of fifteen instrumentalists in both Sydney and Melbourne. Paragraph 24 of the Broadcasting Act, which established the Commission, stated:

> The Commission shall endeavour to establish and utilize in such manner as it thinks desirable in order to confer the greatest benefit on broadcasting, groups of musicians for the rendition of orchestral, choral and band music of high quality.

Charles Moses, the A.B.C's general manager, W. G. James who became Controller of Music, and Bernard Heinze, the musical advisor, seized their chance and were not stopped by a government which must have been surprised at such bold interpretation of the Act. The Sydney and Melbourne permanent ensembles were immediately enlarged to 24 players (who were frequently augmented for special broadcasts) and were named the A.B.C. Sydney and Melbourne Concert Orchestras. By 1936 these had grown to strengths of 45 and 35; Adelaide, Brisbane and Perth had groups of 17 and Hobart a nucleus of 11. By 1937, taking in the members of its dance-bands, brass band and others, the Commission was employing about 320 full-time musicians. The war delayed the process, but in 1946, with subsidies from State governments and city councils, permanent full-size (or almost so) orchestras were established in Sydney and Brisbane, and the others followed fairly closely behind. Given Australia's federal nature, the Commission was almost bound to treat the States even-handedly and not attempt to create a national orchestra of higher quality. In the early 40s the A.B.C. introduced competitions for composers and assisted with musical publication; and in 1942 the Broadcasting Act was amended to require at least $2\frac{1}{2}\%$ Australian content of music played on all stations. This unique case in this period of substantial state support for the arts, we should note, was unusual in world terms; the members of most of the great English and American orchestras had highly insecure conditions of employment until comparatively recent years. Another notable case of State support was the formation in 1945 of the full-time Queensland State String Quartet.

The other extraordinary aspect of the A.B.C's musical policy was its immediate decision in 1933 to finance public concerts and to mobilize subscribers. The Taits had brought many great concert singers to Australia, including Galli-Curci, Chaliapin, and McCormack, but relatively few instrumentalists such as Moiseiwitsch and Heifetz. They continued for a few years to import musicians, including Yehudi Menuhin and Flagstad, but the A.B.C. overwhelmed them. It became a massive concert-promoting agency, introducing an annual stream of 'celebrity' artists, which began in 1934 with Sir Hamilton Harty as guest conductor who was followed by the Budapest String Quartet, Artur Rubenstein, and many more. Another important aspect was the promotion of youth and children's concerts, as partial remedy for the lamentable condition of musical education in the schools; Bernard Heinze made here a highly individual contribution. The continual broadcasting of good music, however, sometimes with commentaries by such attractive personalities as Neville Cardus and A. E. Floyd, was as important an activity as any. The A.B.C. was the major medium through which the development of recordings of reasonable sound-fidelity from about 1930 enabled an immense spread of musical appreciation; and thereby it possibly encouraged the widespread practice again of instrumental skills, which had been lapsing in the previous half-century.[14]

Another feature of the period was the creation in the late 30s of a devoted public for ballet. After Lola Montez introduced the art in the 1850s, it remained little more than an element in lowly variety shows. A Williamson season in conjunction with opera in 1893 was unsuccessful, but the visit of the Imperial Russian Ballet Company in 1913 may be taken as the true birth of ballet in

Australia. In 1926 the Taits brought out Anna Pavlova with a small company; she returned in 1929 and choreographed and presented *Autumn Leaves*, which was inspired by the countryside near Perth. By now several dancing-schools, such as Jennie Brenan's, were operating; after training in Adelaide and Sydney and five years' experience mainly in musical comedy, Robert Helpmann left in 1933 for the Sadlers Wells school, while a few others, like Elaine Fifield, later won overseas scholarships. After another company had toured in 1934, the Taits in 1936 engaged Colonel de Basil's Monte Carlo Ballet Russe Company, with the Danish Helene Kirsova as principal dancer. Another strong de Basil company arrived in 1938 and remained until 1940 when it presented the world première of *Graduation Ball*. Several of the company, including the Czech, Edouard Borovansky, stayed in Australia, as had Kirsova after the 1936 tour. Kirsova in Sydney and Borovansky in Melbourne now began competing to create professional Russian ballet companies. The Taits first presented the Kirsova company in 1942 and Borovansky's in 1943. Frank Tait doubted 'whether the public would accept Russian classical ballets as a local product when names like Toumanova, Riabouchinska and Baronova lingered, but he was willing to take this risk'. Kirsova retired in 1945 and returned to Europe, while Borovansky went from strength to strength. A generation of Australian dancers developed —Dorothy Stevenson, Peggy Sager, Kathleen Gorham, and others. From the mid-40s also, locally composed and choreographed ballets, such as *Terra Australis*, *Ned Kelly*, *The Lifesavers*, *Corroboree*, and *The Black Swan*, were frequently produced.[15]

Grand opera between the wars was almost confined to the rare extravaganzas offered by the Taits. In 1924 they joined with Melba in presenting a company including Toti dal Monte and other Italian singers to perform sixteen operas. Melba announced her retirement on the last night of the season when she sang Mimi in *La Bohème*. Radio listeners also heard the performance and its conclusion. 'Cheers and coo-ees rang through the house at each curtain fall, and reached their peak after the announcement that limbless soldiers had benefited by £18,000 from the performance.' Nevin Tait spoke from the stage: 'We are proud to call Melba an Australian. She is not only a great singer—probably the greatest the world has known—she is a national possession.' The Prime Minister, Stanley Bruce, followed:

Long before Australian soldiers blazoned the name of Australia throughout the world, you were her great ambassadress.

Art knows no nationality. It has no barriers. Tonight, it is not only the people of Australia bidding farewell to Melba, it is the people of the whole civilized races of the world.

Electric lights on a backdrop flashed out, 'Australia's Greatest Daughter Our Melba', to which her response was, 'I was never prouder to be an Australian.'[16] In 1928 Melba sang her very last season when the Taits again imported many stars to sing German as well as Italian operas, with a large supporting cast of Australians. But the Taits lost money and argued to the government that grand opera could never be established without subsidy. Nevertheless in 1931 they backed Bernard Heinze and Claude Kingston in forming a company for a short season of three weeks which actually made money.[17] Otherwise the 30s were almost bereft of opera, though in 1935 Gertrude Johnson returned from Covent Garden to found the National Theatre movement in Melbourne—with a capital of £8.[18] But the establishment of Australian opera was to be delayed until about 1950.

Another art-form to which the A.B.C. made a major contribution was the radio play, which flourished at all levels with very large audiences over the period roughly 1937 to 1960. In the late 30s and 40s when serious local theatre still barely existed, the radio play was almost the only outlet for dramatists and provided several times as much employment for actors as the stage. It is perhaps time for someone to make a serious study of several dramatists who are today little known, such as Sydney Tomholt, Edmund Barclay, G. L. Dann, Max Afford, Catherine Shepherd and Alexander Turner; a few of their plays were published. (And the phenomenon of Gwen Meredith should be noticed. About 1950 it was estimated that about half the radios in use were tuned to *Blue Hills*, of which Mrs. Meredith has by now written some five thousand episodes.) Probably the best and best-known of the radio plays is Douglas Stewart's verse-drama, based on Scott's Antarctic expedition, *Fire on the Snow*.[19]

In the 30s Streeton, J. S. MacDonald and their friends fumed and raged against decadent 'modern art'. Van Gogh had died in 1890, Gauguin in 1903, Cézanne in 1906 and Picasso, Matisse and Braque were becoming elderly men. De Kooning and Jackson Pollock were already at work.

Post-impressionism was a weak, small minority movement among Australian painters of the 20s and early 30s. It had made

some slight impact in Sydney before the 1914-18 war, almost a
decade before Melbourne. Dattilo Rubbo, an Italian teacher and
painter, had seen reproductions of post-impressionist paintings,
and attracted Roland Wakelin (1887-1972), Roy de Maistre (1894-
1968), Grace Cossington Smith (b. 1892) and other young artists
to his school. In 1913 the eighteen-year-old Norah Simpson
brought back from Europe possibly the first coloured reproductions of the post-impressionists. 'We commenced to heighten our
colour,' Wakelin recalled, 'working in stippling touches, and to
make severe cubistic drawings.'[20] When a Wakelin painting was
rejected for an exhibition by the Sydney Royal Art Society in
1916, Rubbo challenged a committee-member to a duel. Wakelin
and de Maistre then developed a theory of colour related to music,
and held an exhibition in 1919 which is one of the landmarks in
Australian art history. That same year they went on to apply their
theory to abstract form and produced the first Australian abstracts
(of which hardly any survive). They then went to Europe for
several years and returned in the mid-20s; in 1926 the moderns,
aided by George Lambert, held an exhibition from which a regularly exhibiting Contemporary Group was formed.[21]

In Melbourne the leading radical influences were William
(Jock) Frater (b. 1890) and Arnold Shore (1897-1963), both stained-
glass craftsmen by trade, who began liberating themselves from
the Meldrum influence. Largely from study of illustrations in
books and journals, they became committed to an aesthetic which
they had no chance to know in depth. Adrian Lawlor gave a sense
of the loneliness of the rebels when he wrote later:

> it is twelve years and more since a group of painters and writers
> —renegades from the complacent 'get-togetherings' of our dud
> suburban intelligentsia—first found fusion under the aegis of
> Post-Impressionism. We were none of us very erudite . . . ;
> but we had the intelligence, and I suppose the will, to under-
> stand that Cézanne and everything that had proceeded from
> him was 'good'.[22]

Gino Nibbi's Leonardo bookshop became a centre for artists concerned with contemporary painting who closely studied the reproductions Nibbi had imported. Little came of the movement in the
20s, but the central figure became George Bell (1878-1966), 'a well-
established academic painter who suddenly went mad and flung
bricks through the window of his own comfortable club'.[23] On his
return from Europe in 1920, he became increasingly plagued with

doubts and eventually was the only Edwardian expatriate totally to reject academic realism. In 1931 he started a school with Shore, in 1934 went abroad again specifically to study modern painting, and on his return attracted the gifted students who joined him in the long war which broke out in the late 30s.

It is not easy to explain why Australian painters and the art public were so backward and out of touch with twentieth century movements. Part of the explanation perhaps lies in the chance that Meldrum and Norman Lindsay—the two leading rebels against the orthodox Establishment—were reactionary in their theories on art. The war thinned out a generation of students and delayed their impact; yet it is curious that the students who went overseas in the 20s brought back so little of post-impressionism and almost nothing of cubism, futurism and non-representational painting. (Bernard Smith comments that the introduction of post-impressionism owed more to women—Grace Cossington Smith, Thea Proctor, Margaret Preston, Ada Plante and others—than to men, and that in painting quality they were at least as good as the men of the period. The similar contemporary prominence of women novelists may also be connected with the effects of the war.) Moreover, the modern movement simply did not produce until the 40s an artist of major stature to inspire a decisive movement, and no important migrant artists arrived before the late 30s to introduce contemporary trends.[24] Meanwhile, the imperialist art Establishment reviled the decadent painting practice of Europe as subversive both of the ordered sway of the British Empire and the eternal Australian verities which Streeton and Heysen had revealed.*

In the late 30s the art world exploded into violent controversy and the Old Guard suffered a terrible drubbing. The two chief events, the attempt to found an Australian Academy of Art in 1937 and the Melbourne *Herald* exhibition of 1939, need to be placed in a context of a steady growth of knowledge and international influences among artists, so that when the crisis came the conservatives simply did not have the numbers. The controversies were most important, perhaps, in their effect on elevating public taste. Bernard Smith sums up:

> During the 1930s Australian art began to show signs of new vitality. Contact with contemporary European art was

---

* Cf. Gulley Jimson in Joyce Cary's *The Horse's Mouth*: 'They knew what modern art can do. Creeping about everywhere, undermining the Church and the State and the Academy and the Law and marriage and the Government— smashing up civilization, degenerating the Empire.'

firmly established; the reactionary opposition in painting and criticism was challenged and defeated by a new generation of artists who broke completely with the traditions of academic naturalism; and a lively curiosity among artists and the public began to replace the complacency that had prevailed during the preceding decade. This curiosity revealed itself in many ways: in the great interest shown in exhibition work from overseas; in the formation of new art schools, centres and societies; in the sense of excitement and interest in experiment prevailing among local art students; in the return of a new generation of students from abroad keenly interested in contemporary work; and in the arrival of artists and scholars from Hitler's Europe.[25]

In Sydney Rah Fizelle's and Grace Crowley's school from 1932 paralleled Bell's in Melbourne. In 1932 also Bell formed the Contemporary Group which acted as a central articulate movement. Several exhibitions of overseas painting, mostly contemporary British, roused interest. In 1931 Keith Murdoch, a patron of modern art, arranged for an exhibition of colour reproductions of moderns in the *Herald* building, in response to provocation by Nibbi. Private owners increased the significance of the occasion by lending originals by Picasso, Matisse, Utrillo, Dufy and Modigliani; and Bell, Frater and Shore gave lectures. Two exhibitions in Sydney in 1935 and 1936 included works by the French masters. In 1937 the Melbourne Gallery actually allowed Bell to organize a Loan Exhibition within its walls—Mrs R. G. Casey lent her Picasso and Sali Herman a van Gogh and a Utrillo—but the director, MacDonald, denounced the show at the opening. The cultural journal, *Manuscripts*, included favourable contributions on cubism and surrealism.[26]

Hence, when the attempt was made to launch an Australian Academy of Art, with the aim of a royal charter, the rot had already gone too far. The plan was to include a sound majority of traditional Australian painters and a few 'sane moderns', post-impressionists who went as far as Cézanne but no further. The chief promoter and spokesman was Robert Gordon Menzies. In April 1937 he was asked to open the annual exhibition of the Victorian Artists' Society and said in his address:

Every great country has its academy. They have set certain standards of art. . . . Great art speaks a language which every

intelligent person can understand. The people who call themselves modernists today talk a different language.

The president of the Society immediately took exception to Menzies' remarks, for he had invited members of Bell's Contemporary
Group to exhibit and many of these artists were present. A de-
lightful controversy followed for several weeks in the newspapers.
Bell denounced Menzies for asserting the right of a layman to
judge art; moreover,

> Academies have been, throughout history, reactionary in-
> fluences. Art is always growing. An Academy sets out to stand-
> ardize art. As soon as that is done art is dead. An Academy
> sets out to be conservative in its very essence. It sets its face
> against a furthering of knowledge gained by experiment.
> Every great artist has been a 'rebel'. . . .

In reply, Menzies made the classically mistaken assertion: 'I am a
typical person of moderate education, I hope reasonably good
taste, and a lifelong interest in the fine arts. . . . I represent a class
of people which will, in the next hundred years determine the permanent place to be occupied in the world of art by those painting
today.'[27] Disagreement about art may have been one of the causes
of enmity between Menzies and H. V. Evatt, who was a conspicuous opener of modernist exhibitions and whose wife was a
student of Bell's. The controversy went on and on through 1937.
Adrian Lawlor's pamphlet, *Arquebus*, which attacked the propo-
sal for an Academy, was a brilliant 'mixture of learning, buffoon-
ery, pastiche and wit'.[28] The promoters of the Academy laboured
under difficulties; for there were enough conservative painters who
were open-minded about modern trends to form a suspicious and
uncooperative group, and in New South Wales the elective Society
of Artists was in effect carrying out the functions of an academy.
Too many of the moderates and conservatives refused to join the
Academy (for reasons which were as complex as only artists could
make them), and eventually the Establishment proved to be in-
sufficiently strong or united to carry it off. The Academy held five
exhibitions, but did not achieve its royal charter and collapsed
during the wartime years.

The Melbourne *Herald* exhibition in 1939—the equivalent of
Fry's London exhibition of post-impressionism in 1910 or the New
York Armory Show of 1913—was a decisive turning-point in public
taste. Murdoch sent Basil Burdett, the *Herald*'s modernist art-

critic, overseas to assemble a comprehensive exhibition of modern French and British painting. Burdett returned with more than 200 paintings including 9 Picassos, 8 Matisses, 8 van Goghs, 7 Cézannes, 7 Gauguins, 5 Rouaults, 4 Braques and works by Bonnard, Chagall, Dali, Derain, Modigliani and Epstein. The exhibition provoked excitement in both Melbourne and Sydney; 40,000 visited it in the Melbourne Town Hall. One consequence was the writing of *Addled Art* by the ageing Lionel Lindsay, who now saw nothing to hope for in a world which seemed to have gone mad. Among other things, he set out to prove that Picasso, Matisse and the surrealists were part of a vast Jewish conspiracy. Another major consequence was the settlement of the dispute between Murdoch, who had just become chairman of the Library and Gallery trustees, and MacDonald (who was a sick man) by the latter's virtual dismissal. A committee of the trustees had selected for possible purchase nine paintings from the *Herald* show, and a van Gogh, a Derain and a Vallotton were eventually bought. MacDonald described the nine paintings as wretched, putrid meat and filth; most modern art was produced by 'degenerates and perverts'.[29] Murdoch worked harmoniously for a decade with the new director, Daryl Lindsay, to bring the Gallery reasonably in line with the modern world.

Another seminal event was the formation in Melbourne in 1938 of the Contemporary Art Society, which spread to Sydney in 1939. It was an attempt to unite all modernist forces and arose directly from Bell's campaign against the Academy. Part of its constitution ran:

> By the expression 'contemporary art' is meant all contemporary painting, sculpture, drawing and other visual art forms which is or are original and creative or which strive to give expression to progressive contemporary thought and life as opposed to work which is reactionary or retrogressive including work which has no other aim than representation.[30]

But very soon there was a schism. Bell and his followers, who were apolitical and mainly interested in 'significant form', came to be tagged as the conservative right wing of contemporary painters—which is an indication of how post-impressionism, which arrived in Australia so tardily, had little chance to flower before it was outdated by later trends. Bell resigned his presidency in protest both at growing political activity and at lay influence in the Society; then in 1940 he and eighty-two sympathisers resigned from the Society itself. Bell has been described as 'arguably the most influential single teacher who ever worked in Australia';[31] his work came to fruition largely in Sydney in the 40s after Russell Drysdale, Sali Herman and others of his students had moved there, partly to escape the venom of Melbourne's art-politics. There remained in the Contemporary Art Society in Melbourne a social realist left wing, and a heterogeneous group variously influenced by abstract art, expressionism, surrealism, cubism, and dada.

Melbourne was the scene of 'the angry decade' in painting—roughly 1937-47—but in other respects painting based on Sydney was just as interesting. In the 20s and early 30s Julian Ashton had been producing more promising students than Bernard Hall in Melbourne. In the years 1938-40 there was a remarkable influx of returning students and of migrants from Europe, who had a wide variety of artistic approaches without, in general, any social commitment. The most notable of them was William Dobell (1899-1970), son of a building tradesman, who became an architectural draughtsman and did not attend Ashton's school until he was twenty-five. He won the overseas scholarship in 1929, studied under Tonks and Steer at the Slade school, and was almost unknown when he returned at forty years of age. He had absorbed, especially, Rembrandt, Goya, Daumier, Renoir and Soutine, and their influences were transformed into a highly personal vision of humanity. He had already painted many London characters and scenes—sometimes affectionately, sometimes acidly, occasionally delighting in the macabre and vulgar. In the early 40s he produced a series of portraits which are a gallery of Australian types, possibly unique in twentieth century world-painting as a sustained effort of portraiture and in quality of characterization. Bernard Smith comments:

> a complete mastery of the traditional techniques . . . are united with a personal gift for characterization equally responsive to the vanity, ugliness, charm, stupidity, sensuality, beauty, obesity, vitality or arrogance of his sitters.

He was not deliberately Australian in his approach, but it is almost impossible not to notice a democratically egalitarian handling of the wide range of subjects. Dobell's portraiture overwhelms his other work, but he was a notable miniaturist and James Gleeson considers some of his New Guinea sketches between 1949 and 1953 to be 'tiny masterpieces'. He became a living 'old master' and suffered from gross overpraise by those who made him a fashionable culture-hero; partly in response, Robert Hughes has summed him up as a 'minor twentieth century mannerist'.[32]

Dobell's winning Archibald Prize portrait of Joshua Smith in 1943 was the occasion of the decisive battle in New South Wales between ancients and moderns, for a group of disgruntled conservative artists took legal action to have the award set aside. Mr Justice Roper had to rule on whether the painting was a portrait in the terms of Archibald's will or whether it was a caricature as the petitioners claimed. Expert witnesses on either side were cross-examined on their definitions of a portrait; Dobell himself stood up well to questioning by Garfield Barwick, K.C. The judge dismissed the action and came close to stating what must be accepted: that the painting was indeed a caricature but also a portrait of the highest quality. The intense public interest made Dobell a notoriety, but he was shocked and bewildered by the bitterness of some of his critics, had a serious breakdown and did not paint again for a year.[33] In the rest of his career he painted relatively few portraits; some of them like *Dame Mary Gilmore* were among his most interesting works, but he had been diverted from an investigation which might have produced quite remarkable results. He always claimed he was essentially a traditionalist, but had tried to keep up with modernism; in doing so, he believed he might have side-tracked himself away from his greatest potentiality.

Russell Drysdale (b. 1912) is a far more important artist, if only because of his immense influence on his successors, whereas Dobell had almost none. Drysdale came of old pastoral families and was intended for the land; his view of the land and people is a countryman's. At the age of twenty-three he placed himself under Bell whom he acknowledges as a teacher of extraordinary ability. Trips to Europe familiarized him with the whole range of contemporary painting. He was the first to make a complete break with naturalistic landscape, unless perhaps preference is given to Peter Purves Smith (1912-49), a close friend from Geelong Grammar days with whom Drysdale studied in Melbourne and Paris, an artist of the greatest promise. The followers of the Heidelberg school had been confining themselves to the pretty country, idealizing and romanticizing, losing visual integrity. Drysdale found reality again with the help of 'ideas drawn from realistic, expressionistic and surrealistic sources'. The 1940 drought in the Riverina and the nightmarish drought in 1944 in western New South Wales gave him crucial inspiration. At the time many thought his subjects were shockingly ugly. He was presenting a landscape which, as Bernard Smith has defined it, was 'alien to man, harsh, weird, spacious and vacant, given over to the oddities and whimsies of nature, fit only for heroes and clowns, saints, exiles and primitive men'. He was experimenting with the forms and possible symbolic qualities of dead trees, roots, rocks, sand, burnt-out farms, corrugated-iron. He took up again the enduring theme of loneliness and melancholy in a hostile environment, and presented a realistic Lawson view of the outback with more affection and less sentiment. His outback women stand calm and dignified, 'strong and patient, rebuffing loneliness'. In less serious vein, the expressive stance of his 'characters' set in the townships are friendly comments on country types. Another of Drysdale's major claims to originality is his long series on Aborigines following his 1951 north Queensland trip, for this was the first important depiction of the Aborigine in modern Australian painting. Drysdale's originality of vision of Australia, his innovatory importance, are unlikely ever to be surpassed.[34]

Brief mention of several artists must suffice to indicate the variety of approach and increase in international influence in Sydney in the 40s. Lloyd Rees (b. 1895) was a painter of the older generation who, alone perhaps, gave new vitality to the old landscape tradition. Strongly influenced by the Italian countryside, his paintings in the late 30s and 40s of the bony folds and wrinkles of hills impress a sense of geological antiquity.[35] Sali Herman (b. 1898), a Swiss, migrated when almost forty and, though he ranged widely for subject-matter, became tagged as the painter of Sydney tenements in happy decorative colour; the *Bulletin* reprimanded him severely for painting slums. Donald Friend (b. 1915) cannot easily be labelled. A fine draughtsman, stylish and urbane, he has been experimental and inventive within a realist framework. A love of the primitive has led him to spend much of his life in Nigeria, Ceylon and Indonesia. One marked trend of the period was a romantic return to European tradition, the classical past, especially Renaissance and Byzantine styles.[36] Jean Bellette's groups of figures in landscape, which often derived from mythology, and Justin O'Brien's religious paintings, influenced by Byzantine and Sienese art, are examples. Most of these painters and many others in Sydney were neo-romantic, decorative and 'had little to say'; but Robert Hughes is surely harsh in brushing off most of their work as 'luxury art' and defining them as 'the charm school'.[37]

There was little 'charming' about art in Melbourne. This had been the headquarters of the art Establishment; this was the city of political extremes, always more open to international ideological influences than Sydney. The sense of having the old guard on the run and the heightened self-awareness and consciousness of crisis produced by the outbreak of war made it inherently likely that an extreme radical movement would develop among the younger artists. After the secession of Bell and the post-impressionists, nearly all the painters of the Contemporary Art Society practised an 'engaged' art. And in such an isolated province, the influence of two recent European migrants who knew what expressionism was about, was crucial. In 1937 Danila Vassilieff (1897-1958) arrived in Melbourne; a Cossack and a Czarist soldier, he had farmed in Queensland in the 20s, then trained himself as an artist in South America, the West Indies and Europe. His paintings of street-scenes introduced a trend which the social realists were to develop, and the liveliness and immediacy of his expressionism had a wide general influence. Vassilieff later became a notable sculptor. Josl Bergner, who had grown up in Poland but was of a Viennese Jewish family, also arrived in 1937 at the age of seventeen. Bergner's importance probably lies not so much in his sombre paintings of social injustice, or in his series on the Warsaw ghetto, but in the impact of his strong personality and his ability to convey to his listeners something of the agony of Europe.

About 1940 surrealism made a wide impact. Several painters had previously made isolated surrealist experiments, but Dali's painting in the *Herald* exhibition caused more argument than any other. James Gleeson made the most sustained attempt to develop this approach (which also became quite a vogue in poetry); and it had a lasting influence on the styles of painters like Nolan, Drysdale, Tucker, Boyd and Perceval. A strong group also formed of social realist painters, of whom Noel Counihan, V. G. O'Connor and Bergner were the most prominent. Counihan (b. 1913) had been a press cartoonist for many years and later developed into a sometimes brilliant portraitist. This faction, following the wartime 'popular front' policy of the Communist Party, persuaded the Society in 1942 to hold an exhibition of Anti-Fascist Art. The working agreement between the social realists and the individualistic expressionists soon broke down in bitter controversy. The social realists broadly maintained that art was art only when it was politics rather than general comment on the human condition. The other school, led by the patron and publicist, John Reed, and Albert Tucker, maintained the need for the artist's creative freedom; moreover, they argued that the Society had been formed in opposition to the naturalistic representation which the social realists continued.[38]

The three major artists who emerged from this Melbourne melting-pot—Nolan, Tucker and Boyd—are characterized by the limited part formal art training played in their development, their intense self-training and acquisition of world intellectual and painting trends, and extraordinary range of experiment.

Sidney Nolan (b. 1917) came from an Irish-Australian working-class family and in his youth took a variety of casual jobs; his chief interest was competitive cycling. By 1938, after some practice in commercial art, he had become a serious painter; most of his works were abstract and others were designed to shock conventional art opinion. Nolan was one of the many part-products of the State Library of Victoria, for it was there that he studied the prints of Picasso, Klee, Miro, and Henri Rousseau, and read omnivorously—Blake, Rimbaud, Verlaine, Joyce. He was also writing verse. About 1940 he was taken up by John and Sunday Reed whose patronage made possible the large volume of his painting in the 40s. Early in that decade he turned deliberately to figurative and representational painting in an attempt to find a fresh approach to familiar subject-matter; the Wimmera landscapes were the chief product. Over the next fifteen years he used Australian history to create mythical emblems which he universalized; they were often in 'sham folk-art style' and nearly always with a strong element of fantasy. His subjects were the Kellys (in two series), convicts, explorers, Eureka, Gallipoli, and drought and desert scenes. He went on to draw inspiration from Italy, Greece, Cambodia and the Antarctic, and became the first Australian painter to win a major European reputation.[39]

Arthur Boyd (b. 1920) possibly surpasses even Nolan in versatility and variety of experimentation. Boyd is highly unusual in Australian art history in that he came of families with a long tradition of 'art, craftsmanship and Christian humanism'. His grandfather, Arthur M. Boyd, and grandmother were painters; his great-uncle, Edward a'Beckett was a portrait-painter; his father, Merric, a potter; his uncle, Penleigh, a painter; his uncle, Martin, a writer; his cousin, Robin, an architect; and his younger brother, David, a painter and potter. As a youth Arthur Boyd painted traditional landscapes and first exhibited in 1937. Study of prints by Rouault, van Gogh and others at Nibbi's bookshop, reading Dostoievsky, and meeting Bergner and other *avant-garde* painters led him towards expressionism, and in 1941 a 'steady stream of powerful and obsessive drawings' began. The mid-40s were rich and prolific years. Surrealist images, 'symbolic of death, grief, illness and violence', characterize the 'suburban' paintings;

in the Hunter and Forest series, the Bush was peopled with sur-realist monsters. The great series of religious paintings, notably *The Mockers* (1945), was influenced by Breugel and, later, Rembrandt. In the years roughly 1947 to 1958 Boyd mainly painted calm, sparse landscapes, particularly his version of the Wimmera; but he had also established a pottery and produced notable ceramic sculptures and ceramic paintings. The *Love, Marriage and Death of a Half-caste* series, exhibited in 1958, was a return to imaginative figures under the influence of Chagall, and was a turning-point. In 1959 he left for London and his painting took new directions; his themes since have included a myth of the outcast, Romeo and Juliet and St Francis. Throughout his Australian career his work continually alternated between the naturalist and imaginative approach. His biographer, Franz Philipp, in stressing Boyd's constant awareness of Australian painting tradition, has described him as a 'traditionalist revolutionary'.[40]

Albert Tucker (b. 1914) left school young, and had a hard time finding regular employment during the depression. He attended classes at the Victorian Artists' Society from 1933 to 1939, and had some contact with the Bell group after his first exhibition in 1935 of fairly conventional portraits, nudes, landscapes and still lifes. He was soon attracted by Vassilieff, whom he came to regard as 'a father-figure for his generation', and was a founding member of the Contemporary Art Society. By 1939 he was coming under the strong influence of German expressionism; Cézanne, Picasso and de Chirico were also guides and he was familiar with the writings of Eliot, Herbert Read and Jung. Work as a medical illustrator in the Army in 1942 added a new dimension of the horror of war. Tucker had had a communist phase in the 30s and his work was based on social protest. But he was a disillusioned Marxist and after keeping on terms with the social realists fell out with them violently in 1943 in defence of the artist's right to individual response. His militant polemical ability made him in most respects the intellectual leader of the *avant-garde* painters of the period. His aggressive energy and independence helped to form a highly individual style in his treatment of urban imagery and his expressionist portraits. In his series from 1943, *Images of Modern Evil*—'The City in Wartime'—he became increasingly surrealist; obsessive symbols of moral degradation demonstrated his outraged protest against the state of the world. Tucker was little appreciated and left Australia resentfully in 1947, saying, 'I am a refugee from Australian culture'. After a period in Paris, when he profited from a study of Dubuffet, he had several years in Italy where he produced a notable series of religious paintings. By the mid-50s he had won a considerable reputation in Rome and New York, but by this time he was turning back to Australian themes; he was developing his 'disc head' or 'Antipodean head', taking up the Bush and explorers and, in part-parody of Nolan, painting a Kelly series. From his return in 1960 'to collect his back pay', he has been stating his versions of Australian myths in numerous landscapes featuring wild life and the recurrent head.[41]

Nolan, Boyd and Tucker were all in their ways reacting violently against the world, lashing out against mass unemployment, totalitarian ideologies, world war and concentration-camps. They were also well aware of the relationship between complacent provincial isolationism and conservatism in art, and were trying to drag Australia into the intellectual twentieth century. A comment by Clive Turnbull in 1947 reflects their attitude:

> For too long, since the time of Roberts and his brethren, artists have been turning away from life and their work has suffered in consequence. They have not been good enough human beings. In the heyday of the Streeton imitators Australian painting sank to its lowest level. Even today one looks at large mixed exhibitions with wonder. After all that the world has suffered in the last 10 years there are still dozens of painters covering the wall with gumtrees and poplars, with slick photographic portraits, nostalgic sketches of tumbledown rural hamlets, and all the rest of the unprofitable stuff. . . . their banality of subject matter, in a time of vast and tragic flux, shows that they lack the mental equipment necessary to produce works of art.[42]

It is remarkable that Nolan, Boyd and Tucker picked up so much of the intellectual framework of modern European painting—having seen only a few dozen examples—from study of a limited range of reproductions, talk with those who had been in Europe, and hard reading. They had to acquire a cultural pattern from fragments. But they became, in a sense, national as well as universal painters. The remarks which Tucker made in 1943 on Nolan's paintings may be applied also to Drysdale, Boyd and Tucker himself:

> we glimpse for the first time since Roberts, McCubbin and the early Streeton, the return of an authentic national vision. . . .

> In a series of courageous portraits and themes of disaster, where Nolan is approaching problems rich in human implications, he is wisely obeying history and pushing back towards the real sources of aesthetic experience—the world of living men.[43]

As with the Heidelberg Impressionists, ideas and techniques from Europe enabled a new Australian vision.

Painting was one area of very exciting advance, especially during the war-years; the other was poetry. By 1946, when H. M. Green's anthology, *Modern Australian Poetry*, indicated the depth of recent achievement, Slessor had collected his work in *One Hundred Poems* (1944), FitzGerald's *Moonlight Acre* (1938) was accepted as a major contribution, Douglas Stewart had published five books of verse, and the first volumes by Judith Wright and James McAuley had just appeared. All five of these poets, incidentally, were from New South Wales. In addition a dozen other poets of substance were making their mark, and fugitive poems by A. D. Hope were appearing. Green fairly claimed that now, for the first time, there was 'a basis for comparison with the work of poets overseas'.[44]

Robert D. FitzGerald (b. 1902), a surveyor by occupation, was of Slessor's generation and emerged with him as a major poet in the 30s. H. P. Heseltine asserts that together they 'thrust Australian verse forward with an imperious force unknown since its foundations', and liberated and gave independence to their successors.[45] FitzGerald's verse reflects the gusto and delight in life of a natural optimist with a heroic view of mankind. Time, the relationship of past and present, has preoccupied him as in 'Essay on Memory' (1938) and in his feeling for historical background in poems like the later 'The Wind at your Door'.[46] Judith Wright (b. 1915) was to become the most popular of the distinguished poets, for her capture of history and landscape and for her femininity. In *The Moving Image* (1946) she evoked the New England landscape, legends and way of life superbly, and in her imagery used the Australian language to communicate more easily perhaps than any of her predecessors. Poems like 'Bullocky' were packed with symbolic suggestion.[47] James McAuley (b. 1917) in *Under Aldebaran* (1946) displayed himself as an austere classicist, a meditative lyricist and a gifted epigrammatic wit. He was to become 'the most ardent upholder of the European tradition in Australia' and the most combative of literary controversialists.[48] Few critics feel sure in claiming that the poetic achievement of Douglas Stewart (b.

New Zealand, 1913) rivals that of his leading contemporaries; but he has been a warm, fluent, melodious poet of abundant inspiration, most successful perhaps with his nature-poems and balladry.[49] And Stewart is the great all-rounder of modern Australian literature, as poet, playwright, short-story-writer, critic and editor for twenty years of the *Bulletin*'s 'Red Page'. None of these leading poets, who established themselves during the war-years, and few of their rivals owed any stimulus either to the Jindyworobak or the *Angry Penguins* movements.

We have already argued that a substantial dissident intellectual class emerged in the 30s. But it was the generation born roughly between 1915 and 1925, which grew up in the depression and was then faced with the shock of war, which rose in total revolt against cultural orthodoxy. The most notable group was the 'anti-Australian' internationalist modernists, such as the expressionist painters and those associated with *Angry Penguins*. As Ian Turner has put it:

> almost overnight there was an Australian *avant-garde*. The blues, sociology, cubism, the collective unconscious, atonal music, the classic German film, primitive sculpture, the Id and the Superego, symbolism, surrealism, expressionism—all were avidly absorbed by young artists and intellectuals for whom *avant-garde* meant a revolt against age and provincialism and bourgeois values, a rejection of the market-place and the subordination of art to ideology, a revelation of the senses and the psyche, even a way of life.[50]

The contents of several Melbourne little magazines of the 30s—Cyril Pearl's *Stream* (1931), H. Tatlock Miller's *Manuscripts* (1931-5), and Mervyn Skipper's *Pandemonium* (1934-5)—indicate that there were forerunners.[51] But youth was the outstanding feature of the contributors to *Angry Penguins* and other wartime experimental little magazines such as *A Comment* (Melbourne, 1940-47) and *Barjai* (Brisbane, 1943-7).

Angry Penguins (1940-46) was founded as the journal of the Adelaide University Arts Association by Max Harris (b. 1921) in association with Donald Kerr and Paul Pfeiffer, two young poets of quality who were shortly to die in the Air Force. The title was taken from a line in a Harris poem: 'drunks, the angry penguins of the night'. The young Harris was something of a nihilist idol-smasher, concerned to shock all established opinion and of course to ridicule the local Jindyworobaks. Much of the surrealist Neo-Apocalyptic verse published was no doubt nonsense. But from 1943 the journal published a phenomenal variety of material; one issue ran to 185 pages of close print. John Reed, with whom Harris formed a publishing firm, became co-editor, and Sidney Nolan was closely associated. *Angry Penguins* became the vehicle for the violent art controversy of the day, and lavishly printed illustrations of paintings. Psychoanalysis and primitive religion were two prominent interests; Freud, Marx, Kafka, Rilke, Proust, Sartre, Croce, Dylan Thomas, Henry Miller were major subjects of concern; while film, jazz and other art-forms were also discussed. Karl Shapiro and Harry Roskolenko, American writers in Australia, were involved. Hal Porter, Peter Cowan, Geoffrey Dutton and other rising writers contributed—indeed, almost anyone with anything to say. Harris summed it all up in retrospect as 'an astounding monolith of obscure cult-ridden subjectivism, incredible in fervour for such a small country as Australia'; and he was right enough in claiming there was important work 'embedded in that solid and useless mass'.[52] Much of it undoubtedly was the pouring-out of half-grasped advanced ideas and styles, but in its time it was immensely liberating and stimulating. And again it is interesting that Harris and Dutton who began as *avant-garde* internationalists, in the long run not only became notable poets but as publicists have been among those most concerned to define the Australian identity.

Sydney had its typical answer to *Angry Penguins*, in satire of experimentalism. Garry Lyle, the founder of a deliberately un-named little magazine (*Number One,* etc., 1943-8), stated in the first issue: 'We are as utterly fed-up with self-conscious national bards as we are with the unoriginal importers of meretricious styles already done to death overseas by their own intrinsic mediocrity.' A. D. Hope was the chief contributor; some of his early verse satirized modern intellectual fashions (or rather half-baked expression of them) and he wrote a notorious review carving up Harris's novel, *The Vegetative Eye*. It is probably not unfair to restate a contemporary opinion that at this stage Hope, and James McAuley and Harold Stewart, the two other rising Sydney poets, 'could not reach past the negative critical attitude. They did not advance their theories past a mere classical revival against romanticism.'[53] Their main blow was the perpetration by McAuley and Stewart of the Ern Malley hoax. Harris published and hailed as a major discovery, in the Autumn 1944 issue of *Angry Penguins*, a series of poems entitled *The Darkening Ecliptic* by Ern Malley, allegedly a motor mechanic and insurance salesman who had recently died at the age of twenty-five; Nolan contributed the cover for the issue. Some weeks later McAuley and Stewart announced in the press that they had concocted the meaningless poems in one afternoon as 'a serious literary experiment' in protest against 'the gradual decay of meaning and craftsmanship in poetry' and against a literary fashion, represented in Australia by *Angry Penguins*, which 'rendered its devotees insensible of absurdity and incapable of ordinary discrimination'. The press and all who hated poetry—and especially those who hated modern poets and artists and all they stood for—seized on the exposure in high glee and Harris became a national butt. The incident also made world-wide news; Ern Malley overnight became the only internationally-known Australian poet. The affair soon took on a new dimension of sorry farce when a witch-hunt developed and Harris was prosecuted—at the instigation of members of Catholic Action, he believes—for an indecent publication. A ludicrous detective was the lone prosecution witness, learned literary critics gave evidence, and Harris was examined for two and a half days. A verdict of indecency, but not of obscenity or immorality, was found, and he was fined £5 and costs.

Harris of course had been credulous. But the poems had been cunningly contrived to appeal to his prejudices, and we may sympathize with his eagerness to discover a young poet who was an 'outsider'. And the poems were by no means all nonsense or meaningless. Some of them, especially the first, made quite a lot of sense, and overall, as Brian Elliott says, although their rational content was incoherent, their drift was intelligible. There were a few striking lines and a sustained satirical purpose.

> [Harris] was really justified because, though not in the way he supposed, it *was* art. At least he saw what few others could see: that, whether for this reason or that, *The Darkening Ecliptic* was a remarkable *tour de force*. Those who will take the trouble to read over again this *jeu d'esprit* will be agreeably surprised with its lightness, its devastating perspicuousness where it was intended to be clear, its grace and wit, its acute satirical sharpness, and the aplomb with which it annihilated its victims while saying virtually nothing.[54]

In the following issue of *Angry Penguins* Harris launched a brave counter-offensive, including a defence by Herbert Read:

If a man of sensibility, in a mood of despair or hatred, or even from a perverted sense of humour, sets out to fake works of imagination, then if he is to be convincing he must use the poetic faculties. If he uses these faculties to good effect, he ends by deceiving himself.[55]

Ern Malley's poems have continued to attract interest over the years for their own sake, and their short-term effect on the practice of poetry in Australia was considerable. On the one hand experimental poets were shocked into reassessment; as Elliott says, a major effect was 'to discountenance all flimsy, wishful and lazy poetical dilettantism'.[56] But another consequence may have been to impose an unfortunate element of cautious restraint on many a young poet.[57]

The challenge and stimulus of war brought a surge of national consciousness and idealism and also a widening of interest in the arts. The editors of existing journals and others founded soon after the outbreak of war were determined that culture should be kept alive. 'Art cannot die, and we in Australia can and will carry on our efforts to preserve, encourage and foster the cultures our enemies would destroy,' *Art in Australia* bravely declared.[58] In the dark days of 1942, Vance Palmer wrote in *Meanjin* a noble statement of faith. 'Battle' concluded:

> I believe we will survive; that what is significant in us will survive; that we will come out of this struggle battered, stripped to the bone, but spiritually sounder than we went in, surer of our essential character, adults in a wider world than the one we lived in hitherto. These are great, tragic days. Let us accept them stoically, and make every yard of Australian earth a battle-station.[59]

Thrown largely on their own resources, Australians showed new interest in their art and letters. The demand for Australian books could not be met, and was not entirely to be explained by printing restrictions, absence of luxury goods on which to spend, and inability to import many English books. The Commonwealth Literary Fund issued a series, 'The Australian Pocket Library'; in 1941 Angus & Robertson began its annual anthologies of short stories and poetry, *Coast to Coast* and *Australian Poetry*. The 'Legend of the Nineties', the age of the brash nationalists, attracted enthusiastic interest. Sales of paintings and visits to galleries increased. A Council for the Encouragement of Music and the Arts worked hard to widen audiences. Hundreds of servicemen, for the first and last time in their lives usually, wrote verse and short stories. The Army Education Service was by far the most successful adult educational experiment there had been; its journal, *Salt*, and its library and gramaphone-record services succoured those starved of culture and roused the interest of thousands who had been unaware of it. *Introducing Australia* (1942) by the American, C. Hartley Grattan, was an important educative influence. Towards the end of the war a quickening, an alertness, a revival of utopian hope and a resurgence of national idealism were clearly discernible. There was also, following the shock of the fall of Singapore, a marked growth of self-confidence and of a sense of independence which reflected military and industrial achievement, such as the speedy manufacture of aircraft and tanks. H. L. Coombs's Department of Post-War Reconstruction envisaged a prominent place for the arts in the new Australia; among other things a Commonwealth Cultural Council and a National Film Board were mooted. 'The Australian cultural scene shows many signs of bursting into bloom as glorious as the adventurous hopeful days of the Nineties,' wrote Lloyd Ross. 'There are many young men and women standing poised before futures that may make this decade an outstanding period in our history.' And he cited as evidence the community centre movement, art festivals, mobile film units, rural concert halls, area schools, residential adult colleges, town planning exhibitions, innumerable discussion groups— and trade unions combining to employ an artist, munition workers learning to paint, music-teachers and verse-speakers visiting factories on request.[60] For a brief period the 'new order' appeared to be easily attainable.

One particular cultural strand developed under the guidance of the Communist Party during the only period when it attracted any substantial intellectual support. The 'workers' art clubs' of the late 30s did not take root, but the social realist wing of modern painting was briefly influential around 1940 and after. The most valuable of the Party's literary enterprises was *Australian New Writing* (1943-6) which included much 'realist' work by young writers and brought to light the outstanding talent of John Morrison, the best of the 'proletarian' writers. The continuing realist writers' groups in the late 40s produced writers such as Frank Hardy. The New Theatre movement presented plays by such writers as O'Casey and Odets and numerous entertaining revues, but contributed little indigenous drama of merit apart from plays by Oriel Gray and Dick Diamond's musical, *Reedy River*. Hostile opponents foolishly attributed Communist identification with Australian nationalism to mere political opportunism, without realizing the genuine historical depth of popular anti-imperialism.

The mainly Jewish refugees from Nazi Europe in the late 30s provided new life. The several thousands who settled in Sydney and Melbourne were to form an important element in audiences for music, drama and opera; they also brought sophisticated knowledge of modern art. The early group was reinforced by Austrian and German refugees, who had been interned in England and then in 1940 transported on the *Dunera*; many of its passengers, such as Henry Mayer and Gustav Nossal, have since become noted scholars. These migrants and refugees of the late 30s and early 40s included the composers George Dreyfus and Felix Werder, the art historians Leonhard Adam, Ursula Hoff and Franz Philipp, the publisher Andrew Fabinyi, the architect Frederick Romberg, and many others who have contributed notably to Australian culture.[61]

There had indeed been a change in the scale of cultural creativeness and participation in the 30s and early 40s, and over the same period both a resurgence of national aspiration and a new openness to international influences. The most striking change and success had been in painting; can any of the arts in any decade rival the painting achievement of the 40s? Literature had grown steadily but not spectacularly since the mid-20s until the emergence of the young poets of the 40s. Musical appreciation had developed enormously, but composition had made little progress; the theatre remained almost moribund. The notion of Australia turning a corner and coming of age may perhaps be argued more easily with regard to public life than cultural, and more convincingly dated in the war years than in the late 30s. The achievements of Slessor and FitzGerald, of Dobell and Drysdale, and others, had given a new distinction to Australian culture. Yet despite the undoubted improvement in quality and scale, cultural development seemed to stop just short of maturity. There was to be a curious sense of unfulfilment and hesitation on the brow of the hill during the decade after the war.

Since the 1939-45 war Australia has fundamentally changed. Sustained mass-migration contributed largely to a steady growth of population from $7\frac{1}{2}$ million in 1946 to 10 million in 1959 to 13 million in 1972. The introduction of more than one million migrants from most European countries—almost as many as came from Britain—basically modified the composition of the population. Mass unemployment was eliminated and social services and central banking regulation of the economy protected the mass of the people from distress, although many serious inequities remained. The 1950s and 60s were a period of sustained economic growth, boom prosperity for many, and crass materialism comparable to the 1850-90 period. Not even the development of nickel and other minerals and oil could halt the march of urbanization based on industrialization and the decline of rural industry; less than one-fifth of Australians live outside cities and large towns. The increasing diversification of an industrial society produced new complexities in class relationships.

Wartime idealism petered out in frustration and disillusion even before the Menzies era. The Cold War, the attempt to ban the Communist Party and the persecution of left liberals, the fabrication of the notion of red Asian hordes swarming down on isolated Australia, and the brilliant Petrov diversion then embittered politics. The Catholic bishops abandoned concern for social justice in favour of anti-communism. The long-standing two or three party system was upset by the breakaway from the Labor party of the largely Catholic Democratic Labor Party which extended Labor's stint in the wilderness for nearly two more decades. However, the breach precipitated the outstanding intellectual development of the 50s—the break-up of monolithic Catholicism and the emergence of dissident liberals from the ghetto. But in general the new generation of young intellectuals of the 50s tended to be quietist and sceptical, though less naive than their predecessors. Almost all radicalism was dead, it seemed; timid, unthinking conformity prevailed. The real cracking of the standard intellectual mould was to come in the 60s when, for example, rigid belief in

White Australia was abandoned by nearly all educated men and women.

Australia almost grew out of the Empire during the 1939-45 war, although sentimental affection for Britain remained as strong as ever, up to and after the royal tour of 1954. After H. V. Evatt's brief flaunting of Australian independence as a small nation at the United Nations, the Menzies governments retreated into relative subservience, pendulating between the United States and Britain. By about 1960, however, it was clear that Australia had almost become an American satellite, although many of the trappings of imperial loyalty remained. But the main props of the British association—defence and foreign policy—had been knocked away; and the proportions of British trade, migration and capital investment had all declined, as had British cultural and technological influence. Contacts with Asian countries were steadily growing. The old Australian isolationism had gone forever, in the sense that modern communications increasingly exposed the continent to international ideas and fashions. At the same time young Australians through the 50s had been accepting their nationality with little sense of any conflict of loyalties between Australia and Britain; however uncertain they were of their destination, they now at least walked naturally upright—neither strutted nor cringed. Only in the mid-60s, perhaps, was it widely recognized that the imperial age was over, that almost nothing remained of the British connection except the residual monarchy and traditional bonds of affection.

Interest in the Australian past and environment had been growing fast since the war. The study of Australian history, its popularity as a university and school subject and the publication of miscellaneous Australiana all developed steadily. Serious writers now had the audience which they had lacked in the 20s and 30s. In the 50s old bush songs, ballads and yarns were collected and published in numerous anthologies, and folklore societies and bush music clubs flourished. By the late 60s National Trusts had many thousand members, New South Wales and Victoria both had well over one hundred local historical societies, and most provincial centres and shire towns demanded their historical park or folk museum. By then even the Governors-General and their wives— the Caseys and Haslucks—were not only Australian but distinguished in arts and letters.

Cultural standards unquestionably improved immensely between 1945 and 1965, although the progression was by fits and starts. Immediately after the war the dilettante student of local culture could without great effort read almost every new book and attend nearly every concert and exhibition. Within less than ten years he was struggling to find time to keep up with current developments in either literature or painting. The growth was more quantitative than qualitative, perhaps; but almost every recent commentator on Australia has written in terms of a cultural breakthrough in the 50s or early 60s. There had been a decline of excitement and discussion in the immediate postwar years. The mid-50s, however, saw a hopeful surge of promised greatness—Patrick White appeared, Nolan and Tucker had established Australian art abroad, Ray Lawler's *Summer of the Seventeenth Doll* was a revelation—but once again there was a lull. Painting and poetry were the main areas of steady advance, and in the 50s musical composition suddenly achieved maturity.

Some time about the late 50s a decisive change in fashion and taste, a recognition that the arts *mattered,* became evident among both the upper middle class and the younger educated generation. Some knowledge of painting, especially, became an essential ingredient of cocktail-party chatter in Toorak and Woollahra, businessmen began decorating their board-rooms with works of art, and over a few years scores of private galleries sprang up to meet the swelling demand by a newly affluent public to purchase paintings. A few leaders of business became prominent patrons of the arts. There were other indications, such as increasing support for film festivals, growing membership of gramaphone-record clubs, the movements for preservation first of Paddington and later of Carlton and other inner-suburban areas, and the mild growth of a continental-bistro-café society. In general there was a significant movement towards direct involvement with the arts away from passive acceptance of a proxy culture. The state was tardily beginning to recognize its responsibility to nurture creative artists. Nevertheless, in 1960 Hugh Hunt could still deplore the 'sense of inferiority which at every turn stunts the growth of the arts in this country. . . . Australia cannot play an active part in international art until it acknowledges its own art; until it becomes conscious of its own artists and ceases to regard them as inferior to those from overseas.'[1]

The contemporary historian must beware of an unconscious Whiggism which underrates the achievements of writers and artists of earlier generations, whose work has become unfashionable. Though aware of this danger, Harry Heseltine in the recent

Penguin Book of Australian Verse has deliberately selected close on three-quarters of the contents from the post-1940 period. A similar judgment might be broadly appropriate in all the arts. The quantity of work of high quality so expands that it now becomes necessary to be far more brief and selective in treatment than hitherto. Lack of perspective and the difficulty of making judgments on those who are still at work make futile any but the broadest and safest assessments of individual significance.

Through the 50s and 60s, the senior established poets—Fitz-Gerald, Judith Wright, McAuley and Douglas Stewart—continued to widen their range of form and subject-matter. They were joined by A. D. Hope (b. 1907) who did not publish his first volume, *The Wandering Islands*, until 1955; he has since won a higher international reputation than any other Australian poet. His main themes have included loneliness, the nature of sexual love and the regenerative power of art. Despair for humanity has been a strong prevailing note, and a minor but well-known portion of his work has been forcefully satirical.[2] Hope has commonly been linked with McAuley as standing for conservative tradition. McAuley has indeed been an explicit conservative in a wider sense, since his conversion to Catholicism in 1952 and his graduation as a leading spokesman of the conservative church. In his essays, *The End of Modernity*, he 'sets the idea of a traditional, ordered and ceremonious way of life' against degraded modern values, and deplores 'the fixation of the Australian cultural matrix at a late nineteenth century level of Progress and Enlightenment'.[3] J. D. Pringle has quite exaggeratedly seen Hope and McAuley in the 50s leading a successful counter-revolution against the Jindyworobaks and the moderns.[4] But poetry in the 40s had become diverse and fragmented in approach, and the second rank of poets who wrote on through the 50s were far too varied to fit Pringle's interpretation. David Campbell, for example, wrote poetry of landscape and rural folk with unselfconscious ease and delight; Harold Stewart was exotic in his use of Oriental themes and symbols; Kenneth (Seaforth) Mackenzie was a sensualist and vitalist; Rosemary Dobson, a detached, polished craftsman, used painting as an inspiration; John Manifold was a balladist, wry satirist and left-wing propagandist; and Francis Webb (b. 1925), who was to influence some of the rising poets of the 60s, displayed brilliant but bewildering talent in his narratives.

Melbourne became a centre of poetry again only in the mid-50s when Vincent Buckley (b. 1925) stood out. A religious (Catholic), introspective and metaphysical poet, 'a curious blend of lyrical and rhetorical qualities',[5] he has displayed an energetic range of subject, emotion and style. Other rising Melbourne poets of the 50s were Chris Wallace-Crabbe, Evan Jones, Alexander Craig and R. A. Simpson. Buckley believed he discerned a new *Bulletin* school landscape orthodoxy, with Campbell as leading practitioner and Judith Wright as unwilling mother-confessor.[6] Wallace-Crabbe defined a 'habit of irony' and a dominant concern for craftsmanship as leading characteristics of the younger poets of the 50s, who were reacting against the 'forthright confidence of their predecessors' in the confusing and 'contradictory post-war years'.[7] There were many other poets of this period—J. R. Rowland and John Blight among them—who demonstrated how much increase in urbanity, range of skills and forms, and intellectual quality there had been. But in general, Hope was happy to report in 1963, there had been 'a return to traditional forms and techniques of verse and a retreat from experimental methods, free verse, surrealist logomania, fragmentary imagism, dislocated syntax and symbolist allusiveness'.[8]

Palmer, Prichard, Dark, Herbert, Davison, Mann, Tennant and other novelists of the 30s continued to write into the 50s (and some of them into the 60s), but relatively few important successors appeared. Martin Boyd (1893-1972) had spent almost all his adult life overseas and had published a family saga, *The Montforts* (1928), and several other minor novels with non-Australian settings. In his fifties and sixties, however, between 1946 and 1962, he published *Lucinda Brayford* and four other linked novels based on his family's experiences as Anglo-Australians over several generations. He has similarities with Henry James both in his subject—the tensions between the old and new worlds—and in his approach to it. Witty and satirical, yet a deadly serious commentator on the trends of civilization, his prose is seemingly so effortless that its quality is often overlooked. Although he has been brushed off by parochial critics or labelled as an elegant minor novelist of manners, his reputation and popularity have been growing; A. D. Hope believes that in the long run he will be regarded as at least as important as Patrick White.[9] (Kenneth) Seaforth Mackenzie (1913-55) was a novelist of unfulfilled talent, but of unusual interest for his poetic prose and the innovatory range of his subject-matter. His two youthful pre-war novels, both of which steam with eroticism, are studies of adolescence and of Jewishness; his two later works are based on the wartime outbreak of Japanese prisoners from Cowra camp and on the notion of Australia as a refuge from Europe.

The commonly accepted view that Australian fiction made dramatic advances in the 50s is largely bound up with the advent of Patrick White. *Tree of Man* (1955) and *Voss* (1957), despite some savage local carping, were immediately accepted as works by a master—a response made easier by their international reception. Australia now had an 'indisputably great' novelist. White (b. 1912) came of grazier families, was sent to an English public school between the ages of thirteen and seventeen, and then three years later to Cambridge where he graduated in modern languages. In the interim he spent unhappy years as a jackeroo, retreating in distaste from people whose conversation was bounded by sheep, horses, sport and the weather; the sourly-titled *Happy Valley* (1939), his first published novel, was the consequence. White remained in England, served with the R.A.F., and after two more novels returned in 1948 to Australia, where he was almost entirely unknown, to farm at Castle Hill near Sydney. White said he was trying 'to discover the extraordinary behind the ordinary, the mystery and the poetry which could alone make bearable the lives of such people' as Stan and Amy Parker in *Tree of Man*.[10] But he is a novelist of ideas, who uses symbolism and allegory and the whole European frame of reference—Christian thought, old Jewry, classical mythology—as no other Australian novelist has. It has been suggested that his novels are 'poems' in the sense that they are 'extremely complex, ambiguous and ironic linguistic structures'. His daring style teeters on the edge, sometimes collapses, but has certainly encouraged verbal experiment by others. In his concern with the 'texture and colour of experience', White has affinities with Drysdale, Nolan and Boyd.[11] The solitariness of the individual and the view that men are self-destructive but redeemed by suffering have been among his main themes. Love, simplicity, humility are the chief virtues; the socially pretentious are scourged with savage comedy. White once described the Australian novel as the 'dreary dun-coloured offspring of journalistic realism',[12] and in doing so was grossly unfair (he had possibly read few Australian novels); but he himself owes almost nothing to any local literary tradition. In his several novels since *Tree of Man*, and in his stories and plays, he has built a remarkable body of work.[13]

Randolph Stow (b. 1935) was probably influenced by White. By the age of twenty-four he had published three novels, of which the first was *The Haunted Land* (1956), all set in the north-west of

Western Australia; his obsessed characters drive themselves to destruction in surroundings which are powerfully and poetically drawn. Most of the new novelists of the 50s, however, worked in straightforward naturalist forms. Several war-novels, including those by T. A. G. Hungerford, Eric Lambert, George Turner and David Forrest (all of whom went on to write other interesting novels), were competent and moving without reaching great heights. The left-wing social realist movement produced several writers of talent. Frank Hardy's *Power Without Glory* (1950), an exposure of Victorian politics, has had more impact on public life than any other Australian novel. Russian-born Judah Waten (b. 1911) first published stories (*Alien Son*, 1952) and a novel (*The Unbending*, 1954) of Jewish migrant experience, and has followed with several novels of social protest. Dymphna Cusack has written nearly a dozen novels, from the early 50s committedly from the left. A new professionalism developed which enabled skilful writers like Jon Cleary, D'Arcy Niland and Olaf Ruhen, who shaped their work for a popular market, to make reasonable incomes. Morris West, the most able and successful of the formula writers (especially in *The Devil's Advocate*) and one of the best-known Australian writers internationally, deliberately rejected Australian settings. George Johnston (1912-70), like Martin Boyd, became prominent in middle age; during and after a career as a leading journalist, he had spent twenty years away from Australia and had written several minor novels. Then in *My Brother Jack* (1964) he began an autobiographical trilogy which was highly evocative of the Australia he had known and an acute study of the relationship between the ordinary man and the artist. His intense love and hate for his country in the end helped to produce emotion-charged and sensitive writing. Few of the postwar generation of novelists have fulfilled themselves; it is salutary to realize that hardly a living novelist under the age of sixty has established himself as a major writer.

It might also be argued that the short story reached its peak in the 40s and has since been in decline. Palmer and Davison were then at their best, and were backed by Gavin Casey, Don Edwards, Brian James, E. O. Schlunke, Dal Stivens, the young Peter Cowan and others. The radical tradition was renewed more strongly in the story than the novel, and it is curious that the charge of neglecting urban themes is truer with regard to short-story writers than novelists. Gavin Casey (1907-64) must be granted a high place in any ranking of Australian writers for the sustained art and in-

FROM DESERTS THE PROPHETS COME

sight of his stories, which were largely set in working-class Kalgoorlie, as well as for his humour and almost unsurpassed development of the folkish tall story. John Morrison (b. 1904), who migrated from England in his youth, is not only a genuine working-class writer but also probably the most successful of all the left-wingers in finding artistic form for his message; his humanity is unassumingly penetrating. In absolute contrast, Hal Porter (b. 1911) is a virtuoso: his glittering stories (*A Bachelor's Children*, 1962) display 'linguistic experiment, sophisticated wit, and a satire which singles out for attack bad taste, ugliness and stupidity'.[14] Porter is also a novelist, poet and playwright, but his most remarkable achievement is *The Watcher on the Cast-Iron Balcony* (1963), the first volume of his autobiography, which is a brilliantly written recollection and reconstruction of the pre-war period. Alan Marshall (b. 1902) similarly is mainly a short-story writer, building on the bush tradition with seemingly artless yarning. But in his fictionalized autobiography of childhood, *I Can Jump Puddles* (1955), he achieved a masterpiece. No other book by an Australian has sold so widely (more than two million copies, including 250,000 in Australia) and it has been translated into more than a dozen languages. The universality of theme and the humility and unsentimentality of author contribute greatly to its phenomenal appeal.

By the 50s literary criticism was coming of age. The chief agents were the two surviving quarterlies. *Southerly*, which was founded in 1939 as the journal of the Sydney branch of the English Association, has confined itself narrowly to Australian literature; *Meanjin* (originally *Meanjin Papers* and since 1961 *Meanjin Quarterly*) was founded in Brisbane in 1940, since 1945 has been sheltered by the University of Melbourne, and has been edited throughout by C. B. Christesen (b. 1911). *Meanjin*, while mainly literary in emphasis, has been a committed journal of ideas covering the broad cultural spectrum and has had a greater impact than any other periodical of its kind. Its chief virtue has been the combination of inward-looking 'nationalism' and outward-looking internationalism, its devotion both to the definition and development of Australian culture and to reflection of world culture in its time, as evidenced especially by its range of foreign contributors and local commentators on world literature. The most important function of such journals is to provide a channel for national literary interchange, a sense of community among writers, and assurance of serious examination of their work—in short, to make possible the development of a literary tradition and to aid its definition. In 1954 *Overland* appeared under the slogan, 'Temper democratic, bias Australian'. It was originally closely linked with the Communist Party and inspired by the need to restate the left-wing tradition and to resist 'Coca-cola imperialism', but its editor, Stephen Murray-Smith, soon broke free from dogma. *Quadrant*, published from Sydney by the Australian branch of the Congress for Cultural Freedom, first appeared in 1956 with James McAuley as editor and supplied hitherto lacking articulate conservative comment in opposition to the trend of *Meanjin* and *Overland*. The Congress has been more conservative, perhaps, than its overseas affiliates, and its Cold War polemics alienated most liberals. *Quadrant* has maintained high literary standards, but its rigid Liberal-D.L.P. orientation became increasingly prominent and its pages were occasionally marred by abusive methods similar to those of its Communist enemies. *Australian Letters* (1958-68), edited by Max Harris and Geoffrey Dutton, was apolitical and claimed to follow 'the principle of cultural self-containedness as against nationalistic or anti-nationalistic tendentiousness'.[15] *Prospect* (1958-64) was a lively Melbourne liberal Catholic cultural journal of affairs. The development over the years of *Westerly* (1956-) from a minor university publication to a substantial literary journal illustrates the new vigour in the cultural life of the smaller capital cities. In addition, a reputable periodical press appeared in 1958 with the foundation in Sydney of T. M. Fitzgerald's fortnightly *Nation* and the weekly *Observer*; in 1961 the latter merged with a reformed *Bulletin* which followed a 'radical right' policy of some intellectual quality. Thus from the mid-50s Australia had for the first time a diverse range of literate reviews and magazines.

The journals to a considerable extent provided a focus for the warlike literary controversy which characterized the 40s and 50s. Writers were now at last numerous and diverse enough to be involved in movements—to the benefit of literature if we agree with Henry James that 'the best things come, as a general thing, from the talents that are members of a group'.[16] However, the Jindyworobaks (and their Sydney offshoot, the Lyre Bird Writers) and the *Angry Penguins* modernists fell apart. The militant left-wing writers held together longer and in the late 40s and early 50s made the Fellowship of Australian Writers a battleground. In the 50s Cold War politics increasingly influenced controversy. McAuley and the group for whom *Quadrant* became a rallying-ground and the left-wing writers argued bitterly over the 'nationalist' issue, the identification of the left with the Lawson-Furphy tradition, and rival versions of literary history. For most writers, however, the issue of 'local content' in literature had become largely irrelevant;

by now they were relatively at ease with their country and its history and were using it as a source, naturally and without strain. By 1960 the 'nationalist' question had almost died out of debate, except as an academic issue. Left-wing writers tended to deplore 'intellectual' poetry and the 'unrealistic' novels by such writers as White and Stow, but were weakening as a coherent movement by the late 50s. In the 60s, no strong literary groups remained, and polemics were mainly confined to attacks on the dominance by academics of criticism.

In the 50s university men did indeed begin to take over criticism. Critical articles accumulated: G. A. Wilkes and Leonie Kramer, the first two professors of Australian Literature at the University of Sydney, have been prominent scholars. But few important biographies or full-dress studies appeared. H. M. Green published his authoritative 1469-page *History of Australian Literature* in 1961, and the Pelican *The Literature of Australia* (ed. Dutton) followed in 1964. Colin Roderick began his scholarly series of Lawson's complete published and unpublished writings. Broad interpretative work, however, attempting to relate literature to the historical context and to define the literary tradition, proceeded only slowly. The combined effect of Vance Palmer's *Legend of the Nineties* (1954), A. A. Phillips's *The Australian Tradition* (1958) and Russel Ward's *The Australian Legend* (1958)—all of which explored the democratic-egalitarian tradition—provoked alternative interpretations. Vincent Buckley in the late 50s stressed the perennial influence of Nietzsche on many major writers and posed 'vitalism' as well as utopian humanism as the two leading lines of influence. Judith Wright (*Preoccupations in Australian Poetry*, 1965) and Brian Elliott (*The Landscape of Australian Poetry*, 1967) set new standards of historical appreciation of poetry. In a productive exchange in *Meanjin* in 1962, H. P. Heseltine asserted that the special concern of Australian writers had been 'the terror at the basis of being', 'the sense of the horror of sheer existence' ('nothing' was the last word in *Such Is Life*), a major concern of modern writing expressed very early in Australia. In reply A. A. Phillips agreed that Australian literature was a literature of loneliness, stressed the affirmative elements in writers like Lawson and Furphy, but saw the chief conflict in Australian writing as being between the 'aristocracy of the especially sensitive' and those traditional writers who were unwilling to forgo their sense of identity with the nation and the common man.[17] Subsequently, among several other basic approaches, T. Inglis Moore has stressed the prevalence of the 'cry of the crow' sombreness of much Australian writing,[18] and Brian Kiernan has found the 'estrangement of the individual from society' and the assumption of the artistic 'outsider' to be the outstanding features of major Australian writing.[19]

After the wartime growth in publishing, the number of publications fell and then barely increased during the 50s. Nevertheless, firms like Cheshire and Rigby consolidated their positions, new houses such as Jacaranda and Lansdowne were founded, and Angus & Robertson opened a London branch. During the decade, locally published educational texts began to predominate over imported, but a high proportion of novels were still published overseas. About 1960, despite all the homes with or without one single bookshelf, Australia still spent more per head on books than any other English-speaking people, bought more than a quarter of British book-exports, and had relatively twice as many bookshops as Britain and four or five times as many as the United States; and almost half the residents in local government areas which had libraries were enrolled as borrowers. Publishing boomed in the early 60s, many more English firms established branches or subsidiaries, and export sales of Australian books became substantial. Australian book-design came to be of outstanding quality. In the mid- and later 60s, however, a spate of international and local takeovers disrupted the industry; other than the university presses, hardly one independent local publisher has survived. Nevertheless, in recent years the output of books, especially of locally written educational texts, has continued to grow.[20] Bookselling, which suffers especially from new competition from library suppliers, has fallen on hard times.

In painting, the decade after the second world war was a slack period of relatively little vitality; discussion 'ground to a halt' and art-publication was almost non-existent. In Melbourne the Contemporary Art Society collapsed in 1947 and Nolan, Tucker and Bergner departed. No matter how much Dobell and Drysdale developed and varied their approaches through the 50s and 60s, they could not possibly sustain the impact of their work of the early 40s. Younger painters tended to turn away from realism and contemporary life; the Cold War period was not propitious for social involvement, and several leading artists withdrew into their work and lived in near-seclusion. The establishment of the Blake Prize in 1951 for religious painting signified one important trend; the prize was appropriately first won by Justin O'Brien. The

Ukrainian-born Michael Kmit also worked in neo-Byzantine style and his flamboyant use of colour markedly influenced others.[21]

Three painters of the older generation—Passmore, Miller and Fairweather, all of whom were tending towards abstraction—stood out in Sydney in the 50s. John Passmore (b. 1904), who was in Europe from 1933 to 1950, became the 'painter's painter' and an inspiring teacher. Cézanne was his guide and he carried out a sustained analysis of form, eventually arriving at the notion of 'total experience': 'that one should paint not only the sum of different angles from which one sees an object, but the implied relationships between different things in one scene: the way they are knit together by something other than form'.[22] Godfrey Miller (1893-1964) had private means and, after lifelong single-minded study and meditation, began to exhibit only in his late fifties. He was influenced by Egyptian and Oriental art, but post-impressionism was his base. He 'set himself to capture a feeling for the essence of things in the flux of changing appearances: to find a pictorial technique capable of celebrating both permanence and change at the same time'; and constructed colour-mosaics on a grid-network of fine lines.[23] The third semi-abstract painter to flourish in the 50s was Ian Fairweather (b. 1891), 'peripatetic, eccentric and picturesque in his habits', 'the very pattern of the wandering hermit',[24] who first came to Australia in 1934 and in 1953 settled on a Queensland island. His work is markedly influenced by Chinese, Indonesian and Aboriginal art, as well as by Modigliani; fluent and inventive, his linework owes something to Chinese calligraphy. As no-one else in Australia, perhaps, he has stated a synthesis of East and West.

Melbourne remained the chief centre of figurative painting, often with direct social content. At least two of the more important figurative artists who emerged in the 50s, however, worked elsewhere. Jon Molvig (1923-70), born in Newcastle like Dobell and several other important painters, settled in Brisbane. He was especially stimulated by German expressionism; his work was powerful and colourful, and his range was wide: landscapes, figures looming against factory chimneys, and portraiture. His 'Industrial Eden' series condemned the mechanical destruction of Australia. Robert Dickerson (b. 1924) was a Sydney factory-worker (and briefly a professional boxer) whose art was largely self-taught and whose technique and range have been limited. But he found a personal mode to express a powerful emotional vision of the loneliness and isolation of contemporary man; his sad and tired figures gaze with haunting eyes on the baffling world around them.

John Brack (b. 1920) is a more biting and satirical critic of urban life, who has submitted city clerks, racegoers, suburban housewives and squabbling children to his penetrating and pessimistic gaze. Charles Blackman (b. 1928) similarly found a highly personal style in his poignant and melancholy paintings of children, young girls especially, which include a strong element of fantasy. All these painters demonstrated a new seriousness in the 50s, in their generally anti-heroic view of mankind as pathetic and defenceless, in contrast to the light-hearted, witty comment on manners by painters such as Dobell, Herman, Friend and frequently Drysdale.[25]

Other Melbourne painters renewed the local landscape tradition. John Perceval (b. 1923), after several years working in ceramics, returned to painting in 1956 and broke away from the Drysdale-Nolan-Boyd reinterpretations of landscape to find a spontaneous, joyful, highly coloured, thickly-painted style. Clifton Pugh (b. 1924) has delighted in Nature, but his is sometimes a menacing Nature—savagery beneath the surface—depicted in a near-surrealist manner; he is also a leading portraitist. Fred Williams (b. 1927), an outstanding etcher, also developed a highly original form of landscape. Critics have claimed that he was 'the one unquestionably major painter' of the 60s, and that in 1972 he was dominating contemporary painting. Patrick McCaughey has remarked that the 'central paradox' of his art is that he is 'a painter who recalls and frequently surpasses the best in Australian landscape painting and at the same time impresses one as the most advanced painter in the country'.[26]

Before the 50s abstract painting had followed a remote erratic path; in the 30s and 40s Rah Fizelle, Grace Crowley, Frank Hinder and Ralph Balson were among those experimenting with cubism and constructivism. The touring 'French Painting Today' exhibition of 1953 helped to stimulate the first postwar generation of Sydney students towards abstraction, and French influence remained far more important on them than American until at least 1960. The 1954 exhibition by the Sydney Group, which included work by Passmore, Kmit, Miller and Balson, showed a leaning towards free expressionistic constructions rather than geometric forms. From 1955 abstract expressionism, tachism and action painting were continuously discussed in the Sydney Contemporary Art Society *Broadsheet*, edited by Elwyn Lynn (b. 1917). The Direction 1 exhibition of 1956 was perhaps the turning-point, the leading critics were converted, and the bandwagon began to roll. Sydney had almost caught up with the latest overseas trends.

John Olsen (b. 1928), a student and colleague of Passmore, was the focus; he was hailed overnight as a master and, says Bernard Smith, 'gave a new energy and character to Sydney painting'. In the mid-50s he became committed, with Passmore, to painting as a 'total expression' and saw landscape 'not as scenery but as environment'. Olsen was abroad between 1956 and 1960, mainly in France, Spain and Majorca, and on his return carried out some of his best work, taking special delight in Australian vulgarity. Virginia Spate has remarked that he found 'a new and compelling image of Australian nature as something wild, untamed, joyful and, above all, alive.'[27] Lynn (who introduced texture or matter painting in 1959), Thomas Gleghorn, Leonard Hessing, Stanislaus Rapotec, John Coburn, Frank Hodgkinson and William Rose, and in Melbourne Donald Laycock and Ian Sime, were other abstract painters of the period.

Abstract expressionism was immensely liberating to its devotees: 'what excited them all was the sense of discovery made possible by the new informal techniques by means of which they might give birth to a new personal symbology'.[28] And at least the art of Olsen and some of his associates contained images of environment and was not entirely non-figurative; indeed they gave abstract expressionism in Australia a regional character. However, Robert Hughes has remarked, 'most local abstraction was only a remote gloss on what had been painted before in Europe or America. One detail of a de Kooning, seen in black and white in *Art News*, could (and did) supply enough forms for three exhibitions in Sydney.'[29] And Bernard Smith made a famous gibe:

> Abstract expressionism brought new vigour, new life and a new cause to be fought for, to a rather stuffy art world. But in the process a good deal of Sydney's art began to look like a provincial expression of American painting; aesthetically, the city was anxious to become, it seemed, a kind of southwestern suburb of San Francisco.[30]

Certain that History was on their side, the exclusive Sydney painting brethren damned all other forms, especially Melbourne figurativism, with evangelical fervour. They made an extraordinary study in mob psychology.

In reaction, an Antipodean group was formed of seven painters —Blackman, Arthur and David Boyd, Brack, Dickerson, Perceval and Pugh—in conjunction with Bernard Smith who wrote the manifesto for their Melbourne exhibition of August 1959. The manifesto was essentially a formal protest, not against abstraction as such, but 'against the clamorous pretensions of the multitude of new converts to abstract expressionism':[31]

> the existence of painting as an independent art is in danger. Today tachists, action painters, geometric abstractionists, abstract expressionists and their innumerable band of camp-followers threaten to benumb the intellect and wit of art with their bland and pretentious mysteries . . . we are witnessing yet another attempt by puritan and iconoclast to reduce the living speech of art to the silence of decoration.

The 'image, the recognizable shape, the meaningful symbol' was the basic unit of the artist's language; it communicated, because it could refer to experiences the artist shared with his audience. The manifesto explicitly denied any attempt to lay down a national style; however,

> Our experience of life must be our material. We believe we have both a right and a duty to draw upon our experience both of society and nature in Australia for the materials of our art. . . . We live in a young country still making its myths. . . . In the growth and transformation of its myths a society achieves its own sense of identity. In this process the artist may play a creative and liberating role. [Nevertheless] our final obligation is neither to place nor nation. So far as we are concerned the society of man is indivisible.

The combative tone aroused those who mistakenly assumed that all abstract art was being attacked and that the Antipodeans were essentially cultural nationalists. There is a case for Franz Philipp's view that it was all a 'mock Armageddon'[32] in that the frontier between the image and the non-image was becoming increasingly fluid. But the manifesto, among other things, was an 'attempt to defend an indigenous tradition against the uncritical acceptance of currently fashionable overseas modes'[33] and, as such, was misunderstood by those who, like so many interested in the arts, have assumed that interest in indigenous traditions necessarily implies parochialism or chauvinism and lack of concern with the world's best.

The general movement, among young painters especially, was towards abstraction in some form. There was another trend, however, set by a group of symbolist painters (mainly in Melbourne) who had little in common either with the Antipodeans or the abstract expressionists. Leonard French (b. 1928) was the most prominent among them. In Europe between 1949 and 1952 he was influenced by Celtic and folk art. His concern with myth and the problem of the hero was reflected in his *Iliad* and *Odyssey* paintings, and his interest in religion in the *Genesis, Campion* and *Seven Days* series. Most of his art is based on geometrical devices, and mastery of the techniques of gilding, enamelling and glazing has enabled him to produce major works in ceramics and stained glass.[34] Other leading painters of 'portents, totems, presences and memories'[35] include Roger Kemp and Lawrence Daws.

Until recent years, sculpture in Australia was one of the relatively neglected arts, confined to isolated workers; the better of them like Bertram Mackennal (1863-1931), of 'full-blown Edwardian charm', usually moved to England. The 30s and 40s were an especially bad period when there were few public commissions. About 1950, however, Lyndon Dadswell was an important sculptor and teacher in Sydney, Robert Klippel was a pioneer of abstract form, and the Boyds and Perceval were working productively in ceramics. In the 50s and 60s major public commissions became more frequent and, although the demand for domestic sculpture remained small, public appreciation markedly grew. Nearly all the work has been 'international' in approach and usually derived from the English school; the Australian scene or past has inspired very little.*[36] Art-potting was similarly neglected —Merric Boyd (1889-1959) was almost a lone figure—but also developed in the 50s. H. R. Hughan, Ivan McMeekin and Peter Rushforth have achieved most, perhaps; all of them have close links with contemporary English tradition. The Kent Collection at the National Gallery of Victoria, one of the finest collections of Oriental ceramic art outside Europe, has been a stimulus.

In the late 50s and early 60s there was a passing vogue in England for Australian painting. Nolan had blazed the trail in 1949 with an exhibition in Paris; encouraged by Kenneth Clark, he and Drysdale then showed in London late in 1951 and early in

---

* There is little writing which enables sculptors to be placed in perspective. Important twentieth century artists, other than those mentioned above, include (in rough chronological order) Web Gilbert, Rayner Hoff, Paul Montford, Orlando Dutton, Ola Cohn, Daphne Mayo, Danila Vassilieff, Gerald Lewers, Margel Hinder, Andor Meszaros, Tom Bass, Clement Meadmore, Victor Greenhalgh, Stephen Walker, Lenton Parr, Norma Redpath, Clifford Last, Inge King, Vincas Jomantis, Carl Duldig and Robertson Swann.

1952. Nolan and Tucker exhibited widely in Europe throughout the 50s. A dozen painters were represented in 1953 in a Coronation selection of Australian art, the first general exhibition in England since 1923. In 1957 a retrospective Nolan exhibition in London introduced him to fame. Then, on the initiative of some of the Antipodeans who were anxious to gain overseas showing, a representative collection was gathered and exhibited at the Whitechapel Gallery in 1961. The critical and public response was enthusiastic, the nature of Australian painting was widely discussed, and a new market grew in England. 'This was painting stripped of European graces; stripped of aesthetic refinements; and deeply concerned with purpose and meaning,' wrote the *Guardian* critic. But when the Commonwealth government followed in 1962 with an official representative exhibition, chosen with conservative taste, at the Tate Gallery, it was widely recognized as bearing 'all the hallmarks of national pride and culture politics'. As in the case of Mexican art in the 30s, the interest aroused had been mainly in the exotic—the most peculiarly Australian painting—and it soon waned.[37]

Through the 50s, as affluence grew, knowledge of art and possession of paintings became an adjunct to gracious living, a status symbol. Gallery societies, formed first in Melbourne, attracted many thousand members; art became fashionable, to the material profit of the artist. Establishment approval, with all its snobbish aspects, yet helped considerably to educate taste and widen public support. Local government authorities, despite bitter protests from philistine ratepayers, established provincial galleries and art prizes, and public relations officers of major companies sometimes persuaded their employers to offer generous awards, so that through the 60s the number of prizes grew towards the hundred. Several generous institutional scholarships ensured that more of the best young artists could acquire overseas experience. From early in the 60s many scholarly and popular art publications were produced. From the mid-50s, also, a new class of art-dealers arose in response to growing recognition of the investment-potential of paintings; dealers now did much to form public taste and the one-man exhibition and sale through the dealer-agent tended to replace distribution through sales at exhibitions of art societies—indeed, the N.S.W. Society of Artists collapsed in 1965 after a history of seventy years. In the 60s art was almost to become big business: throughout the twentieth century the painters had maintained a higher degree of public support than any other artists. A relatively large number of professionals and semiprofessionals now made good livings; and in quantitative terms at least, and in the middle range of quality, Australian painting had made a spectacular advance.[38]

The drama was kept alive by the amateur and semi-professional repertory theatre. In Sydney for most of the 40s four groups struggled bravely to present regular shows—Doris Fitton's Independent Theatre (founded in 1930 and in good health still), Kathleen Robinson's Minerva (1940-50, on a professional basis), May Hollinworth's amateur Metropolitan (1942-52) and the New Theatre (which the press, on political grounds, refused to review). In Melbourne Brett Randall's Little Theatre (later St Martin's) was the main group after Gregan McMahon retired in 1940. John Alden toured with his Shakespearian company from 1948, and most of the universities had strong dramatic societies. In the later 40s the young Peter Finch and Leo McKern departed from Sydney and Keith Michell from Adelaide to pursue their distinguished acting careers in England. The tour by Laurence Olivier and Vivien Leigh with the Old Vic Company in 1948 stimulated a whole generation who had had no opportunity to see first-rate classical theatre; the Stratford Memorial Theatre Company, led by Anthony Quayle, toured in 1950 and Quayle returned in 1953 with a strong company, while the Old Vic toured again in 1956 and 1961.

Radio had produced a score of good dramatists who (although given minimal publicity) were accepted and respected by the listening-public; some of them also tried their hands at writing for the stage. They were encouraged by the voluntary Playwrights' Advisory Board of Sydney which from about 1940 acted as a clearing-house, gave criticism, negotiated amateur productions and helped to publish a few plays. Its play-competitions and those of the A.B.C. and some little theatres produced a lively response. But the works of promising dramatists, like Dymphna Cusack, Alexander Turner, George Dann, Betty Roland, Henrietta Drake-Brockman and Dorothy Blewett, were performed, if at all, by repertory groups or amateur societies without the try-out and revision process normal in the professional theatre; and these authors had no financial incentive to write for the stage. Australian stage-plays were identified with the makeshift and amateur. Similarly, the commercial-theatre-public demanded 'star' actors; the local actor had no opportunity to achieve a 'star' reputation; so 'stars' had to be imported.[39]

Douglas Stewart's verse-play, *Ned Kelly* (1942), was a turning-point in its (limited) dramatic success and its intellectual quality. H. G. Kippax writes of it:

> Here all the birds in the bush of the 'Australianist' legend come home to roost—the underdog and his fight against society; the ambiguous rebel seen as lawless hero; the collision between the capitalist enterprise of the cities, and its conformist compulsions, with the private enterprise of the bush; the epic themes of endurance and of wandering in vast, hostile landscapes. And for the first time an Australian playwright rose to them. . . .[40]

The next landmark was the production by Doris Fitton in 1948 of Sumner Locke-Elliott's *Rusty Bugles*, after it had been rejected by several commercial and amateur managements. It was essentially an anti-war protest, but its significance lay in its richly comic use of the vernacular and in its popular success; it had the good fortune to be temporarily banned for its swearing content, was then taken up commercially, and ran for six months in Melbourne alone.[41] Locke-Elliott had already achieved his ambition of emigrating to the United States.

Many of those present at the University of Melbourne Union Theatre on 28 November 1955 for the first night of *Summer of the Seventeenth Doll* felt like cheering the performance (but behaved with regrettable decorum and lack of abandon). Ray Lawler (b. 1922) had written 'the play which will always be considered as the beginning of the Australian national theatre', according to J. D. Pringle.[42] One critic 'compared the experience with that felt by the Irish when they heard the first plays of Synge and O'Casey at the Abbey Theatre or by the Americans at the first plays of Eugene O'Neill'.[43] The sad irony is that Lawler for many years had been writing English historical plays, of which a couple had been played by repertory societies, and had little confidence in *The Doll's* prospects. But it demonstrated that contemporary Australian life could stimulate authentic drama, and it was also a popular success. The theme was the relevance of mateship and the old dream to modern Australia, but the universal elements were strong enough for the play to be seen as 'a parable for modern man' and to be performed successfully in England and France and by a negro company, with transposed locale, in the United States. It was the first play to be taken overseas by an Australian company. Lawler had instructed his fellow-practitioners in dramatic engineering and especially in how to write Australian dialogue.

Richard Beynon, Peter Kenna, John Hepworth, Alan Seymour and others quickly followed with 'slice of life' plays which examined peculiarly Australian attitudes with 'a disconcerting blend of disenchantment and compassion'; the combination of melodrama and humour in many of them perhaps owed something to Arthur Miller and O'Casey. Seymour in *The One Day of the Year* probed at an exposed nerve from the opening line: 'I'm a bloody Australian and I'll always stand up for bloody Australia'; Kippax has justly remarked that 'Alf Cook is, as an archetype, as relevant to Australian self-criticism as Archie Rice, say, is to Englishmen or Willie Loman to Americans.'[44] The play was performed widely in France; as many Frenchmen have seen it as Australians.

In sum, it was a remarkable development over five years—but there were obvious limitations. The dramatists had moved from rural to immediately relevant urban themes, as the radio playwrights had not. But most of these plays had glaring technical deficiencies as well as striking merits; they were confined to vernacular naturalism and stressed violence and low life; tended to take the theatregoer on guided tours of aspects of the contemporary scene; were curiously uneasy in their handling of middle-class characters; missed crucial aspects of contemporary life, such as social mobility; and were unadventurous in use of poetic language.[45] Patrick White was the chief deviant force in writing non-naturalistic drama: firstly with *The Ham Funeral*, produced in 1961 though written fourteen years earlier and inspired by an anecdote and painting by Dobell, then with the underrated *The Season at Sarsaparilla* (1962). But White's plays of ideas received a hostile reception both from an offended Establishment and a philistine press and a curiously luke-warm response from the more educated public. Ric Throssell, David Ireland, Ray Mathew, J. P. McKinney and others were also producing work which was rarely performed but adventurous in style and structure.

In the early to mid-6os there was a disappointing lull in a promising movement; the playwrights did not continue to produce. Lawler, Beynon, Seymour, Mathew and others were working in England—with appropriate recognition of talent. Another generation of actors, similarly, such as Diane Cilento and Zoe Caldwell, were making famous careers elsewhere, and were usually angry about the lack of career-prospects in Australia but convinced that competent theatrical management could attract a loyal public. There had been a warm response to self-critical Australian plays which explored the question of identity, but the audience was still relatively small. It was partly a generational gap, as Hugh Hunt remarked: the middle-class, middle-aged theatre-going public was not inclined to tolerate anything but 'sophisticated upper-class comedy and the comedy-thriller'—a demand for thought was considered a denial of entertainment.[46] This audience had little sympathy for a questioning examination of the Anzac tradition or of relations between Old Australians and New, or for depiction of 'sordid slum-types'.[47]

The 50s at least saw in the Elizabethan Theatre Trust a public movement to sustain the theatrical arts and also some puny support from public funds as, in line with developing notions of nationality, the call for a 'national theatre' was heard. In collaboration with the British Council the Chifley government in 1949 invited Tyrone Guthrie from England to advise on how best to develop theatrical resources. Guthrie advised against any national theatre building for the moment; but as the best means of developing talent and taste he recommended establishment of a permanent touring company which would best be formed in London where most trained Australian actors, designers, managers, producers and technicians were to be found. Guthrie later wrote:

> The suggestion that Australian taste might not be entirely perfect and that Australia might, in certain matters, be a decade or two behind certain other communities, aroused a tremendous head of steam. Persons who would not otherwise have given a snap of their fingers to support a national theatre felt a passionate eagerness for Australia to possess such an institution, and a passionate rage against the sneering, bloody Pommy who dared suggest that the time was not quite yet.

Labor lost office and, as Guthrie put it, 'the Menzies government took a traditionally conservative view of Art, and the report fell upon stony ground'.[48] Guthrie himself might have been captured, but went to Canada and formed the famous Stratford (Ontario) Shakespeare Festival Theatre.

Reacting against governmental apathy, H. C. Coombs of the Commonwealth Bank, J. D. Pringle of the *Sydney Morning Herald* and Charles Moses of the A.B.C. took the lead in launching in 1954 the Elizabethan Theatre Trust to commemorate the Queen's visit by fostering indigenous drama, opera and ballet. Modelled on the Arts Council of Great Britain, the Trust was organized as a private company, but with federal representation. However, the public response to the appeal for funds and the small subsidies grudgingly granted by the Commonwealth and State governments were totally inadequate; one consequence was the fatal compromise of presenting a large proportion of 'thoroughly popular entertainment' in order to maintain 'high standard opera and drama'.[49] Under the executive director, Hugh Hunt, a former director of the Old Vic, the immediate policy was to form a national company based on the Newtown, Sydney, theatre and not to work through the weak 'little theatres'; however, the Union Theatre Company (which became the Melbourne Repertory Company), under the direction of John Sumner, was subsidized. A few leading actors, like Ron Haddrick, were attracted back to Australia and the Trust made possible the full-time employment of many more actors than hitherto; in conjunction with the University of New South Wales, the National Institute of Dramatic Art was established as a full-time training school in the Old Tote theatre. But the drama company had to be disbanded as too expensive, and policy was switched to the occasional gathering of ad hoc companies and support of regional theatre companies. The Trust achieved much (and more, as we shall see, in opera and ballet), but its vacillating policies caused wide dissatisfaction. Hunt departed in 1961, having firmly implied his view that the Trust was too much controlled by Establishment figures who were preoccupied with fund-raising and following fickle majority taste in the hope of making ends meet.[50]

The Trust was, indeed, impossibly limited in resources and could not hope to fulfil its intention of providing drama and opera in all States. Kippax has summed up the leading features of its first ten years as

> the middle class preoccupation with the conspicuous culture of Britain and its standards and judgments; the businessman's amateur approach to art; his concept of art as a commodity to be manufactured and distributed; his expectation that an under-capitalized enterprise would be capable of paying artists and creative talents even the modest rewards which he regards as their deserts. . . . Above all, there is the grandiosity of the cultural forms envisaged, the result, one feels, of a materialistic philosophy impatient with the need for the organic growth of art and its institutions from regional, realistically modest roots.[51]

Yet it must be said that, largely because of the Trust, the amount of serious theatre was far greater in 1964 than in 1954.

The Trust did not succeed in establishing a national theatre company; but, after many vicissitudes, it did establish national opera and ballet companies. It built on a remarkable surge of interest in opera about 1950 which arose partly from a conscious determination, in the A.B.C. and elsewhere, once symphony orchestras had been set up on a sound basis, that development of opera should be the next objective. Gertrude Johnson's National Theatre Company in Melbourne gave many future stars their first opportunity and in 1949 it produced a remarkable series of nine standard operas. The New South Wales Conservatorium, under Eugene Goossens, gave fine performances of three operas in 1950, and in the next three years in Sydney Clarice Lorenz's National Opera of Australia began to rival the National Theatre in Melbourne. Operatic movements became active in all the smaller states, and J. C. Williamson's presented touring Italian companies in 1949 and 1955. From 1949 the public regarded the Mobil Quest (and others) as great sporting occasions; early winners of the Mobil included Joan Sutherland, Ronal Jackson and Donald Smith. The existing, largely voluntary, at best part-professional institutions could arrange only temporary companies for youngsters and veterans. The Trust, it was hoped, would provide a career for the best singers in a national company. It started bravely in 1956 with four Mozart operas, and the touring seasons in 1957 and 1958 were also successful. But financial losses in 1958 demoralized the Trust, the company and the sympathetic public which still did not realize that top-class opera pays for itself nowhere in the world. The 1958 loss, largely attributable to touring expenses to the outlying States, was a mere $140,000. The company was suspended in 1959 and many of the best singers left to take up foreign contracts. The next few years witnessed further discontinuity and erratic standards until consolidation from about 1966. In 1965 Joan Sutherland and Williamson's staged a Melba-type season. Several of the best of the recent composers have written operas, but few of them have been staged; probably the most noteworthy are Larry Sitsky's *The Fall of the House of Usher* and George Dreyfus's *Garni Sands*.[52]

Ballet, like opera, developed remarkably in the postwar period. The Borovansky company lasted until the late 50s; Laurel Martyn founded the Melbourne (Victorian) Ballet Guild in 1946 on an audience-subscription and school-touring basis, and it survives still; the National Theatre movement in Melbourne maintained a professional company between 1949 and 1953 and presented predominantly Australian ballets. In Sydney in the early 50s, the Sydney Ballet Group, the Polish-Australian Ballet, the Bodenwieser Ballet and the Sydney Dance-Drama Group were all at work —also the West Australian Ballet Company from 1953, the Brisbane Ballet Theatre from 1954 and the Studio Theatre in Adelaide. From overseas, the Ballet Rambert toured in 1948, the Royal Ballet in 1956, the Bolshoi in 1959 and 1961, the New York City in 1961, the American Dance Theatre in 1962 and the Fonteyn-Nureyev combination in 1964. The Trust delayed its entry into the field of ballet until 1962 but the national company then formed, mainly under the direction of Peggy van Praagh, and the supporting Australian Ballet Foundation kept leading dancers in Australia on a professional basis and, if the company did not quite triumph, it has developed exciting qualities; it toured overseas in 1965 and 1967. Kathleen Gorham, Elaine Fifield, Marilyn Jones and Garth Welch were among the leading performers. Of the many local ballets in the postwar years, such as *The Sentimental Bloke, Just for Fun, The Display, The Melbourne Cup* and *Jazz Spectrum*, Laurel Martyn's *Sylvia* (1963) is possibly the most notable.[53] In the late 60s about half the ballets presented by the national company were Australian compositions. The fact that there are today about 700 private ballet-schools in Australia indicates the phenomenal popularity of the dance.

In 1953 a leading English critic, Arthur Jacobs, summed up the state of music in Australia. It was remarkable that a country with a population of nine million could support six professional symphony orchestras, but their quality varied greatly: the Sydney orchestra, under Eugene Goossens, was 'in the same class as the premier orchestras of Europe and America' but nowhere near the top; there was a marked lack of first-rate conductors; the 10,000 or more subscribers to the Sydney concerts were comparable with the Manchester audience in numbers; since chamber-music was poorly developed, the A.B.C. 'might have pushed too far the cult of the symphony orchestra'.[54] Between 1948 and 1956 Goossens, who also directed the Conservatorium, certainly raised the standard of the Sydney orchestra which in the 60s also profited from the direction of the American, Dean Dixon. The Melbourne orchestra did not lag far behind, but it both suffered and profited from a long run of short-term distinguished overseas conductors.

It has commonly been said that in the 50s the A.B.C. control of music became middle-aged and relatively conservative in outlook, that there was some resting on laurels. Broadcasting of music tended to become static in approach with little attention to contemporary music, local solo performers suffered from the attention given to visiting celebrities, and numerous resignations from the orchestras indicated wide discontent with bureaucratic control. On the other hand, the monopolistic position of the A.B.C. inevitably made it the target of 'random antipathies as well as of reasoned opposition'.[55] The success-story of concert-promotion and widening of popular support continued: through the 60s the A.B.C. was promoting about 800 concerts a year and extending country and suburban performances; famous American, English, Polish, Czech, Israeli and Japanese orchestras made visits; the Sydney orchestra made its first overseas tour to England in 1965 and the Melbourne orchestra followed to Canada in 1967. In 1967 a National Training Orchestra was established and in the same year the creation by the Elizabethan Trust of an orchestra for opera and ballet introduced a welcome element of competition. The A.B.C. had promoted a massive development of taste for good music since the 30s; in the mid-60s nine million records a year were being sold of which about one quarter were of 'classical' music. By this simple test of consumption and appreciation, Australia was competing at world level.

Tours soon after the war by the Boyd Neel String Orchestra and the Griller Quartet roused interest in chamber music. Already in 1946 Richard Goldner, a pre-war Austrian refugee, had founded the Musica Viva Society of Australia. Its effort to establish a professional chamber group in Sydney brought financial collapse in 1952 and suspension of activities. The Queensland State Quartet was defunct and now no full-time professional group existed. Musica Viva rebuilt its fortunes from 1955 on the basis of importing overseas groups for subscription-concerts; among them have been the Pascal Quartet, the Budapest Quartet and most of the world's illustrious ensembles. By the mid-60s the Society was increasingly employing local professional groups such as the Sydney String Quartet, the Glickman Trio, the Austral Quartet and the Elder Quartet, and programming a growing number of Australian compositions. The Sydney and Melbourne branches of the International Society for Contemporary Music in the early 60s were giving many concerts, acting as a clearing-house for new ideas, and helping to eliminate the time-lag in musical awareness.[56]

Musical composition provides a most striking illustration of cultural flowering and maturing—a quick transformation in the 50s and 60s from poverty to near-affluence. Writing as late as 1957, Felix Werder described the musical heritage as 'purely transplanted' and compared the situation to pre-Heidelberg painting. It was futile to attempt to continue to produce a cosmopolitan music; following popular European composers meant remaining fifty years behind the advance-guard of contemporary music; Australian music had to be built on individual reaction to environment.[57] Roger Covell describes earlier twentieth century musical creation as normally out-of-date by two or three generations. Composers were crippled by the prevailing, rule-bound, conservative 'English organist' tradition, by the limited range of available experience and ideas, and by the colonial requirement to imitate— to write 'fluent and grammatically acceptable music in established idioms'. But Australian musical conservatism was also just a local accentuation of the conservative characteristics of English music.[58]

We have discussed the two major early figures, Grainger and Hill. Arthur Benjamin we shall rule out, for he left Australia in his 'teens (though he returned for two years to the Sydney Conservatorium) and identified himself entirely with English artistic traditions. A broad public was first made aware that Australian composers existed when in 1946 the music from the ballet *Corroboree* by John Antill (b. 1904) was performed. While it owed something to Stravinsky it was highly original, and most significant as the first important modern use of Aboriginal inspiration. Antill has composed other ballets, a symphony, an oratorio and an opera and, as an A.B.C. employee, has also been almost 'a kind of musician-laureate for state occasions'.[59] Margaret Sutherland (b. 1897), according to Covell (on whose judgments we rely), 'really naturalized the twentieth century in Australian music' during a period from the 20s to the 50s when many of her younger contemporaries 'found it impossible to shake off allegiances to superannuated styles'. Her work is in varied fields although much of it is for chamber groups: 'it is spare, lithe, quick-thrusting music for the most part, clean in outline, deft but not fussy in the play of counterpoint, seemingly . . . cool and detached in emotion'.[60] Dorian Le Gallienne (1915-63) worked within the limited range of styles of English music between the wars. In 1967 Covell considered his Symphony in E of 1951, partly in the idiom of Vaughan Williams, to be 'still the most accomplished and purposive symphony written by an Australian'; the dexterous, cheerful *Sinfonietta* of 1956 is Le Gallienne's best-known work. Clive Douglas

and Robert Hughes are the most prominent of the other composers of the generation producing mostly in the 40s and 50s.

Felix Werder (b. 1922), when he arrived from Berlin and London in 1941, was already a precocious composer who had inherited
the Austro-German and Hebrew musical traditions. Highly prolific, he has worked freely in varied forms and combinations of
instruments; Bartok, Hindemith and Schoenberg have especially
influenced him, and he has also been a radically provocative
critic. The distinguished group of composers who mostly began
work in the mid-50s were younger than Werder, had benefited in
their youth from the accessibility of broadcast music (including
some which was reasonably up-to-date) and, in comparison with
earlier composers suffered little from lack of opportunity to acquire taste and knowledge. Two of them, Donald Banks (b. 1923)
and Malcolm Williamson (b. 1931), after graduating at Melbourne
and Sydney universities, from 1950 studied with leading teachers in
Europe (and in Banks' case in the United States), and have since
followed highly successful careers in England while retaining a
strong sense of Australian identity. Banks possibly acquired his
high professionalism and clarity of aim from the wide variety of
work he performed for film and television while making his way;
he became something of a composer's composer for 'his mastery of
orchestral device and the unfailing logic of his musical construction'. His *Horn Concerto* (1966) has high claims for consideration
as a potential classic. Williamson has written prolifically, both in
avant-garde and conservative styles, for both 'serious' and 'popular'
audiences, always with 'enormous technical assurance'. His compositions include piano concertos, symphonic work, cantatas with
organ, hymns and ballet-music, nearly all of which have strong
melodic content. He is sure that his music is 'characteristically
Australian' although he has 'never tried to make it so'; he has
certainly retained a strong interest in Australia, as his evocative
pieces on Sydney, his settings of poems by McAuley, and his music
for the Helpmann-Nolan ballet, *The Display*, demonstrate. The
Tasmanian, Peter Sculthorpe (b. 1929), was early acclaimed as a
master and had a dazzling progress of scholarships, prizes and
commissions during and after his period at the University of Melbourne and a later year at Oxford; his career illustrates the comparative advantages open to his generation. He has taken the relationship of nationality to music more seriously perhaps than
any of the recent composers, as his *Irkanda* and *Sun Music* series
demonstrate; some of his works show not only the influence of
Aboriginal music but convey a general sense of 'loneliness and

haunted melancholy' which many of his audience have recognized as relating to their country. Japan and Mexico have also influenced his work. Richard Meale (b. 1933) has been independent, unconventional, highly intellectual and uncompromisingly modern in approach; his music 'serves as a kind of rallying standard for strong, even violent musical partisanship'. Strongly influenced by Oriental and Spanish music, his major works have included a *Flute Sonata, Homage to Garcia Lorca* and *Nocturnes*.[61]

It would be tedious to continue to summarize inadequately the contribution of other distinguished contemporary composers. They include George Dreyfus (b. 1928), Larry Sitsky and Nigel Butterley (b. 1936).[62] Finally to cite Covell, most kinds of music being written in the world today are being written in Australia; the time-lag between the world and Australia has almost been eliminated; a few of the better composers are confidently 'attempting to find a synthesis of styles true to themselves and the society (local and international) for which they are writing'; some of them, like Sculthorpe and Meale, are reaching out to Asia; and their work 'can be measured against the general run of accomplished composition in Europe and America without apology'.[63] In 1950 to have forecasted such an advance would have seemed crazy.

One minor aspect of music, which deserves mention for its singularity, is the development of Australian jazz (largely traditional New Orleans) as a small minority movement since the 40s. It has been unusual for jazz to take such a firm root outside America and to develop a local tradition. What was extraordinary, however, and probably unique in Australian cultural history, was the colonization of jazz in eastern Europe (and its revival in Britain) by the Graeme Bell band in the late 40s—that is, the transmission of an art-form by Australia from America to Europe.

Television was introduced in Sydney and Melbourne in November 1956 under a Broadcasting and Television Act which was broadly based on the recommendations of a royal commission of 1954. The commission had laid down as objectives 'programmes which will have the effect of raising the standard of public taste' and make 'the best use of Australian talent'. But the Commonwealth government was mainly concerned to use television for political advantage and issued commercial licences largely to friendly newspaper-proprietors who knew that the high-sounding objectives, which were to be policed by the Broadcasting Control

Board, did not need to be taken very seriously. The commercial channels broadly assumed that TV was simply entertainment and, in pursuing the highest profitability, pitched their levels at the lowest common denominator. Even when their managements were willing to use locally written film-serials or documentaries, the costs were prohibitory compared with the trivial sums paid for dumped syndicated American material which was used roughly eight times as much as English productions. 'Australian content' was confined almost entirely to news, sport, variety artists, panel-programmes and women's sessions. The A.B.C. met the challenge reasonably well: in the first eight years of television it produced 180 live plays of which about one-quarter were locally written. Its documentary, educational and news programmes steadily improved in quality.[64] But from the mid-60s the A.B.C. was seduced into 'playing the ratings game' and a regrettably large proportion of its programmes at peak viewing-hours have been as trashy as the commercial offerings. The net overall result has been a standard of television which ranks low on the world scale.

In the mid-50s, before television, fourteen commercial radio production companies were providing regular work for about 600 actors. TV almost wiped out this avenue, for commercial radio dropped almost all live dramatic programmes; employment for actors in theatre and TV did not make up the loss for several years. Film-production still languished through the 50s despite the enterprises of Charles Chauvel, Chips Rafferty and Cecil Holmes. American and British companies continued to make occasional films in Australia, but the Australian 'industry' produced *no* feature-film for ten years before Tim Burstall's *Two Thousand Weeks* in 1968. In the 40s and early 50s only two newsreel companies and the Commonwealth Film Unit (formed in 1946) were providing any training or continuous employment for technicians. Documentary film-production, sometimes of fine quality, increased during the 50s, and television, slowly and tardily, made increasing demands for local work through the 60s.[65] Moreover, dogged and persistent underground film-makers continued to practise their art.

The generation of Annear, Haddon, Dods and Griffin, which included most of the outstanding innovators in Australian architecture, had few immediate successors. In domestic architecture the widespread uninspired adoption from America in the 20s of the Californian bungalow and Spanish mission styles was followed in the 30s by the modern revolution. 'The general ideology that gained acceptance,' writes J. M. Freeland, 'was a compound of bits and pieces from the main contending schools in Europe and America. . . . Because its adherents so little understood in any depth the tenets of what were mutually exclusive philosophies, it succeeded only in being crassly superficial', streamlined, quick and slick.[66] At the same time there were some neo-Tudor excesses and a mild Georgian revival. A few young architects, such as Roy Grounds (b. 1905), Sydney Ancher and Walter Bunning, were returning to the environment and with inventive simplicity were using open pergolas and verandahs with low-pitched and flat roofs and rediscovering 'the colonial virtues of sunlight and shadow'.[67] After the wartime hiatus, catching-up with international fashion was signified by the influence of the first flat-roofed box on thin pipe columns designed by Harry Seidler (b. 1923), a Vienna-born migrant student of Walter Gropius at Harvard. The young postwar architects crusaded for functionalism and finally overwhelmed conservative resistance, but in ransacking the world for ideas and in striving to be original they usually merely followed international trends.[68]

Architectural historians, Robin Boyd especially, give little comfort. There has been no, and perhaps cannot be any, consistent national style; Australian flavour is almost involuntary. In general, a fifteen-year time-lag of international fashion prevails, but a few rebels recognise a challenge and refuse to be swamped entirely by imported ideas; a weak tradition, based on the colonial Georgian, survives. In the past twenty years there have been little more than Australian versions of mid-twentieth century mannerisms, rebels have been fewer, eclecticism has increasingly given way to Americanism: 'as far as Australia is concerned [now] the only modern architecture in the world is modern American architecture', identified with 'new international style'.[69] Yet such generalizations do less than justice to a solid body of high-quality domestic and smaller public building in recent years. Freeland, for one, has found in the best work of the 60s, in contrast to 'the glossy slickness and impersonal detachment' of the 50s, a sensitive and deep architecture, timeless but uniquely mid-twentieth century, 'thoroughly and distinctly Australian', appearing to be neither Colonial nor exotic.[70] And it must be conceded that, in the 50s and 60s, thousands of outer suburban houses have been built in harmony with the environment, when it has been possible to avoid the razing policies of developers or where home-owners—

a new phenomenon from the 50s—have actually planted gums and other natives.

In the cities, in the first half of the twentieth century—fortunately, on the whole—there was relatively little rebuilding and few new public buildings. Those there were, such as the major office-blocks at Canberra, were often in the tradition of 'British brutalism'. From about 1955, however, the business areas of the central cities of Sydney, Melbourne and the other capitals have been largely rebuilt with boxes in modern international style— 'sleek, glossy cliffs of glass', 500 feet and more tall. Seidler's Australia Square Tower is the most distinctive. New universities are almost indistinguishable in architectural style and layout from those of other continents. Taking into account all considerations of prestige, the decision to build an 'Opera House' on Sydney Harbour reflected the growing respect for the arts in the period. Joern Utzon's winning design of 1957 envisaged one of the greatest architectural shapes in an 'international era of great shapes', but it was 'an architectural dream that turned into a political nightmare' which lasted for sixteen years. Nevertheless, despite the cost, the necessary and unnecessary amendments to the design, and all the personal agony involved, 'the world's architecture was advanced and enriched' both by the final splendid product and the advances in technology which were required to achieve it.[71] Melbourne had to emulate Sydney, from 1960 the planning of Roy Grounds's Arts Centre proceeded smoothly, and the first stage, the massive bluestone Gallery, was opened in 1968.

The cause of city planning had languished throughout the interwar period. A new era at last began with the adoption of the 'Cumberland' plan of 1948 for Sydney, the Board of Works plan for Melbourne in 1954 followed by the impressive revision of 1967, and the imaginative replanning of Canberra by the National Capital Development Commission from 1957.

Scientific research expanded immensely in the postwar years. The Council for Scientific and Industrial Research (which in 1949 became the Commonwealth Scientific and Industrial Research Organization) had already branched out from its emphasis on primary industry to industrial research; between 1936 and 1939 divisions in industrial chemistry, aeronautics and radiophysics, and a National Standards Laboratory had been established. Under the leadership of D. F. Martyn (1906-70), radiophysics became probably the outstanding area of Australian scientific excellence;

the giant radiotelescope at Parkes from 1961 has been the major
tool. Work relating to primary industries has also grown in scale;
the application of myxomatosis to exterminate rabbits in the 50s,
work on trace elements, forest products, plant and animal diseases
and pests, and the introduction of new grasses and legumes have
been some of the successes. Under the able leadership of Rivett
and Ian Clunies Ross (1899-1959), C.S.I.R.O. earned enormous respect from primary and industrial interests, and more than any
other force tended to break down the 'practical man's' idiotic
suspicion of 'theorists'. Industry was slowly persuaded to under-
take its own research rather than run to C.S.I.R.O. with every
piffling problem. In the war and postwar years, research sections
of the departments of Defence, Supply and Health also gained
strength; the Bureau of Mineral Resources was set up in 1946 and
the Atomic Energy Commission in 1952. State departments of
Agriculture and Mines continued their limited research activities.

The universities had had little opportunity to develop scientific research, and during the postwar decade university scientists
tended to resent the support for and success of C.S.I.R.O. Since
then co-operation and harmony have grown, and with the development of the Australian National University and the ploughing-in
of Commonwealth finance after the Murray report in 1957, university research has vastly expanded. Medical research has produced Australia's two Nobel Prize winners—Macfarlane Burnet
(b. 1899) and J. C. Eccles (b. 1903), both of them university men.
The growth of research is also demonstrated in the proliferation
of specialist scientific societies and journals; C.S.I.R.O. alone was
producing eight journals in the early 60s. The Australian Academy of Science, based initially on the dozen Fellows of the Royal
Society, was founded in 1954. Growing concern with preservation of
the environment led to the establishment in 1964 of the Australian
Conservation Foundation, in which Francis Ratcliffe, a former
director of C.S.I.R.O's Wild Life Survey, took the lead; but the
objective of a national biological survey remains unfulfilled. An
informed visitor late in the 60s found that, in spite of all
funding limitations, Australia ranked about tenth in the world,
absolutely, in scientific achievement, and was responsible for
about one in sixty scientific breakthroughs. And, at least until
very recent years, despite all talk of the 'brain drain', Australia
has been a net importer of scientists, although it is doubtful
whether the rate of import has kept up with national growth. The
new class of scientists has won social esteem and some influence

on government, but remains largely a cultural class apart with little meaningful communication with practitioners of the traditional culture.[72]

The 'educational explosion' of the 50s and 60s in the longer term involved a steady enlargement of the proportion of the community interested in the arts or matters of intellect. Prosperity and the determination of many parents who married during the depression that their children must grasp the security of higher educational qualifications led to startling growth in the proportion of children staying at school until sixteen or seventeen. The schools were already having to handle a much larger population (the result of a higher birth-rate and heavy migration), bricks and mortar and teacher recruitment necessarily dominated educationists' attention, and the quality of education inevitably suffered. Between 1950 and 1970 in Victoria, for example, the number of high schools multiplied by five, and the number of students taking the final school-year by more than fifteen. Reputable school libraries came to be accepted as a normal requirement rather than an addition; similarly, few municipalities by the 60s failed to provide a well-stocked local library.

The first shock-waves hit the universities in the later 50s. Tardily, the Murray committee was appointed as the authoritative agency to recommend in 1957 necessary Commonwealth finance for expansion. It is a measure of governmental hostility to higher education and its products that Sir Robert Menzies had to summon all his personal authority to force the issue in Cabinet. Several new universities were founded; between 1955 and 1970 the number of university students rose from 30,000 to 120,000 and of full-time teaching staff from 2,000 to 7,000.

Opportunities for basic work in the Humanities and Social Sciences as well as the Sciences thus greatly expanded and a large new intellectual class was institutionalized. By the 60s a Ph.D. was in most cases becoming the normal prerequisite for appointment to a university lectureship. Commonwealth power of the purse and the States' enforced hand-to-mouth financing was regrettably reflected in the near-full-time research position of members of the Institute of Advanced Studies at the Australian National University and the sparse opportunities for research at all other universities. Whatever its shortcomings, the A.N.U. attracted home highly distinguished men like W. K. Hancock, the historian, and Marcus Oliphant, the physicist; made massive contributions to new areas of research such as Pacific Studies; and fostered works of the highest excellence, such as J. A. Passmore's *Perfectibility of*

Man, Charles A. Price's *Southern Europeans in Australia* and D. J. Mulvaney's studies in Aboriginal prehistory. The teaching universities could also produce some men determined enough to write part-time master-works, such as J. A. La Nauze's *Alfred Deakin,* Manning Clark's histories, or S. L. Goldberg's *The Classical Temper: a study of James Joyce's* Ulysses.[73] The beginning of publication in 1966 of the multi-volume *Australian Dictionary of Biography,* a massive co-operative scholarly enterprise based on the A.N.U., was a national cultural landmark. In almost every field of study, it must be stressed, the work of the past twenty years far outweighs all that went before.

And yet the talent concentrated in the academic class contributed much less than might have been expected, despite all the remarkable advances in scholarship and the general competence of professional training. The older generation tended to live a vicarious English intellectual life with little sense of commitment to the local scene; the next generation faced the deep distrust of conservative governments for the leftish products of the 30s and 40s. The old and some of the new universities maintained ramshackle hierarchic structures which inhibited educational innovation and a sense of policy-responsibility among those junior to the unduly powerful professoriat. The Social Sciences (other than Economics) long remained backward: Sociology and Anthropology belatedly arrived in most universities in the 60s, and no university fully committed itself to Australian studies. Interdisciplinary ap-approaches amounted to little more than pious professions: the tyranny of the disciplines was such that few academics were confident enough to attempt more than specialist studies. The influential books on contemporary Australia were written by journalists—J. D. Pringle's *Australian Accent* (1958), Donald Horne's *The Lucky Country* (1964) and Craig McGregor's *Profile of Australia* (1966).

Australia has always been short of independent intellectuals outside the universities—men of letters and publicists such as F. W. Eggleston and Brian Fitzpatrick, or Geoffrey Dutton and Max Harris in a later generation, or prominent journalists with freedom to comment such as T. M. Fitzgerald or Bruce Grant, or other professional men of wide-ranging ideas like Robin Boyd. In the early 60s the depressing situation was evident of an intellectual class concentrated in the universities, largely alienated from the society around it, ideologically unsophisticated, and rarely closely involved with creative culture.[74] A decade later the situation was more encouraging. A few university departments of

Music, Fine Arts and English Literature were more closely concerned with creative activity; and, partly because of the emergence of new important issues of less immediate party-political significance such as pollution and city-planning, academics were appearing more prominently in areas of public controversy.

Robin Boyd once remarked that 'Australia's is a special kind of philistinism . . . which puts art and ideas of any kind deliberately and firmly to one side to let the serious business of living proceed without distraction'.[1] In few countries have the artist and man of ideas been so required to justify their existence. Cultivated visitors have recoiled, only too often, from 'a barbarous, uncivilized land of cultural yahoos'.

The old Australian anti-intellectual resents and is suspicious of the life of the mind, is hostile to discussion about first principles and to those who raise awkward questions, query assumptions or rock the boat. He assumes that the university of life is the only one that matters, and the best school is the school of hard knocks. He tends to believe that intellectuals and artists are conceited, effeminate and subversive of authority and moral values—that academics are impractical or 'theoretical' and professors absentminded.* If he is middle-class he tends to believe artists are parasites, if he is working-class that they are merely entertainers of the wealthy. If he is a politician he has often vigorously cultivated a philistine image. He is all too closely in sympathy with C. J. Dennis's 'Bloke' talking about his first-born:

* An extract from *Victorian Parliamentary Debates*, 1964:
Floyd (A.L.P.): I have not been to the university.
Bolte (Lib.): Of course not. You are just as good as I am and you did not go to the university.
Floyd: I went to the university of adversity.
Bolte: You went to the university of life.

Hugh Stretton (*Ideas for Australian Cities*, pp. 188-9) has commented on a recent South Australian Minister for Local Government and Planning, an estate-agent well known for his attacks on anything 'theoretical': 'All his working life he has done business from an address on Light's town plan near the symmetrical city squares and greenbelt parklands. He has negotiated thousands of Torrens titles to land chosen . . . by Light's over-riding planning authority, and surveyed to the novel requirements of the systematic colonizers. Throughout the years when the Minister was himself selling land, the buyers' numbers and prosperity owed a good deal to Keynesian central economic management, to the assisted migration scheme, and to Wainwright's industrialization theory. But anything theoretical is wrong!'

Doreen she says 'e's got a poet's eyes;
But I ain't got no use for those soft guys;
I think we oughter make 'im sumpthin' great—
A bookie or a champeen 'eavyweight.

As in the case of the United States, attitudes to the artist and intellectual have been shaped historically by the pioneering values of European migrants to 'new' countries, the prevalence of the 'business ethic', egalitarian assumptions, the evangelical tradition, and educational assumptions and practices.[2]

Pioneer communities prize the physical virtues. The man most valued is the one who can turn his hand to anything; there is no time or felt need for education, culture or reflection, which are luxuries for the days when the urgent tasks have been done. In primitive communities the migrant largely discards what refinement he has; his children often have little chance to acquire any. Early Australian history is full of contemptuous remarks about impractical new chums or educated men who could not swing a pick for more than ten minutes, make a damper, pitch a tent, or in general make do. Here are some of the origins of the mystique of practicality, the assertion of the value of the practical man as against the theorist, the assumption that a practical man can tackle anything without special training—'the omnicompetence of the common man' in the 'populistic dream'.[3] Experts were mistrusted; and when they were proved to have been wrong, as Professor McCoy so soon was when he confidently asserted in the late 1850s that quartz-mining at depth could never be profitable, the error was seized on with glee; in the following half-century McCoy's mistake must have been quoted innumerable times against the universities.[4] The kind of business ethic which came to prevail was typical of raw societies in its near-exclusive emphasis on material success: self-made merchants, manufacturers and retailers regarded with contempt the life of the mind and any education which was not highly utilitarian. In new societies, as E. G. Wakefield remarked, values and manners tend to be imposed from the bottom not the top. Moreover, as de Tocqueville knew, there are aspects of the democratic, egalitarian outlook which encourage both suppression of potential élites and the educating down of the rich and educated. In Australia, until the last half-century, the identification of intellect and art with political conservatism sharpened the common man's hostility. And, being rejected, artists and intellectuals were encouraged to believe that their true home was in Britain.

Two of the chief characteristics of Australian religious history have been the strength of Protestant evangelicalism and Irish Catholicism, both of which have displayed strong anti-intellectual and anti-artistic tendencies. The revealed truths which evangelicals defend are not open to argument; nor is their cast of mind sympathetic to the artist's aims. The Church of England in Australia has never been intellectually strong. Until recent years, the Catholic church was largely cut off from the rest of the community, its adherents were relatively culturally impoverished, inoculated against liberal notions of free discussion, and isolated from intellectual movements in the church elsewhere and from intellectual life in Australia. There can be few countries in which the churches have contributed so little to intellectual and cultural life.

Moreover, it may be that historically State departments of education have tended to be authoritarian, conformist and excessively utilitarian in approach, that as A. G. Austin has argued, 'the community's obsession with practicality strongly influenced both the curriculum and the methodology of the schools' which have conspicuously failed to be self-critical.[5] There is also a strong case for arguing that, historically, the universities have not been much more than technical training-shops and have failed to convey to most of their graduates what a university is or what humane discourse is. In short, anti-intellectualism has displayed itself within the educational system almost as much as anywhere. There are fascinating contradictions in this area: few populations have ever displayed such strong belief in the right to education and in the virtues of education—only to a certain point, perhaps—as seen classically in the yearning of the old-style workingman for education for his children, and yet also such dislike and disregard of the educated.

Things have markedly changed in recent years: the old philistine anti-intellectual Australian is almost on the defensive. 'Against a background of mass indifference and hostility,' Pringle was writing in 1958, 'everywhere men and women of great ability and strong creative gifts are emerging.'[6] Donald Horne has detected, since the late 50s, a kind of intellectual seepthrough'.[7] 'The artists have begun to provide an alternative to the sterile ethos of materialism,' writes Craig McGregor. 'They have begun to offer a critique of Australian society and its preoccupations, to advocate contrary theses and demonstrate different scales of priorities.'[8] In 1967 Robin Boyd defined 'a new kind of split in our society: the emergence of an intellectual or cultural opposition to

the Australian conservative—who is the ex-frontierman, gone in-
doors behind a cluttered desk'.

> Australia is divided—not into halves, but into two uneven
> sections—by a jagged, vertical crack. . . . On the larger side is
> the modern Australian who believes in the long-established,
> still popular, anti-intellectual Australian values, who is con-
> vinced that the Australian state and rate of progress are satis-
> factory. On the other is the modern Australian who sees so
> many shortcomings in Australian social development that he
> is on the point of despair. . . . He denies the need for Aus-
> tralia to continue a life overbalanced on the materialist side.
> He refuses to believe in an infinite projection of economic
> security and physical comfort and spectator sports as the goal
> of living. . . . he sees the promise of a new Australia actively
> creating or intelligently receptive to ideas expressive of this
> country's special condition.[9]

Younger-minded Australians revel in Barry Humphries' celebration of our cultural gaucheries. And the censors, in despair have almost abandoned their task (Queensland, and now Victoria, apart).
  Censorship of literature has been the outstanding example of
repressive anti-intellectualism and a perennial battleground. Before the 30s there were curiously few attempts to ban books; in
1928 almost the only books excluded by Customs were Balzac's
Droll Stories and cheap editions of Boccaccio and Rabelais. From
1929, however, 'the Federal Government tried to preserve Australia from all books which in any way—cleverly or stupidly,
wittily or pompously—questioned, betrayed or attacked what they
took to be the values of the patriotic family man and woman'.[10]
James Joyce's *Ulysses* was the turning-point; Defoe, Aldous Huxley, Orwell, dos Passos, Hemingway, Colette and, of course, Norman Lindsay were honourable successors. By 1936 about 5,000
books had been prohibited by Customs. Almost all communist or
near-communist writings, from the *Communist Manifesto* on, were
banned but, after a massive campaign of protest, political censorship was largely abandoned in the late 30s. The years 1944 to 1946
saw some of the most notorious prosecutions of authors. Max
Harris was fined for indecency for the Ern Malley issue of *Angry
Penguins*, the publishers of Lawson Glassop's war-novel, *We Were
the Rats*, were fined for obscenity, and Robert Close was actually
jailed for three months in Victoria for his 'gross assault on
morality' in *Love Me Sailor*. Barnard Eldershaw's *Tomorrow and*

Tomorrow was mutilated by the censor.[11] (In these years, also, William Dobell after the Archibald case suffered greatly from mob-curiosity. Even at his home at Wangi, he said, frequent visitors and holiday-makers 'used to come around saying "This is where the mad artist lives".')[12] The unsuccessful prosecution in 1950 of Frank Hardy for criminal libel in *Power Without Glory* perhaps falls into a different category. Meanwhile the Commonwealth had also been ruthlessly censoring films, while imports of prints of Modigliani nudes were barely distinguished from Port Said photographs. Gradually, with the help of advisers, governments came to allow some distinction between literature and pornography, and the number of banned books dwindled in the 40s and 50s. Numerous occasional incidents followed, however. In 1964 in Sydney the editors of *Oz* were sentenced to six months (but their appeal was upheld); and in 1965 Michael Brown was charged with exhibiting indecent paintings, was sentenced to three months, and on appeal was fined and bound over.[13] Free-ranging satire was still not to be tolerated. Attempts to ban such works as *The Trial of Lady Chatterley*, *The Group* and *Portnoy's Complaint*, however, merely inflated their readership. By 1970, under the rule of a sophisticated Minister of Customs in Don Chipp, Commonwealth book-censorship had almost been eliminated, while State governments had become ultra-cautious in launching prosecutions.

In the 60s the Commonwealth government at last began to give something like adequate recognition to the arts. Federal aid had begun as early as 1908 when Alfred Deakin established the Commonwealth Literary Fund to provide a few pensions for impoverished writers. From the late 30s the Fund slowly widened its activities, especially by providing two or three small grants for fellowships for writers. We must recognize that indirectly, through the A.B.C., the Commonwealth provided massive support for music and radio-drama from the mid-30s. State governments' votes for galleries and museums and subsidies for orchestras remained niggardly throughout the 50s and, other than providing an inadequate subsidy for the Elizabethan Trust, the Commonwealth could not be moved to further action. The Massey commission of inquiry into the arts in Canada in 1951 and the subsequent lavish funding of the Canada Council stimulated many groups and individuals in Australia to bring pressure to bear on government in the 50s and early 60s. Why should not creative artists share in boom prosperity, they asked, while real-estate speculators were making fortunes? Why shouldn't the arts be protected as every industry was, or generously subsidized as in Britain and every European country? The protestors cited the Massey commission's test of civilization—'the extent to which the nation's creative artists are supported, encouraged and esteemed by the nation as a whole.'[14] Sir Robert Menzies remained obdurate. But eventually in the mid-60s the grants to the Opera and Ballet companies and the subsidies to theatrical companies were increased, and the Literary Fund was enabled to extend its activities. A Commonwealth fund for composers was established, as a parallel to the Literary Fund, in order to aid 'the writing, performing, publication and recording of new works'. In 1968 the Australian Council for the Arts was created, to allocate public funds for the performing arts instead of the Elizabethan Trust, which had found its dual role of entrepreneur and judge of which bodies were worthy of support increasingly embarrassing. The new era of governmental patronage began that year when the Council was granted $1.66 million; the vote rose to $5.7 million in 1972. Under the guidance of H. C. Coombs and Jean Battersby, the Council laid down a policy of concentrating its support; in theatre, it built up one large fully professional company in each State, but recently it has been able to spread its support more widely. The Trust continues in a limited entrepreneurial and servicing role. About 1970 the Commonwealth at last began to develop an Overseas Cultural Relations programme. State and broad community support have also since 1960 backed the grand biennial Adelaide Festival of the Arts and the modest annual Perth Festival.

Expatriation has continued, but probably at a much reduced rate. There are still refugees who have fled permanently from a native-land they have found oppressively constricting—and 'provincial, complacent, authoritarian, racist, anti-intellectual, mindlessly conformist, and tastelessly materialistic'.[15] They are usually unaware that battle has been joined in recent years and that the tide has perhaps turned. They confirm the prejudices of the many educated Englishmen whose contempt for Australia has tended to sharpen in recent years. There are also still many unwilling expatriates, whose talents are recognized overseas but not at home, who are angrily impatient with the hidebound conservatism still prevalent in many areas of Australian industrial and professional life. 'What is happening to Australia is natural selection in reverse,' one bitter scientist has remarked.[16] Actors, writers and technicians in the theatre, television and film industries are the most conspicuous group for whom Australia has failed to cater. Nevertheless, compared with twenty or forty years ago, the problem has diminished, for there are now relatively few areas where ability cannot command adequate opportunity. But in some fields the artist of great talent will always have to leave for long periods, simply in order to compete at international levels.

The novel has suffered a decline in the past decade. Almost the only major occasions have been the publication of White's two most recent novels, the Johnston trilogy, Davison's last work and the arrival of Thomas Keneally (b. 1935). Since 1964 Keneally has published seven novels of widely varying quality; the best of them have been *Bring Larks and Heroes*, *Three Cheers for the Paraclete* and *The Chant of Jimmy Blacksmith*.[17] Peter Mathers, Barry Oakley and David Ireland are among the few other novelists of promise. David Martin's three novels in the 60s revealed a writer of cosmopolitan background and a penetrating eye; and Thea Astley and Elizabeth Harrower have also won solid reputations. The growth of satire, statements of a tragic view of the world, studies of the artist and commitment, and direct treatment of sex (at last) have been among recent trends.

Poetry has fared far better. The major writers of the older and middle generations continue in a varied range of style and subject; poetry in Australia remains in excellent health. Gwen Harwood, Bruce Dawe, Bruce Beaver, Thomas Shapcott, Les Murray and Rodney Hall are among the newer voices. Aided by the Commonwealth Literary Fund, more volumes of poetry are being published than ever before; in recent years the reputable newspapers have taken to publishing poems regularly; and *Poetry Australia* (1964-) and *Poetry Magazine* (1965-, now *New Poetry*) are other important outlets.[18] A strong movement among the young, however, has rejected all tradition and is firmly anti-academic. The practitioners of 'contemporary', 'new' or 'underground' poetry have absorbed recent stylistic influences from overseas, notably from the work of Ginsberg, William Carlos Williams and Charles Olson. Much of it is mere apeing of overseas fashion, some of it is lively and intelligent. Like most young painters, few of them have any interest in the local scene as inspiration, except possibly as stimulus for political verse. They publish in numerous mimeographed or offset partisan magazines, though some regard their work as purely for the moment and hence disposable. The most welcome aspect of the movement is the popularity of poetry-readings and the extent of appreciation by the young.[19]

The decline of the novel, though not of poetry, is a world-wide phenomenon, for the visual media have attracted away the potential audience. The cinema has been a major rival; although people may not read much less than formerly, the highly literate give less attention to literature and everyone's attention-span has shortened. That Keneally is almost the only younger serious writer who can live by his work is an indication of the novel's declining appeal; only the most optimistic and dedicated can continue to write in such a situation. At least half a dozen of the more promising novelists of the 50s have abandoned the task. Yet literary awards attract hundreds of entries (1,000 novels in one case in 1970, to the confusion of the judges); the Society of Authors has topped the thousand in membership, and the ranks of the Fellowship of Australian Writers have been swollen by hundreds of tyro members. Aboriginal writers, such as Kath Walker and Colin Johnson, have appeared. An extensive literature for children has grown. The literary-based culture is by no means dead.

Since the late 60s there has been a revolution in Australian drama, brought about by an alternative theatre in protest against the debased standards of the commercial theatre, 'the powdered clutch of the theatre-going middle class', and the genteel, elevated outlook of the Repertory movement. David Williamson has remarked:

> established Australian theatre has been convinced until recently that nothing worth showing will ever originate in Australia. This in turn is due to the fact that there has been in Australia a cultural élite who preferred overseas theatre and films because they are convinced that there is nothing here worth writing about or investigating.[20]

'Australia is not a European nation with a European history', Bob Ellis has been reported as saying,

> but rather a 'barbaric, working-class, provincial, ignorant nation of understimulated slobs', with a history it was largely unaware of and a cultural present which possessed little in common with the local reality. To write an Australian play was not a matter of shanghaiing Greek myths into the environment of Boggabri but of starting with what you have and building on it.[21]

A score of new young playwrights have had several dozen plays produced, mostly in the makeshift improvised 'theatres'—La Mama, the Pram Factory, the Claremont in Melbourne, the Jane St, Nimrod, Head and Hand and Mews Theatres in Sydney, the Q Theatre in Adelaide and others. They have aimed at a 'theatre that would mirror (and with any luck, subvert and change) contemporary Australian life and a drama whose forms would evolve from Australian myths and social mores'.[22] They have returned to the traditions of the nineteenth century theatre at its most popular and least respectable, and write comic, colloquial, antiauthoritarian, satirical and sometimes savage plays, often in free, highly informal shape. Australian history has been ransacked for subjects and, among others, Macquarie, several explorers, Henry Parkes, Archbishop Mannix, John Norton and King O'Malley have lived again. Alexander Buzo, Jack Hibberd, David Williamson and, of the older generation, Dorothy Hewitt are among the more successful and prolific authors.

The new writers nearly all have a university background and have been involved in student protest. Betty Burstall's La Mama café-theatre in Carlton, close by the University of Melbourne, has been one workshop where dozens of plays have first been tried out. The Australian Performing Group, which has an outlook of conscious nationalism and community orientation with a determination to present 'plays of and for the people',[23] grew out of this centre. There are, of course, derivative elements: overseas experimental and alternative theatre has inspired liberation from traditional forms, and Brecht, 'black comedy' and the documentary movement in England have had some influence. The sheer determination and total commitment of so many of those working full-time in the new movement, who are now given all-important subsidies by the Council for the Arts, promise future greatness. Most remarkable of all in the historical context has been Williamson's statement: 'It's very heartening for an Australian writer to find people want Australian drama so badly.'[24]

In recent years the number of promising plays being written has outstripped the resources of theatres and professional companies available to present them. Overall attendances at theatre, opera and ballet have been steadily increasing. A new professionalism is evident in companies like the Melbourne Theatre. The number of professional actors, who may now fall back on a booming entertainment industry in pubs, clubs, restaurants and discos, has also grown considerably.[25] The National Institute of Dramatic Art about 1970 could accept only some 40 of 400 applicants, and nine out of ten of its graduates were professionally employed.

The outrageous deficiency long remained the lack of state support for a film industry, although Australia relatively (in the mid-60s) had the fourth highest film attendance in the world; of all the advanced countries only Australia (and the United States!) had failed to apply state assistance. Through the 60s the number of experimental film-makers, especially in the universities, quickly grew. Their demands for opportunity eventually, late in the decade, won such wide public backing that prime ministerial promises followed. A limited measure of support has since been given, but we await adoption of a more comprehensive plan which might remedy an outstanding area in Australian life of frustration of talent.

In painting the 60s saw remarkable expansion and spread of diversity, and increasingly close and quick reflection of international trends.[26] The new generation of artists and critics rejected abstract expressionism as well as Antipodean-type painting. Pop art had a limited impact from the early 60s—the Subterranean Imitation Realists were the first—and encouraged the concentration on sex, violence and satire which came to characterize the younger figurative painters, among whom Brett Whiteley (b. 1939) is outstanding. A total break with the local past came in 1965-6 when young artists returning from overseas introduced the urban international New York-derived style of colour painting—hard-edge, optical or colour-field. The 1967 visiting exhibition of contemporary American painting encouraged rejection of the 'tiring style' of expressionism. Sydney Ball, Dale Hickey and the group associated with the Central Street Gallery, Sydney, have been among the leading practitioners; but the ruck of the work has been totally derivative. Meanwhile, the Melbourne emblematic symbolists pursued their 'concern with time, change and eternity',[27] and the figurative expressionists of the 40s and 50s continued to work productively, though perhaps without making many new departures. Naturalistic involvement with landscape continues, as in the case of the Western Australians, Robert Juniper and Guy Grey-Smith, to inspire satisfying and original work.

Australian art is best regarded as all art carried out in Australia, whether inspired entirely by place or not at all. Much of it reflects place, history and contemporary Australian society; much of it is merely the working of international styles with no relation to place, although such work may be to some extent a variant on an international style, affected by local group-influences and traditions. Almost all development in Australian art has been shaped by the application of an international theory or technique by artists born overseas, or trained there and returning, or else inspired by overseas examples. Time-lag arising from distance, not isolation, has been the leading feature—a wide lag early in the twentieth century becoming progressively narrower. But the innovation from overseas may not be immediately productive; it has to find 'a creative point of accommodation with the sluggish provincial tradition',[28] as the impact of Impressionism, Post-Impressionism, Expressionism and Abstract expressionism demonstrate. Franz Philipp has remarked that 'there are two types of cultural provincialism: unawareness and over-awareness of the "centre", a hedged complacent identity and a loss of it in a desperate attempt to keep up with the Joneses of the international art scene'.[29] Unawareness was dominant in the earlier twentieth century; over-awareness has come to be a drawback of ultimate tardy international consciousness. Both types have their clichés: gum trees or red deserts, simple imitation from the art-magazines. In the 40s and 50s, it may be argued, this provincialism was largely broken down when a variety of leading painters were working in full consciousness both of modern world-painting and universal issues, and of their Australian surroundings.

Bernard Smith has indicated a basic change in the 60s from provincial to nascent metropolitan art situations, in Sydney and Melbourne at least. Postwar migration has produced cosmopolitan art communities; artists and critics have travelled overseas much more freely, overseas artists and critics have frequently visited Australia and there have been many visiting exhibitions. By 1970, Smith writes, Sydney and Melbourne had begun to develop

> communities directed towards *avant-garde* art and susceptible to drives and pressures similar to those operating in Milan, Tokyo, San Francisco, Amsterdam and Los Angeles. . . . the climate of thought and experiment was directed towards international aesthetic issues and artistic problems, away from a concern with regional culture.[30]

On the other hand, as it was rejected by the new *avant-garde*, figurative expressionism (the *avant-garde* art of the 40s) 'began to be absorbed within the popular traditional art of Australia', as general understanding of it grew. The relatively popular audience finds pop art or sophisticated products of international design or popular international furniture-store art-reproductions inadequate; it seeks from art not only 'pure aesthetic response but a sense of personal and national identity'. The expressionists provided the prototypes of a new popular art (as practised for example by Ray Crooke or Pro Hart) which expresses folk taste. A cleavage has developed between 'one group dedicated to experiment, to internationalism, to a metropolitan-type culture . . . based upon a young, urbanized and . . . other-directed, highly mobile élite group' and another group, usually older, often suburban and rural, who desire to 'draw some sustenance and a sense of identity from [Australian] legends and history'.[31]

The serious painter who draws inspiration from his national surroundings and who is not content to work exclusively in an international mode will survive. For whereas the artist in advanced societies has almost invariably cut himself off ruthlessly from any national identification, Australia remains a society seeking self-definition and many painters will still attempt in some degree to be the voice of their tribe. And, however international Australian artists may intend to be, they will continue to need the particular stimulus and 'critical edge' which local experience can provide.

The many continental European migrants, who mostly arrived after the 1939-45 war, have had relatively little impact on creative culture, except in painting. Scores of artists have come, from most European countries, but predominantly from eastern and central Europe.* As teachers as well as practising painters, they have helped to educate a generation to accept modern art and have reinforced the trends to expressionism and abstraction. Naturally, in view of their background, they have tended to be hostile to social realism and national tendencies, and have helped to tip the balance of Australian painting against concern with local life and tradition.[32] In literature (omitting Judah Waten who was a child-migrant) David Martin is alone, as novelist, poet and critic, in having made a substantial contribution in a language not native to him. A little work has appeared in the migrant-language press, and a selection of poems by Russian migrants has recently been translated and published.[33] It will be interesting to see whether, in the next generation, any ethnic sub-literatures develop as in the United States. In music, Werder, Dreyfus and Sitsky have made important contributions and many Europeans have been out-

---

* They include: prewar, Bergner, Herman, Hirschfeld-Mack, Haefliger, Orban, Vassilieff; postwar, from Poland, Feuerring, Halpern, Ostoja-Kotkowski; from the Ukraine, the Dutkiewicz brothers, Kmit; from Baltic countries, Abolins, Salkauskas, Senbergs, Zusters; from Austria, Cassab, Hessing, Kahan; also the dealers Komon (Czech) and Mora (French).

standing instrumentalists. They have, moreover, provided solid audiences for music, opera and theatre.

Perhaps the greatest qualitative change of all over the past decade has been the improvement of the press.[34] The foundation in 1964 of the *Australian*, which became the first daily to achieve wide national distribution, inspired the *Sydney Morning Herald*, Melbourne *Age* and Canberra *Times* to better their standards. In 1970 a Sunday quality press appeared with the foundation of the *Sunday Australian* and the *Review*; the latter immediately became a focus of younger generation intellectual dissent, and in 1972 amalgamated with *Nation*. In 1971, also, the weekly *National Times* was established. Regrettably, the *Australian* in seeking wider circulation has dropped sadly in standard and the *Sunday Australian* has amalgamated with the lower-level *Sunday Telegraph*. Nevertheless, despite the dangerous concentration of ownership, the daily and weekly press is now comparatively varied in opinion and is much closer to fulfilling its proper critical function. Cartoonists like Petty and Tanner have carried on the great black-and-white tradition. The press also gives more attention to the arts (and publicity for artists) than ever hitherto. In conjunction with TV, it has thrown a new harsh light on public affairs and has canalized the anger and shame with which most educated Australians have regarded the poverty of national government.

The speed of change over the past decade indicates unpredictable cultural developments. Terry Smith has listed some of the novelties of current art:

'expanded cinema', participatory art, environmental, process art; a fascination for new technologies, untried materials and systems, for mixing media; ephemerality, spontaneity, chance; the invention of processes that all are welcome, and able, to use or adapt.[35]

The rise of new information techniques, the development of the media as a general cultural communicative force and a widening gulf between word-oriented teachers and audio-visually oriented students, and the growing popularity of the social sciences as against the humanities are some of the background features. Some fashionable young heretics even believe that the present age is so different and the speed of change so great that there is nothing to be learned from the past. The 'sexual revolution', Women's Lib, Gay Lib, the hippy drop-out movement, drugs, the new radical social critique and other aspects of the counter or alternative culture, all in various ways imply rejection or re-evaluation of traditional cultural forms.

The sense of national independence and self-reliance has perhaps increased in recent years after a long period when fear and the long habit of dependence on a great power held Australia back from full nationhood and inhibited development of an identity. In the period roughly between 1950 and 1965 Australia was a threatened, constricted society, communicating with the world only to a small extent. Then in the mid-60s it seemed as though there could be no resistance to American economic, ideological and cultural takeover. The considerable intellectual and cultural development during the postwar years was hardly reflected at all in national policies or in the rhetoric of national spokesmen.

The British influence has continued to decline, although some traditional veneration for English intellectual authority, in contrast to respect for American technological expertise, properly remains. American and Japanese economic penetration has continued unabated but, even before the change of government in 1972, Australia seemed to be much less inclined to go 'all the way' in foreign policy with the United States. The American influence on Australia at first was most marked in life-styles and popular culture, becoming prominent in the 20s via popular music, films, comics, advertising techniques and household gadgetry. The pace accelerated after the 1939-45 war when the Australian entertainment, advertising and hotel industries largely succumbed to many of the most meretricious aspects of American life which were flaunted as everything most luxurious and enviable. Juke-boxes, disc-jockeys, Colonel Sanders, neon-advertising, shoddy popular television, used-car lots, drive-ins and featuristic motels have added new dimensions to the natively created Australian ugliness.[36] But by the 50s and 60s the best of American culture was for the first time having a substantial impact, notably in architecture, painting and increasingly in literature. The world, we are now told, is a global village, culture is linear: moon-landings, sporting events and assassinations are seen on TV as they happen, or almost so, student protest and black power movements are immediately reproduced, while the latest book is syndicated world-wide in the week of publication and works of art are almost instantaneously disseminated through magazine-reproductions. America, 'where the action is', is the fount. And yet, while it has obviously shortened, the time-lag to Australia remains important in many fields.

Vietnam may possibly in the long run be seen to have saved Australia, in that this traumatic experience has provoked resistance to blind Americanization and has perhaps enabled independent assessment of Australia's political and cultural future. And when a true sense of regional consciousness develops, Australian artists increasingly will reach out to Asia, in ways which Fairweather and Friend, Sculthorpe and Meale, have already indicated.

It is simplest, and it takes us far, to see Australian cultural history, firstly, in terms of simple growth, in terms of what might reasonably have been expected from a scattered population of one million in 1860, three million or so in 1900, six million in the 1930s, and eleven or twelve million in the 1960s; or from two cities of half a million in 1900, and from two cities of two million and three others approaching half a million in the 1960s. But growth progresses geometrically, as it were, not in simple proportion: large communities have all the advantages. The bigger the city, the greater the stimulus from diversity of occupation and opinion. At certain stages of growth, organization of cultural societies becomes possible, and later of specialist and conflicting societies and rival group-movements; the individual artist is no longer isolated and stunted but develops in a context of debate and challenge. And more important, at a certain stage of growth the size of the cultural market develops to the point where professionalism or semi-professionalism instead of spare-time amateurism become possible. Until well into the twentieth century, moreover, the Colonies or States remained considerably isolated from each other; a national audience hardly ever existed, artists were barely acquainted with the work of colleagues over the borders; distance further reduced the possible impact of limited activity and prevented the combination of scattered talents. Similar aspects of growth apply within the various cultural fields: only at a certain stage could any sense of an achieved body of work or of the beginning of a tradition or traditions in local writing or painting be recognized, or later a surrounding body of critical scholarship begin to develop. And only at a certain stage of growth could a diverse intellectual class, with its supporting institutions of varied societies and publications, appear.

It is not just a question of simple growth, however; it is also a process of maturing, and growing out of a colonial situation. There is a standard description often made of the process in new countries of European settlement like the United States, Canada and Australia. An early period of imitation, of working in the styles of the parent civilization, is followed by a stage of national assertiveness which celebrates the local subject-matter and values of the new nation struggling to be born; then an uneasy period of clash between the nativists and those holding fast to the values of the imperial source; and finally, when something like mature nationhood has been achieved, a reconciliation in which a relaxed sense of nationality is combined with openness to international influences. In Australia the process is seen clearly in literature and painting, but more obscurely in music, drama and architecture which tend to lag behind and to reflect the broad trends only weakly. The main stages of political growth out of Empire towards independence have their artistic echoes.

It took almost a century for any real nationalist movement to appear; in literature and art, writers and painters used the European styles and subject-matter they knew, or with vision blurred by old associations or traditional language produced European versions of Australian scenes. In the late 8os and 9os the *Bulletin* writers and Heidelberg painters closely reflected the new patriotism and political idealism of the nationalist movements of the day; their vision of and literal recording of Australia were probably only made possible by their individual consciousness of *being* Australians in the new sense. The disappointing delay in the development of both literature and painting in the first quarter or third of the twentieth century is closely related both to the delayed development of Australian independence, because of the swing back to Empire for ideological and geographical-strategic reasons, and to the continuation of extraordinary cultural isolation. The clash between those content with local self-sufficiency and those concerned mainly to import culture was reflected in the excesses of P. R. Stephensen, the Jindyworobaks and the gum-tree painters on the one hand and the Australia-rejecting *Vision* school and the internationalist modern painters and *Angry Penguins* movement on the other. The Vance Palmer-*Meanjin* 'nationalist-internationalists' held the key to the future. When, in the 4os, the political movement to national independence again gathered momentum, and in the following twenty years a broader conception of nationality allied with internationalism emerged, so in the arts there was on the whole a harmonious reconciliation of

Australian traditional approaches and natural use of Australian subject-matter with international techniques and world-views. Patrick White and Sidney Nolan could be and were both national commentators and modern international artists. They and their successors are no longer tortured by the 'complex fate' of being culturally colonial Australian artists.

Growing out of a colonial situation, however, did not involve any reduction in world influences but rather an altered relationship. Australian culture must not be seen as an isolated growth. Australia, obviously, has a continuous history along with the rest of the world; many of its cultural movements and products are simply Australian versions of English or European or world trends —the Gothic revival in architecture, romanticism and realism in the novel, 'modern' art. Much (but by no means all) of the cultural development in Australia in the past two generations has been a world or western world phenomenon—radio and records enabling wider appreciation of music, the free library movement, the larger proportion of the young undertaking higher education, state patronage of the arts. Moreover, an international movement or a change in the parent culture sometimes precipitated a breakthrough of a specifically Australian creative kind: the ideas and techniques of Impressionism partly made the Heidelberg vision possible, just as study of European literature and contemporary painting and the principles of abstract art were part of the background to Drysdale's and Nolan's Australianism. In literature, as extreme cases, Brennan and White probably owed nothing to any Australian literary tradition or to earlier Australian writers. The poetic influences on nearly every poet have been overwhelmingly international: even Paterson wrote in a currently fashionable international mode, Slessor owed a little to McCrae but perhaps to no other Australian poet. 'Art for art's sake' and Nietzsche were the inspirations of the *Vision* school. In a sense nearly all Australian literature and culture is an extension of European civilization (bar American influences). Forms and techniques are nearly all internationally derived.

But of course there is something new as well as something borrowed. White gained much of his inspiration from Australian history and suburbia, Slessor from Sydney Harbour and Captain Cook, Drysdale and Nolan from desire to say something important about their country. The setting is only part of subject-matter, but the novelist and often the poet have to depict what is there, get the scene and society (and language) right, and have something to say about it. The artist increasingly becomes partly a product of his

Australian predecessors; he discusses his craft with his fellows; he is part of movements which, even if foreign in origin, will have developed local emphases; he is more immediately stimulated by new local work of original power; he is influenced by the particular tendencies of his Australian audience; even if he would, he cannot escape being a product of the Australian cultural climate. His inspiration comes partly from his particular experience in Australia and from his thinking about the problems of his art in an Australian context of discussion. Those who do not choose to use 'the giant springboard of the past', including their particular past, court failure.

J. H. Davidson has recently observed that the rising generation 'takes Australian culture in its stride [and] may shortly come to take it as its primary point of reference. . . . they feel less and less constraint and pick and choose from what overseas has to offer. . . . they regard Australia as a fully autonomous society. . . . In short, it's their metropolis.'[37] A more frequent view is that the local culture is too weakly based for much autonomy to be preserved or to develop in the face of incessant instantaneous exposure to international culture, and that most creative artists do not recognize any 'national' responsibility. It may be, however, that the continuing crisis-urgency—increasingly sensed in recent years—of defining and preserving national identity may encourage and reinforce a sense of commitment to the local culture. As A. A. Phillips has argued, there are advantages in being 'proudly provincial', while remaining open to international influences. Provincialism may possess freshness and flavour; metropolitanism may be mere imitativeness. The provincial can be a refreshing 'barbarian' and act as a counter-force to modishness.[38]

The great open question is how strong is Australia's sense of such a provincialism and how dogged will be the drive for cultural self-determination. In 1969 a *Times Literary Supplement* reviewer stressed the urgency of self-scrutiny:

> Why can not the standards be absolute, the culture international? Well, the answer is that although it is true that culture in the ideal is unified and without boundaries, only the countries with scads of cultural background can afford to say so. In the underdeveloped countries . . . a national culture is a political necessity, and like all political necessities looks less like politics and more like an absolute condition of existence as you get closer to where the existence is led. It is quite possible that in Australia in the near future *liberty will*

simply lose the ability to describe itself, unless its permanent definition, which is embodied in the creative values of culture, can be maintained in the national consciousness.[39]

It is this argument which the art-critic, Robert Hughes, and others who believe that nationality is or should be irrelevant to art, refuse to face.[40] As A. D. Hope has put it, 'our native literature' (and art, drama and music)

> has something important to contribute in the very fact that it is *native*: that the civilization, the way of life and the problems of this country are our own problems and that it is through literature that a civilization expresses itself, through literature its values and its tendencies become conscious and its creative force becomes eloquent and evident.[41]

The nation principle, as the basis of world organization, remains as strong as ever, however much national cultures are diluted by international influences. Though the area of possible impact may be smaller than hitherto, the writer and artist still have the potential vital function of defining, preserving and developing the creative values and distinctive quality of civilization of their country.

If still from deserts the prophets come. . . . There has not been much savage and scarlet yet, perhaps, but those who continue to talk in terms of a cultural desert are surely blind and masochistically determined to do a perish. There were many pioneer explorers and there have been many since who have helped to civilize and enrich the Australian wasteland. They have often been driven by baffled and angry disenchantment with the discrepancy between the high promise of the Australian dream and what History has made of it.[42]

APPENDIX: A NOTE ON MELBOURNE AND SYDNEY

In 1962 in one of his most provocative essays, Manning Clark suggested that the 'main confrontation' of intellectual belief then was between two schools of secular humanists, based broadly on Melbourne and Sydney:

> One has been the product of liberalism, secularism, Marxism, Australian cultural chauvinism, and, further back, the Enlightenment, the Levellers, the Independents, and the character Renan detected in the founder of the Christian religion. . . .
>
> The other has also been the product of liberalism and secularism, but looks to Joyce, Nietzsche, Vico, Dante, Socrates, and Heraclitus as its teachers and prophets. . . .
>
> Both talk a lot about culture, but where the one believes in the uplifting and spiritual role of culture in the civilization of the masses, the other believes in culture for the elect, and dismisses all proposals to transmit culture to the masses not only as chimerical but because they are bound to lead to a barbarization of culture and a lowering of standards. The one believes in the perfectibility of mankind, and bends its efforts to creating the material environment in which man is at last freed from the plagues of war [and famine]. The other ridicules such a future as progressivism or meliorism. . . . The one believes in pity and brotherly love for suffering humanity. The other believes pity is the first cousin to disdain. . . .
>
> The one believes in enlightenment and happiness for all. The other is indifferent to the fate of the uneducated masses, and believes in the cult of gaiety and beauty for the few great souls who are capable of them. . . . One drinks to the future of mankind; the other drinks to the acceptance of life. . . .

'In politics, the one supports all left-wing causes [but] would call himself a liberal lefty to distinguish himself from the commissars.' The other fears international communism, is a pluralist in domestic politics, and 'would call himself a liberal righty to make sure people do not confound him with the philistines and the money changers.' In education the one is influenced by humanitarianism, Pestalozzi, Freud and Dewey; the other points to the 'lowering of standards which such values have caused'.

The one casts a man in an heroic role in his struggle against ignorance, and his environment: the other casts men in a tragic role. The one makes for the real and the epic in literature; the other, at its best, makes for the noble and the tragic in literature. The one is concerned with morality: the other is concerned with standards in culture.[1]

It is relatively easy to make the case for a longstanding radical intellectual tradition which has characterized Melbourne. (But it would be as well to take into account the legal-conservative tradition of Latham, Dixon and Menzies.) If moral earnestness and striving for human perfectibility are the tests, those three remarkable nineteenth century political intellectuals—David Syme, George Higinbotham and C. H. Pearson—set the pace. Their products—Alfred Deakin, H. B. Higgins, Isaac Isaacs and others—made a peculiarly Victorian contribution to national politics in offering a brief alternative to the representatives of Capital and Labour. The economic collapse of Victoria at the close of the century and the State's large proportion of Nonconformists (compared to New South Wales) are additional factors which encouraged a greater degree of doctrinaire political involvement than elsewhere. (Melbourne's demonstrations and processions have almost always been relatively far more numerously attended than those elsewhere.) The Labor Party has been weaker in Victoria, but the intellectual left far stronger since the heyday of the Victorian Socialist Party before the 1914-18 war. Clergymen like the Congregationalist Llewellyn Bevan, Charles Strong of the Australian Church, and the Unitarian Frederick Sinclaire fitted in closely with the radical intellectual politicians. John Curtin and Maurice Blackburn were classical Melbourne men, just as Jim Cairns is. The Y Club of the 1920s was part of the tradition. The Melbourne University Labour Club carried it on; its founders in the mid-20s—Lloyd Ross, the communist Ralph Gibson, and Brian Fitzpatrick (historian, one-man Council for Civil Liberties and perhaps the most Melbourne man of all)—exemplify the school. W. Macmahon Ball and Geoffrey Sawer are typical Melbourne academics, who were followed by the graduates of the Melbourne History Department, especially after the arrival in

1937 of R. M. Crawford (an atypical Sydney man). And, in their obverse way, who could be more Melbourne men than Mannix and Santamaria? And Melbourne, of course, has been the home of liberal Catholic dissidents.

Culturally, perhaps the decisive move was the farewell to narrow restrictive Melbourne in favour of Bohemian Sydney by Norman Lindsay and Hugh McCrae about 1900. (Tom Roberts and Streeton had already made the move.) Vance Palmer naturally gravitated to Melbourne to join the serious-minded O'Dowd, Esson and Wilmot; Nettie Palmer and Katharine Prichard were pure Melbourne products. The attempt to intellectualize the *Bulletin* school was made in Melbourne; in Sydney, its home, it was perverted to reaction or remained merely a declining popular movement. Meanwhile Norman Lindsay developed his vitalist, politically conservative influence in Sydney. Melbourne ultimately produced the major realist writers—Waten, Morrison, Hardy. Who could be more Sydney than Slessor, Hope, McAuley and White (and, indeed, Brennan)? What could be more typically Melbourne than *Meanjin* (Christesen arrived from Brisbane in 1945) or *Overland*, or more typically Sydney than *Quadrant*?

The contrast is seen at its most extreme in the art world where Melbourne was the city of violent extremes. In the late 30s both cities were thrown open to international artistic influences, but in Sydney the artists took an apolitical turn while in Melbourne they tended to be deeply committed. In the late 50s again, Sydney was captured by international abstractionism, while Melbourne inevitably produced an 'Antipodean' protest. Half traditional joke, half serious, the longstanding argument cannot be brushed aside.

The alleged Sydney tradition was less deeply rooted and of a briefer span than Melbourne's. Nevertheless, the conjunction of Norman Lindsay and John Anderson, the philosopher, combined with historical factors which have not yet been defined, produced a characteristic outlook, in the 30s and 40s especially, which was broadly as Clark describes it. It is probably true, as Vincent Buckley has said, that the freethinking, libertarian, sceptical anticommunist Anderson 'had more direct influence on [Sydney's] intellectual temper than any other single man has had on an Australian centre'.[2] Sceptical élitism was the characteristic attitude—usually non-political, but occasionally actively anti-communist. But it was barely predominant: Sydney had its Evatt, Mary Gilmore and Bishop Burgmann and has indeed in the last decade provided more intellectual-type Labor politicians than Melbourne. The paradox has been that historically, until about 1960, the independent schools of Melbourne dominated secondary education and their rebellious products took the lead in intellectual and cultural life; whereas in Sydney graduates of high schools, which overall were of higher quality than the independent schools, have dominated and have tended to take more conservative positions. The weird small group of Sydney Libertarians of the 50s and 60s, inspired by doctrines derived from Anderson, Marx, Sorel, Freud and Reich, in a philosophic freethought tradition, was a remarkably original provincial cult.[3] The conflicting traditions have now probably almost entirely worked themselves out. Melbourne's remains faintly discernible, perhaps; but the beliefs and actions of the younger generations of intellectuals and artists in both cities are shaped in new patterns.

BIBLIOGRAPHY AND NOTES

The leading critical works on which much of this book has been based are as follows:

Literature

H. M. Green, *A History of Australian Literature*, 2 vols., Sydney, 1961

E. Morris Miller, *Australian Literature from its Beginnings to 1935*, 2 vols., Melbourne, 1940. Extended to 1950 and ed. by Frederick T. Macartney, Sydney, 1956

Geoffrey Dutton (ed.), *The Literature of Australia*, Melbourne, 1964

Judith Wright, *Preoccupations in Australian Poetry*, Melbourne, 1965

A. A. Phillips, *The Australian Tradition*, Melbourne, 1958

Brian Elliott, *The Landscape of Australian Poetry*, Melbourne, 1967

John Barnes (ed.), *The Writer in Australia. A Collection of Literary Documents 1856 to 1964*, Melbourne, 1969

T. Inglis Moore, *Social Patterns in Australian Literature*, Sydney, 1971

G. A. Wilkes and J. C. Reid, *The Literatures of the British Commonwealth. Australia and New Zealand*, Pennsylvania, 1970

The files of *Meanjin Quarterly*, *Southerly*, *Australian Literary Studies*, *Quadrant*, *Overland* and other periodicals contain many important articles to which it has been impracticable to refer in the following notes.

The Pelican *Literature of Australia* (ed. Dutton) contains invaluable lists of the leading works by and commentaries on writers to 1964. Hence, in the following notes, I have referred only to works which have been of outstanding assistance to me, full-scale biographies where they exist, and the more important critical work since 1964.

Painting

Bernard Smith, *Australian Painting, 1788-1970*, Melbourne, 1971

Alan McCulloch, *Encyclopedia of Australian Art*, Melbourne, 1968

Robert Hughes, *The Art of Australia*, Penguin, 1970
William Moore, *The Story of Australian Art*, Sydney, 1934

Music

Roger Covell, *Australia's Music, Themes of a New Society*, Melbourne, 1967

Drama

Leslie Rees, *Towards an Australian Drama*, Sydney, 1953. (A revised edition is to be published shortly under the title, *The Making of Australian Drama*.)

Architecture

J. M. Freeland, *Architecture in Australia. A History*, Melbourne, 1968
Robin Boyd, *Australia's Home. Its Origins, Builders and Occupiers*, Melbourne, 1952
Robin Boyd, *The Australian Ugliness*, Melbourne, 1960

General

A. L. McLeod (ed.), *The Pattern of Australian Culture*, Melbourne and Ithaca, N.Y., 1963, has some useful chapters. The only general historian of Australia who has paid any sustained attention to the development of culture is C. Hartley Grattan in his *The Southwest Pacific to 1900* and *The Southwest Pacific since 1900*, Ann Arbor, 1963. (Grattan is the only important modern foreign observer of Australia.)

For short biographies of nearly everyone mentioned in this book before the 1930s, see *Australian Dictionary of Biography* (ed. D. Pike) and P. Serle, *Dictionary of Australian Biography*. For writers, see also the works referred to above by Green, Morris Miller and Macartney, and L. J. Blake, *Australian Writers*, Adelaide, 1968. For artists, see the works referred to above by Bernard Smith, Hughes, Moore and McCulloch.

1   FOUNDATIONS pre-1850

1   J. Tuckey, *Account of a Voyage to Establish a Colony at Port Phillip in Bass's Strait*, London, 1805, p. 190
2   Green, *History of Australian Literature*, i, p. 7
3   Pp. 3-6 based on Bernard Smith, *European Vision and the South Pacific 1768-1850*, Oxford, 1960

4   *Memoirs of James Hardy Vaux*, London, 1819, i, p. 205, quoted by Smith, *European Vision*, p. 120

5   J. E. Smith, *A Specimen of the Botany of New Holland*, London, 1793, p. 9, quoted *ibid*, p. 124

6   *Ibid*, p. 123

7   Quoted by A. J. Marshall, *Darwin and Huxley in Australia*, Sydney, 1970, p. 44

8   Paragraph based on D. J. Mulvaney, 'The Australian Aborigines, 1606-1929: Opinion and Fieldwork'. *Historical Studies. Selected Articles*, ed. J. J. Eastwood and F. B. Smith, Melbourne, 1964 (Cook quoted p. 9).

9   Quoted by Kathleen Fitzpatrick, *Australian Explorers*, London, 1958, p. 2

10 Alan Moorehead, *Cooper's Creek*, London, 1963, pp. 10-11

11 Charles Sturt, *Narrative of an Expedition into Central Australia*, London, 1849, ii, p. 90

12 Quoted by J. H. L. Cumpston, *Thomas Mitchell*, London, 1954, pp. 176-7

13 See several articles on early Science by M. E. Hoare in *Records of the Australian Academy of Science* (1967-   ) and his ' "All Things are Quaint and Opposite". Scientific Societies in Tasmania in the 1840s', *Isis*, Summer 1969. Kathleen Fitzpatrick, *Sir John Franklin in Tasmania 1837-1843*, Melbourne, 1949

14 Pp. 9-11 based on Bernard Smith, *European Vision and the South Pacific* and *Australian Painting*, chs. 1-2

15 *Sydney Gazette*, 28 July, 1829, quoted by Smith, *European Vision*, pp. 191-2

16 Lionel Lindsay, *Conrad Martens. The Man and his Art*, Sydney, 1920 (enlarged edition 1968)

17 Pp. 11-13 based on J. M. Freeland, *Architecture in Australia*, chs. 2-4

18 Morton Herman, *The Early Australian Architects and their Work*, Sydney, 1954, ch. 6; Franz Philipp, 'Notes on the Study of Australian Colonial Architecture', *Historical Studies —Australia and New Zealand*, vol. 8, no. 32, May 1959; see also Freeland, p. 37

19 Freeland, pp. 47-8, 50, 72

20 *Ibid,* pp. 75-83

21 Robin Boyd, *The Australian Ugliness*, Melbourne, 1960, p. 35

22 Freeland, pp. 84-8.

23 Freeland, pp. 19, 60-65; see also Hugh Stretton, *Ideas for Australian Cities*, Adelaide, 1970, pp. 1, 142; and Geoffrey Dutton, *Founder of a City*, Melbourne, 1960
24 Bernard Smith, *European Vision*, ch. 10
25 *Historical Records of New South Wales*, vol. 1, pt. 2, p. 333
26 Smith, *European Vision*, pp. 133-8, 168-73 (Péron and O'Hara quoted p. 170)
27 Nora Barlow (ed.), *Charles Darwin's Diary of the Voyage of H.M.S. 'Beagle'*, Cambridge, 1933, p. 377
28 Mrs Charles Meredith, *Notes and Sketches of New South Wales*, London, 1849, p. 84
29 Peter Cunningham, *Two Years in New South Wales*, ed. David S. Macmillan, Sydney, 1966 (1 ed. 1827), p. 115
30 John Oxley, *Journal of Two Expeditions to the Interior of New South Wales*, London, 1820, p. 123, quoted Smith, *European Vision*, p. 176
31 H. M. Hyndman, *The Record of an Adventurous Life*, London, 1911, pp. 122-3
32 Clarke, Preface to A. L. Gordon, *Sea Spray and Smoke Drift*, Melbourne, 1876
33 F. Péron, *A Voyage of Discovery to the Southern Hemisphere*, London, 1809, p. 109, quoted Smith, *European Vision*, p. 169
34 Judith Wright, *Preoccupations in Australian Poetry*, p. xii
35 Smith, *European Vision*, pp. 157-9
36 Clarke's Preface to Gordon's *Sea Spray and Smoke Drift*. I owe the point to Judith Wright.

2 TRANSPLANTATION

1 Grattan, Preface to George Nadel, *Australia's Colonial Culture*, Melbourne, 1957, p. xi
2 Pp. 19-25 based closely on Michael Roe, *Quest for Authority in Eastern Australia 1835-1851*, Melbourne, 1965, and Nadel, *Australia's Colonial Culture*.
3 Quoted by Roe, *Quest for Authority*, p. 51
4 Anthony Trollope, *Australia*, ed. P. D. Edwards and R. B. Joyce, Brisbane, 1967 (1 ed. 1873), p. 445
5 Paul F. Bourke, 'Some Recent Essays in Australian Intellectual History', *Historical Studies*, vol. 13, no. 49, October 1967, p. 98
6 Rev. John McGarvie, quoted by Nadel, *Australia's Colonial Culture*, p. 242

7   Roe, *Quest for Authority*, p. 6
8   Nadel, *Australia's Colonial Culture,* p. 265
9   *Ibid*, ch. 5
10 Rev. David Mackenzie, *Ten Years in Australia*, London, 1851, p. 44, quoted *ibid*, p. 88
11 Quoted by Roe, *Quest for Authority*, p. 155
12 Geoffrey Serle, *The Golden Age. A History of the Colony of Victoria, 1851-1861*, Melbourne, 1963, pp. 47-51, 371-2
13 Quoted by H. E. Barff, *A Short Historical Account of the University of Sydney*, Sydney, 1902, p. 7
14 *Ibid*, pp. 5-6; see also Geoffrey Blainey, *A Centenary History of the University of Melbourne*, Melbourne, 1957
15 See the two articles by David McVilly, *La Trobe Library Journal*, nos. 7-8, 1971
16 Barry Papers, La Trobe Library
17 Leonard B. Cox, *The National Gallery of Victoria 1861-1968*, Melbourne, [1970], chs. 1-2
18 H. M. Hyndman, *Record of an Adventurous Life*, London, 1911, p. 100
19 C. W. Dilke, *Problems of Greater Britain*, London, 1890, pp. 187, 488
20 Francis Adams, *Australian Essays*, Melbourne, 1886, p. 6
21 J. A. Froude, *Oceana*, London, 1886, p. 180
22 Asa Briggs, *Victorian Cities*, London, 1963, p. 305

3   LATER COLONIAL c.1850-1885

1   Judith Wright, *Preoccupations in Australian Poetry*, Introduction, quotes from pp. xi, xiv
2   Cecil Hadgraft, *Australian Literature*, London, 1960, p. 4
3   Green, *History of Australian Literature*, i, p. 138
4   T. Inglis Moore, *Social Patterns in Australian Literature*, p. 150
5   Wright, *Preoccupations in Australian Poetry*, ch. 1; J. Normington-Rawling, *Charles Harpur, an Australian*, Sydney, 1962
6   Green, *History of Australian Literature*, i, p. 143
7   Elliott, *The Landscape of Australian Poetry*, pp. 118-19
8   Wright, *Preoccupations in Australian Poetry*, ch. 2; Elliott, *Landscape*; T. T. Reed (ed.), *The Poetical Works of Henry Kendall*, Adelaide, 1966; A. D. Hope, 'Henry Kendall: a Dialogue with the Past', *Southerly*, 1972, no. 3

9 Elliott, *The Literature of Australia*, Dutton ed., p. 241
10 Elliott, *The Landscape of Australian Poetry*, ch. 5; Leonie Kramer, 'The Literary Reputation of Adam Lindsay Gordon', *Aust. Literary Studies*, vol. 1, no. 1, June 1963
11 Oscar Wilde, *Reviews*, London, 1910, pp. 370-71
12 Phillips, *The Australian Tradition*, pp. 60-62; John Barnes, *Henry Kingsley and Colonial Fiction*, Melbourne, 1971; Coral Lansbury, *Arcady in Australia*, Melbourne, 1970, pp. 118-22
13 Brian Elliott, *Marcus Clarke*, Oxford, 1958; Stephen Murray-Smith, Introduction to *His Natural Life*, Penguin, 1970
14 Phillips, *The Australian Tradition*, pp. 36-7, 62-6; Hadgraft, *Australian Literature*, pp. 49-52
15 Green, *History of Australian Literature*, i, p. 246
16 Colin Roderick, *In Mortal Bondage. The Strange Life of Rosa Praed*, Sydney, 1948
17 Hughes, *The Art of Australia*, p. 51
18 Pp. 38-40 based on Bernard Smith, *Australian Painting*, ch. 3
19 Smith, p. 62
20 Wright, *Preoccupations in Australian Poetry*, p. 12
21 McCubbin, quoted by Brian Finemore, *Australian Impressionists*, Melbourne, 1968, p. 8
22 Smith, p. 117
23 James Smith, quoted by L. B. Cox, *The National Gallery of Victoria*, Melbourne, 1970, p. 60
24 Pp. 40-43 based on Covell, *Australia's Music*, pp. 7-24
25 W. A. Carne, *A Century of Harmony: the Official Centenary History of the Royal Melbourne Philharmonic Society*, Melbourne, 1954
26 Covell, pp. 237-8
27 *Ibid*, pp. 20-21
28 R. E. N. Twopeny, *Town Life in Australia*, London, 1883, pp. 217-18
29 Sir Frederick H. Cowen, *My Art and my Friends*, London, 1913, pp. 191-215
30 Kenneth Hince, *Australian*, 1971
31 Covell, p. 5
32 Adam Cairns, *The Dangers and Duties of the Young Men of Victoria*, Melbourne, 1856, p. 12
33 Viola Tait, *A Family of Brothers*, Melbourne, 1971, chs. 7-8
34 D. E. Bandmann, *An Actor's Tour*, New York, 1885
35 A. L. McLeod, 'Theatre', *The Pattern of Australian Culture*; Alec Bagot, *Coppin the Great*, Melbourne, 1965; Paul

McGuire, *The Australian Theatre*, Melbourne, 1948

36 Leslie Rees, *Towards an Australian Drama*, chs. 1-4

37 Pp. 46-8 based on Freeland, *Architecture in Australia*, chs. 5-8

38 Robin Boyd, *The Australian Ugliness*, pp. 35-7

39 *Ibid*, pp. 41-2

40 Pointed out by N. Pevsner, cited in McLeod (ed.), *Pattern of Australian Culture*, p. 384

41 Australian Council of National Trusts, *Historic Homesteads of Australia*, Melbourne, 1969; Robin Boyd, *Australia's Home, passim*. E. Graeme Robertson, *Victorian Heritage. Ornamental Cast Iron in Architecture*, Melbourne, 1960; *Ornamental Cast Iron in Melbourne*, Melbourne, 1967

42 Freeland, *Architecture in Australia*, pp. 109-10, 117-20, 206-9

43 Margaret Willis, *By their Fruits. A Life of Ferdinand von Mueller*, Sydney, 1949

44 M. H. Walker, *Come Wind, Come Weather. A Biography of Alfred Howitt*, Melbourne, 1971

45 John Tregenza, *Professor of Democracy. The Life of Charles Henry Pearson*, Melbourne, 1968

46 For Hearn and Syme as economists, J. A. La Nauze, *Political Economy in Australia*, Melbourne, 1949

47 W. A. Osborne, *William Sutherland. A Biography*, Melbourne, 1920

4 THE GROWTH OF CULTURE IN COLONIES

1 Henry James, *Hawthorne*, London, 1879, p. 3

2 Frederick Sinnett, *The Fiction Fields of Australia*, ed. Cecil Hadgraft, St Lucia, 1966, quotes from pp. 28-9, 31, 33-4

3 See W. K. Hancock's discussion of de Tocqueville, *Australia*, London, 1945 (1 ed. 1930), pp. 223-7

4 Quoted by Wright, *Preoccupations in Australian Poetry*, p. 5

5 Badham, *Sydney University Review*, 1882, p. 163, quoted by Green, *History of Australian Literature*, i, p. 134

6 P. F. Rowland, *The New Nation*, London, 1903, p. 148

7 Van Wyck Brooks, *The Writer in America*, Avon Books, 1964, p. 73

8 Green, *History of Australian Literature*, i, pp. 135-7

9 Lawson, 'Pursuing Literature in Australia', quoted by Denton Prout, *Henry Lawson. The Grey Dreamer*, Adelaide, 1963, p. 175

10 John Holroyd, *George Robertson of Melbourne*, Melbourne, 1968; Wallace Kirsop, *Towards a History of the Australian Book Trade*, Sydney, 1966

11 Rosa Praed, quoted by John Barnes, *The Literature of Australia*, ed. Dutton, p. 158

12 P. H. Newby, *Listener*, 20 August 1951

13 Emerson, quoted by J. K. Ewers, *Meanjin Papers*, 1946, no. 4, p. 334

14 R. M. Crawford, *An Australian Perspective*, Melbourne, 1960, p. 53

5   NATIONAL INSPIRATION c.1885-

1 Brian Fitzpatrick, *The Australian People 1788-1945*, Melbourne 1946, p. 217

2 Randolph Bedford, *Naught to Thirty-Three*, Sydney, n.d., pp. 89-90

3 *The Lone Hand*, July 1907

4 Vance Palmer, *The Legend of the Nineties*, Melbourne, 1954, ch. 5; Russel Ward, *The Australian Legend*, Melbourne, 1958, pp. 205-9; S. E. Lee, 'The Bulletin—J. F. Archibald and A. G. Stephens', *The Literature of Australia*, ed. Dutton; Sylvia Lawson, 'J. F. Archibald', *Aust. Dictionary of Biography*, vol. 3

5 Wright, *Preoccupations in Australian Poetry*, pp. 50-51; ch. 3 in general

6 Edgar Waters, 'Ballads and Popular Verse', *The Literature of Australia*, ed. Dutton, quotation from p. 265; John S. Manifold, *Who Wrote the Ballads?*, Sydney, 1964; Douglas Stewart and Nancy Keesing ed., *Australian Bush Ballads*, Sydney, 1955, and *Old Bush Songs*, Sydney, 1957; Elliott, *Landscape of Australian Poetry*, ch. 9; Covell, *Australia's Music*, ch. 3

7 Manifold, *Who Wrote the Ballads?*, pp. 107-8

8 Green, *History of Australian Literature*, i, p. 367

9 Clement Semmler, *The Banjo of the Bush*, London, 1967; Judith Driscoll, 'A Thaw on Snowy River', *Aust. Literary Studies*, vol. 5, no. 2, October 1971; H. P. Heseltine, 'Banjo Paterson: A Poet nearly Anonymous', *Meanjin Quarterly*, 1964, no. 4

10 R. H. Croll, *I Recall. Collections and Recollections*, Melbourne, 1939, p. 58

11 Ken Levis, 'The Role of the "Bulletin" in Indigenous Short-Story-Writing during the Eighties and Nineties', *Southerly*, 1950, no. 4

12 Green, *History of Australian Literature*, i, p. 538

13 A. A. Phillips, *Henry Lawson*, New York, 1970; Denton Prout, *Henry Lawson. The Grey Dreamer*, Adelaide, 1963; Stephen Murray-Smith, *Henry Lawson*, Melbourne, 1962; various editions by Colin Roderick

14 Quoted by Prout, *Henry Lawson*, p. 81

15 Bruce Nesbitt, 'Literary Nationalism and the 1890s', *Aust. Literary Studies*, vol. 5, no. 1, May 1971

16 Wright, *Preoccupations in Australian Poetry*, pp. 51-6

17 A. D. Hope, *Meanjin Papers*, 1945, no. 3, pp. 226-7

18 Phillips, *The Australian Tradition*, ch. 2 (quote from p. 21); Miles Franklin, *Joseph Furphy. The Legend of a Man and his Book*, Sydney, 1944

19 Vance Palmer (ed.), *A. G. Stephens. His Life and Work*, Melbourne, 1941

20 Phillips, *The Australian Tradition*, p. 38

21 Rudd, quoted by John Barnes, *The Literature of Australia*, ed. Dutton, p. 166

22 Wright, *Preoccupations in Australian Poetry*, pp. 77-9

23 Phillips, *The Australian Tradition*, p. 38

24 Prichard, *Meanjin*, 1953, no. 4, p. 419

25 Victor Kennedy and Nettie Palmer, *Bernard O'Dowd*, Melbourne, 1954; Hugh Anderson, *The Poet Militant: Bernard O'Dowd*, Melbourne, 1969; Wright, *Preoccupations in Australian Poetry*, pp. 71-7 (quote from p. 71); Vincent Buckley, *Essays in Poetry*, Melbourne, 1957, pp. 11-12; Green, *History of Australian Literature*, i, pp. 501-10 (quote from p. 510); Elliott, *Landscape of Australian Poetry*, pp. 184-98

26 Pp. 71-9 based on Bernard Smith, *Australian Painting*, ch. 4; see also Alan McCulloch, *The Golden Age of Australian Painting*, Melbourne, 1969; Brian Finemore, *Australian Impressionists*, Melbourne, 1968; Ursula Hoff, 'Reflections on the Heidelberg School', *Meanjin*, 1951, no. 2; Elwyn Lynn, 'Australian Image. Art and the Innocent Eye', *Meanjin Quarterly*, 1963, no. 1; Ann Galbally, *Arthur Streeton*, Melbourne, 1969

27 Smith, *Australian Painting*, p. 68

28 Roberts, quoted by William Moore, *The Story of Australian Art*, Sydney, 1934, i, p. 70

29 Quoted by R. H. Croll, *Tom Roberts, Father of Australian Landscape Painting*, Melbourne 1935, p. 18
30 Clive Turnbull, *Art Here*, Melbourne, 1947, p. 17
31 James Smith, *Argus*, 17 August 1889
32 Roberts, quoted by Finemore, *Australian Impressionists*, p. 4
33 Robert Hughes, *The Art of Australia*, pp. 54-6; Bernard Smith, *Place, Taste and Tradition*, Sydney, 1945, p. 119; Hoff, 'Reflections on the Heidelberg School', p. 125
34 Smith, *Australian Painting*, p. 79
35 Julian Ashton, *Now Came Still Evening On*, Sydney, 1941, p. 102
36 R. H. Croll (ed.), *Smike to Bulldog*, Sydney, 1946, pp. 40, 63-4
37 Roberts, quoted by Croll, *Tom Roberts*, p. 340
38 Hoff, 'Reflections on the Heidelberg School', p. 128; see also her 'The Phases of McCubbin's Art', *Meanjin*, 1956, no. 3
39 Finemore, *Australian Impressionists*, p. 8
40 Ursula Hoff, *Charles Conder. His Australian Years*, Melbourne, 1960
41 Anne Humffray, 'Tranquillity and Tempest: the Paintings of Walter Withers', *The Gallery on Eastern Hill*, ed. C. B. Christesen, Melbourne, 1970
42 Bernard Smith, *Australian Painting*, p. 82
43 Lorna Stirling, 'The Development of Australian Music', *Historical Studies. Australia and New Zealand*, vol. 3, no. 9, p. 58
44 Covell, *Australia's Music*, p. 6; pp. 79-83 are based closely on this work
45 Stirling, p. 72
46 Covell, *Australia's Music*, pp. 88-103 (quotes from pp. 91, 95, 96, 97, 103)
47 *Ibid*, p. 104
48 Freeland, *Architecture in Australia*, pp. 192-3, 202
49 Bernard Smith, 'Architecture in Australia', *Historical Studies*, vol. 14, no. 53, pp. 90-91
50 Robin Boyd, *Australia's Home*, p. 212
51 *Ibid*
52 Freeland, *Architecture in Australia*, p. 204
53 H. Desbrowe-Annear, 'The Recognition of Architecture', *Domestic Architecture in Australia* (special no. of *Art in Australia*), Sydney, 1919, p. 21. In the following discussion,

I am indebted to ideas expressed in essays by Conrad Hamann of Monash University.

54 Freeland, pp. 238, 243

55 Robin Boyd, *The Australian Ugliness*, Melbourne, 1960, p. 101

56 Freeland, p. 238

57 Robert J. Haddon, *Australian Architecture*, Melbourne, 1908, p. 39

58 Boyd, *Australia's Home*, p. 60

59 J. P. Birrell, *Walter Burley Griffin*, Brisbane, 1964; Freeland, *Architecture in Australia*, pp. 245-7; Boyd, *The Australian Ugliness*, pp. 12-15

60 A. G. Mitchell in *English Transported*, ed. W. S. Ramson, Canberra, 1970, p. 2; see also W. S. Ramson, *Australian English*, Canberra, 1966; G. W. Turner, *The English Language in Australia and New Zealand*, London, 1966; S. J. Baker, *The Australian Language*, Sydney, 1966 (1 ed. 1945)

6 DELAYED DEVELOPMENT c.1900-1930

1 Graham McInnes, *The Road to Gundagai*, London, 1965, p. 283

2 Pp. 91-8 based on Bernard Smith, *Australian Painting*, chs. 5-6; Hughes, *The Art of Australia*, chs. 3-4

3 Smith, p. 165

4 L. B. Cox, *The National Gallery of Victoria, 1861-1968*, Melbourne, 1970

5 Smith, p. 107

6 Hughes, *The Art of Australia*, pp. 83-6

7 *Ibid*, p. 103

8 Lloyd Rees, *The Small Treasures of a Lifetime*, Sydney, 1969, p. 121

9 Hughes, *The Art of Australia*, p. 89; Colin Thiele, *Heysen of Hahndorf*, Adelaide, 1968

10 Smith, pp. 168-70, 195

11 J. S. MacDonald, 'Arthur Streeton', *Art in Australia*, October 1931

12 Kenneth Slessor, *Bread and Wine*, Sydney, 1970, p. 92

13 Phillips, *The Australian Tradition*, pp. 70-71

14 Vincent Buckley, *Essays in Poetry*, Melbourne, 1957, p. 12

15 Mario Muner, 'Christopher Brennan: his Personality and the

Unity of his Poetry', *Meanjin Quarterly*, 1971, no. 1. There is a large critical literature on Brennan in the periodicals.

16 Wright, *Preoccupations in Australian Poetry*, pp. 98, 100

17 Robert D. FitzGerald (ed.), *The Letters of Hugh McCrae*, Sydney, 1970

18 *The Poems of Shaw Neilson*, ed. A. R. Chisholm, Sydney, 1965, p. 15; Wright, *Preoccupations*, ch. 8; Hugh Anderson and L. J. Blake, *John Shaw Neilson*, Adelaide, 1972

19 These remarks on Wilmot owe something to unpublished work by David Walker; Vance Palmer, *Frank Wilmot*, Melbourne, 1942; Frederick T. Macartney, *Furnley Maurice*, Sydney, 1955

20 H. J. Oliver, *Louis Stone*, Melbourne, 1968

21 There is a series of articles on Richardson, including two by Dorothy Green, in *Meanjin Quarterly*, 1969-70

22 John Alexander, 'D. H. Lawrence's *Kangaroo*: Fantasy, Fact or Fiction?', *Meanjin Quarterly*, 1965, no. 2; Michael Wilding, ' "A New Show": the Politics of *Kangaroo*', *Southerly*, 1970, no. 1

23 Jack Lindsay, 'Australian Poetry and Nationalism', *Vision*, no. 1, May 1923, pp. 33-4

24 Wright, *Preoccupations in Australian Poetry*, pp. 132-4

25 Vincent Buckley, *Essays in Poetry*, pp. 15, 17. See also, for the *Vision* movement, Elliott, *The Landscape of Australian Poetry*, ch. 12, and John Tregenza, *Australian Little Magazines 1923-1954*, Adelaide, 1964

26 Douglas Stewart, 'Norman Lindsay's Novels', *Southerly*, 1959, no. 1, p. 3

27 Vincent Buckley, 'Utopianism and Vitalism in Australian Literature', *Quadrant*, no. 10, 1959, p. 50

28 T. L. Sturm, 'Kenneth Slessor's Poetry and Norman Lindsay', *Southerly*, 1971, no. 4

29 Kenneth Slessor, *Bread and Wine*, Sydney, 1970, pp. 111-12

30 Quoted by Evan Jones, *The Literature of Australia*, ed. Dutton, p. 100

31 Jack Lindsay, 'Norman Lindsay: Problems of his Life and Work' and Jack Allison, ' "Futurity": Norman Lindsay's Creative Stimulus', *Meanjin Quarterly*, 1970, nos. 1 and 3; Norman Lindsay, *My Mask*, Sydney, 1970; Lionel Lindsay, *Comedy of Life*, Sydney, 1967, ch. 12

32 Jack Lindsay, quoted by Richard Fotheringham, 'Expatriate Publishing: Jack Lindsay and the Fanfrolico Press', *Meanjin Quarterly*, 1972, no. 1, p. 57 and see subsequent

articles on Stephensen's and Partridge's presses, *ibid*, nos. 2-3

33 Viola Tait, *A Family of Brothers*, Melbourne, 1971, *passim*, quotes from pp. 131, 215, 214

34 Foreword, *ibid*

35 Alfred Buchanan, *The Real Australia*, London, 1907, pp. 138-42

36 Brodzsky, *The Lone Hand*, 1908, quoted by Leslie Rees, *Towards an Australian Drama*, Sydney, 1953, pp. 57-8

37 Dennis Douglas and Margery M. Morgan, 'Gregan McMahon and the Australian Theatre', *Komos*, 1969

38 Quoted by Vance Palmer, *Louis Esson and the Australian Theatre*, Melbourne, 1948, p. 3

39 Esson, 'Irish Memories and Australian Hopes', *Aust. Quarterly*, June 1939, quoted by Rees, *Towards an Australian Drama*, pp. 58-9

40 Palmer, *Louis Esson*, pp. 27-8

41 H. G. Kippax, 'Drama', *Australian Society*, ed. A. F. Davies and S. Encel, Melbourne, 1965, p. 197

42 Kippax, Introduction to *Three Australian Plays*, Penguin, 1963, pp. 12-13

43 Green, *History of Australian Literature*, i, p. 683

44 Quoted by Rees, pp. 79-80. Pp. 106-13 have been based on Rees and Palmer.

45 Hal Porter, *Stars of Australian Stage and Screen*, Adelaide, 1965, gives the fullest account of theatrical activity

46 Seymour Hicks, "*Hullo Australians*", London, 1925, p. 206

47 Arnold Haskell, *Waltzing Matilda*, London, 1943, pp. 146-7, 149

48 Quoted, A. H. Chisholm, *The Making of a Sentimental Bloke*, Melbourne, 1946, p. 126; see also Alexander Porteous, '*The Sentimental Bloke* and his Critics', *Aust. Literary Studies*, vol. 1, no. 4, December 1964

49 Flora Eldershaw, 'The Landscape Writers', *Meanjin*, 1952, no. 3, p. 219

50 Vane Lindesay, *The Inked-in Image: a Survey of Australian Comic Art*, Melbourne, 1970

51 R. F. Cooper, ' "And the Villain still Pursued Her". Origins of Film in Australia, 1896-1913', M.A. thesis, Aust. National University, 1971; E. Reade, *Australian Silent Films*, Melbourne, 1970

52 John Baxter, *The Australian Cinema*, Sydney, 1970, p. 58; articles by Colin Bennett in the *Age*

7 LITERATURE AND THE NATIONAL PROBLEM

1 Vance Palmer, *Louis Esson and the Australian Theatre*, Melbourne, 1948, p. 96
2 Flora Eldershaw, quoted by John Barnes, 'The Man of Letters', *Meanjin*, 1959, no. 2, p. 196
3 A. D. Hope, 'Vance Palmer Reconsidered', *Southerly*, 1955, no. 4; Harry Heseltine, *Vance Palmer*, St Lucia, 1970
4 Hume Dow, *Frank Dalby Davison*, Melbourne, 1971
5 R. G. Geering, *Christina Stead*, Melbourne, 1969
6 Marjorie Barnard, *Miles Franklin*, Melbourne, 1967
7 Margaret Dick, *The Novels of Kylie Tennant*, Adelaide, 1966
8 Heseltine, *The Literature of Australia*, ed. Dutton, p. 183
9 Chris Wallace-Crabbe, *The Literature of Australia*, ed. Dutton, p. 342
10 Vivian Smith, 'The Ambivalence of Kenneth Slessor', *Southerly*, 1971, no. 4 (Slessor Memorial Number), p. 256
11 Dymphna Cusack, T. Inglis Moore and Barrie Ovenden (ed.), *Mary Gilmore: a Tribute*, Sydney, 1968
12 Alan Moorehead, *Rum Jungle*, London, 1953, pp. 9-12
13 *Ibid*, pp. 19-21
14 Graham McInnes, *Humping my Bluey*, London, 1966, p. 154
15 Philip Lindsay, *I'd Live the Same Life Over*, London, 1941, pp. 115, 131, 146
16 Vance Palmer, 'Fragment of Autobiography', *Meanjin*, 1958, no. 1, p. 3
17 Vance Palmer, *Louis Esson and the Australian Theatre*, pp. 11, 33
18 Jack Lindsay, *The Roaring Twenties*, London, 1960, p. 197
19 Phillips, *The Australian Tradition*, p. 82. Jack Lindsay, 'The Alienated Australian Intellectual', *Meanjin Quarterly*, 1963, no. 1, p. 55
20 Patrick White, 'The Prodigal Son', *Australian Letters*, vol. 1, no. 3, April 1958
21 J. D. Pringle, Preface to George Johnston, *A Cartload of Clay*, Sydney, 1971, p. 7
22 Vance Palmer, 'An Australian National Art', John Barnes ed., *The Writer in Australia*, pp. 168-9
23 *Fellowship*, May 1916
24 I owe much in this paragraph to unpublished work by David Walker

25 Richard Fotheringham, 'Expatriate Publishing: P. R. Stephensen and the Mandrake Press', *Meanjin Quarterly*, 1972, no. 2

26 P. R. Stephensen, *The Foundations of Culture in Australia*, Sydney, 1936, pp. 11-128

27 Rex Ingamells, 'Conditional Culture', John Barnes ed., *The Writer in Australia*, pp. 249-51, 264

28 *Jindyworobak Review 1938-1948*, Melbourne, 1948; Elliott, *The Landscape of Australian Poetry*, pp. 236-49

29 Vance Palmer, *Louis Esson and the Australian Theatre*, p. 83

30 Norman Bartlett, *Australian Writers Speak*, A.B.C. broadcasts, Sydney, 1943, pp. 54-5

31 R. C. Bald, *Manuscripts*, no. 3, 1930, in *Twentieth Century Australian Literary Criticism*, C. Semmler ed., Melbourne, 1967, p. 8

32 Manning Clark, *Meanjin Papers*, 1943, no. 3, p. 40

33 Palmer, *Louis Esson and the Australian Theatre*, p. 86

34 Nettie Palmer, 'Australia—an International Unit', *Meanjin Papers*, 1944, no. 1, p. 7

35 Quoted by Margaret L. Macpherson, *I Heard the Anzacs Singing*, New York, 1942, p. 6

36 C. Hartley Grattan, *Australian Literature*, Seattle, 1929, p. 38; see also his 'A Garrulity about Australian Literature since 1927', *Meanjin Quarterly*, 1965, no. 4

37 H. S. Canby, *A New Land Speaking*, Melbourne, 1946, p. 13

38 Bruce Sutherland, 'An American Looks at Australian Literature', *Meanjin*, 1952, no. 2, p. 152

39 Phillips, *The Australian Tradition*, pp. 89-94

40 H. G. Kippax in *Australian Society*, ed. A. F. Davies and S. Encel, Melbourne, 1965, p. 196

41 Nettie Palmer, quoted by Esther Levy, *Meanjin*, 1959, no. 2, p. 231

42 Leonard Mann, 'A Double Life', *Southerly*, 1969, no. 3, p. 168

43 K. S. Prichard, 'Some Perceptions and Aspirations', *Southerly*, 1968, no. 4, pp. 235-6, 244

44 Douglas Grant, *Purpose and Place. Essays on American Writers*, London, 1965, p. 92

45 G. H. Wilkins, *Undiscovered Australia*, London, 1928, quoted by C. H. Grattan, *The Southwest Pacific Since 1900*, Ann Arbor, 1963, p. 103

46 Constance Rourke, *The Roots of American Culture*, New York, 1942, pp. 45, 284, vi

47 H. H. Richardson, Foreword to C. H. Grattan, *Australian Literature*

48 Louis Esson, Introduction to *Australian Writers Speak*, pp. 9-10

49 Tom Roberts, quoted by Bernard Smith, *Australian Painting*, p. 90

50 Russel Ward, 'Colonialism and Culture', *Overland*, no. 31, 1965

51 Green, *History of Australian Literature*, ii, p. 849

52 A. D. Hope, 'Standards in Australian Literature', *Australian Literary Criticism*, G. K. W. Johnston ed., Melbourne, 1962, p. 6

53 Vincent Buckley, 'Towards an Australian Literature', *Meanjin*, 1959, no. 1, p. 59

54 Hope, 'Standards', p. 11

55 Cf. G. K. W. Johnston, *Australian Literary Criticism*, p. viii

56 F. D. Davison, 'Vance Palmer and his Writing', *Meanjin*, 1948, no. 1, p. 12

57 Judith Wright, *Preoccupations in Australian Poetry*, p. xviii

58 Geoffrey Dutton, *The Literature of Australia*, p. 8

59 Quoted by Van Wyck Brooks, *The Pilgrimage of Henry James*, London, 1928, p. 48

60 Howard Mumford Jones, *The Theory of American Literature*, Ithaca, N.Y., 1948, pp. 131-2

61 Quoted by Van Wyck Brooks, *The Confident Years 1885-1915*, New York, 1955, p. 466

62 Alfred Kazin, *On Native Grounds*, New York, 1942, p. ix

63 James McAuley, *Farrago*, 1 March 1971

8   A COMING-OF-AGE c.1935-1950?

1 James Bryce, *Modern Democracies*, New York, 1921, ii, p. 251

2 Gordon Greenwood, *Australia*, Sydney 1955, p. 255

3 R. M. Crawford, *An Australian Perspective*, Melbourne, 1960, pp. 68-9

4 *Petition to the Government of Victoria . . .*, London, [1901]

5 George Currie and John Graham, *The Origins of C.S.I.R.O.*, Melbourne, 1966; E. Scott, 'The History of Australian Science,' *Aust. Journal of Science*, vol. 1, no. 4, 1939

6 J. B. S. Haldane, quoted by F. L. McDougall, *The Crucial Problem of Imperial Development*, London [n.d.], p. 8

7 K. S. Cunningham, *Australia*, C. Hartley Grattan ed., Berkeley, Cal., 1947, p. 349

8 John A. Passmore, 'Philosophy', *The Pattern of Australian Culture*, A. L. McLeod, ed.

9 R. M. Crawford, *The Humanities in Australia*, A. Grenfell Price ed., Sydney, 1959, pp. 148-56; John M. Ward, 'Historiography', *The Pattern of Australian Culture*, McLeod ed.

10 I. Moresby, *Australia Makes Music*, Melbourne, 1948

11 Covell, *Australia's Music*, p. 236; pp. 155-7 are based on this work. John Hetherington, *Melba*, Melbourne, 1967

12 Covell, pp. 25-6, 141-3

13 Viola Tait, *A Family of Brothers*, Melbourne, 1971, ch. 15

14 Covell, *Australia's Music*, pp. 108-30

15 Tait, *A Family of Brothers*, ch. 28 (quote from p. 224); A. L. McLeod, *The Pattern of Australian Culture*, pp. 342-4

16 Tait, *A Family of Brothers*, pp. 96-7

17 Claude Kingston, *It Don't Seem a Day Too Much*, Adelaide, 1971, p. 153

18 Covell, *Australia's Music*, p. 239

19 Leslie Rees, *Towards an Australian Drama*, Sydney, 1953, chs. 8-10; John Thompson, 'Broadcasting and Australian Literature', *Literary Australia*, Clement Semmler and Derek Whitelock ed., Melbourne, 1966

20 Wakelin, quoted by Hughes, *The Art of Australia*, p. 116

21 Hughes, ch. 5; Bernard Smith, *Australian Painting*, pp. 171-7. Pp. 159-72 are based closely on Smith, chs. 6-8, and to some extent on Hughes, chs. 5-7

22 Adrian Lawlor, *Arquebus*, Melbourne, 1937, p. 12

23 Hughes, *The Art of Australia*, p. 128

24 Smith, *Australian Painting*, pp. 198-203

25 *Ibid*, p. 205

26 *Ibid*, pp. 205-15

27 *Ibid*, pp. 216-17

28 *Ibid*, p. 218

29 L. B. Cox, *The National Gallery of Victoria 1861 to 1968*, Melbourne, 1970, p. 164; J. S. MacDonald, *Australian Painting Desiderata*, Melbourne, 1958

30 Quoted by Smith, *Australian Painting*, p. 218

31 Hughes, *The Art of Australia*, p. 132

32 Smith, *Australian Painting*, pp. 255-64 (quote from p. 263); James Gleeson, *William Dobell*, London, 1964, (quote from

p. 168); Hughes, *The Art of Australia*, pp. 182-90, 201-03 (quote from p. 203)

33 Smith, pp. 264-71
34 Smith, pp. 242-51, (quotes from pp. 244, 251); Geoffrey Dutton, *Russell Drysdale*, London, 1964; Hughes, pp. 190-201
35 Lloyd Rees, *The Small Treasures of a Lifetime*, Sydney, 1969
36 Daniel Thomas, *Sali Herman*, Melbourne, 1962; Robert Hughes, *Donald Friend*, Sydney, 1965
37 Hughes, *The Art of Australia*, pp. 170-72
38 Smith, pp. 230-39, 276-8; Hughes, pp. 135-50
39 Smith, pp. 280-83; Hughes, pp. 160-67, 221-7; Kenneth Clark, Colin McInnes, Bryan Robertson, *Sidney Nolan*, London, 1961; Elwyn Lynn, *Sidney Nolan. Myth and Imagery*, London, 1967
40 Franz Philipp, *Arthur Boyd*, London, 1967; Smith, pp. 283-7; Hughes, pp. 155-8, 231-5
41 Smith, pp. 278-80; Hughes, pp. 150-55, 228-31; Christopher Uhl, *Albert Tucker*, Melbourne, 1969
42 Clive Turnbull, *Art Here*, Melbourne, 1947, p. 34
43 Albert Tucker, *Angry Penguins*, September 1943
44 H. M. Green, *Modern Australian Poetry*, Melbourne, 1946, p. vii
45 H. P. Heseltine (ed.), *The Penguin Book of Australian Verse*, 1972, p. 45
46 Elliott, *The Landscape of Australian Poetry*, pp. 288-303; Wright, *Preoccupations in Australian Poetry*, ch. 11; Leonie Kramer, 'R. D. FitzGerald—Philosopher or Poet?', *Overland*, no. 33, December 1965; articles in *Southerly*, 1966, no. 1, and 1967, no. 4
47 Elliott, pp. 316-20
48 Elliott, pp. 331-5; Wright, ch. 12
49 Elliott, pp. 313-15
50 Ian Turner, *The Literature of Australia*, Dutton ed., p. 52
51 John Tregenza, *Australian Little Magazines 1923-1954*, Adelaide, 1964, ch. 3
52 Max Harris, *Direction*, no. 1, May 1952, quoted *ibid*, p. 73
53 Harry Hooton, *Number Three*, quoted *ibid*, p. 75
54 Elliott, *The Landscape of Australian Poetry*, p. 259
55 Quoted by A. Norman Jeffares, 'The "Ern Malley" Poems', *The Literature of Australia*, Dutton, ed., pp. 408-9
56 Elliott, p. 261
57 The best discussions of *Angry Penguins* and of the Ern Malley incident are by Elliott, Jeffares and Tregenza, *op.*

cit; see also Max Harris, 'Angry Penguins and After', *Quadrant*, no. 25, 1963

58 *Art in Australia*, March 1941, quoted Bernard Smith, *Australian Painting*, p. 226

59 *Meanjin*, no. 8, 1942, p. 6

60 Lloyd Ross, 'Building Community and Nation', *Meanjin*, 1945, no. 1, pp. 5-6

61 Ursula Wiemann, 'German and Austrian Refugees in Melbourne 1933-1947', M.A. thesis, Univ. Melbourne, 1965

9 RELATIVE ABUNDANCE c.1950-1965

1 Hugh Hunt, *The Making of Australian Theatre*, Melbourne, 1960, p. 22. For postwar cultural development in general, C. Hartley Grattan, *The Southwest Pacific since 1900*, pp. 225-32

2 Elliott, *The Landscape of Australian Poetry*, pp. 321-31; Wright, *Preoccupations in Australian Poetry*, ch. 13

3 James McAuley, *The End of Modernity*, Sydney, 1959, p. 62

4 J. D. Pringle, *Australian Accent*, ch. 7

5 Chris Wallace-Crabbe, 'The Habit of Irony? Australian Poets of the 'Fifties', *Meanjin Quarterly*, 1961, no. 2, p. 170

6 Vincent Buckley, 'A New Bulletin School?', *Port Phillip Gazette*, Autumn 1954

7 Wallace-Crabbe, 'The Habit of Irony'; cf. Judith Wright, 'Australian Poetry since 1941', *Southerly*, 1971, no. 1

8 A. D. Hope, *Australian Literature 1950-1962*, Melbourne, 1963, p. 4

9 *Ibid*, p. 12; Dorothy Green, 'From Yarra Glen to Rome: Martin Boyd, 1893-1972', *Meanjin Quarterly*, 1972, no. 3; *Southerly*, 1968, no. 2 (Martin Boyd Special Number)

10 Patrick White, 'The Prodigal Son', *Aust. Letters*, vol. 1, no. 3, 1958, p. 39

11 Brian Kiernan, *Images of Society and Nature*, Melbourne, 1971, pp. 147, 95

12 White, 'The Prodigal Son', p. 39

13 G. A. Wilkes (ed.), *Ten Essays on Patrick White*, Sydney, 1970. There are dozens of critical articles and theses on White in recent years which it is impracticable to list.

14 Harry Heseltine, *The Literature of Australia*, Dutton ed., p. 219

15 Max Harris, 'Angry Penguins and After', *Quadrant*, no. 25, 1963, p. 10

16 Henry James, *Hawthorne*, London, 1879, p. 31

17 Vincent Buckley, 'Utopianism and Vitalism in Australian Literature', *Quadrant*, no. 10, Autumn 1959; H. P. Heseltine, 'The Literary Heritage' and A. A. Phillips, 'The Literary Heritage Re-assessed', *Meanjin Quarterly*, 1962, nos. 1-2

18 T. Inglis Moore, *Social Patterns in Australian Literature*, ch. 7

19 Brian Kiernan, *Images of Society and Nature*

20 See periodical articles by Andrew Fabinyi in *Meanjin Quarterly*

21 Pp. 189-96 based largely on Bernard Smith, *Australian Painting*, and to some extent on Robert Hughes, *The Art of Australia*

22 Hughes, p. 208

23 Smith, pp. 302-3; J. Henshaw, *Godfrey Miller*, Sydney, 1965

24 *Ibid*, p. 304; Hughes, p. 289

25 Smith, p. 306; Ronald Millar, *John Brack*, Melbourne, 1971; Ray Mathew, *Charles Blackman*, Melbourne, 1965

26 Patrick McCaughey, *Age*, 26 August 1972; Smith, pp. 413-14; John Brack and others, *Fred Williams. Etchings*, Sydney, 1968. For Pugh, see Noel Macainsh, *Clifton Pugh*, Melbourne, 1962

27 Smith, p. 354; Hughes, pp. 259-67; Virginia Spate, *John Olsen*, Melbourne, 1963, p. 1

28 Smith, pp. 358-9

29 Hughes, p. 251

30 Smith, p. 321

31 *Ibid*, p. 328

32 Franz Philipp, *Arthur Boyd*, London, 1967, p. 10

33 Smith, p. 330. Manifesto quoted pp. 329-30

34 *Ibid*, pp. 373-81

35 *Ibid*, p. 380

36 Lenton Parr, *Sculpture*, Melbourne, 1961; McLeod, *The Pattern of Australian Culture*, pp. 376-8

37 Smith, pp. 345-7

38 *Ibid*, pp. 342-4

39 Rees, *Towards an Australian Drama*, ch. 12

40 H. G. Kippax, Introduction to *Three Australian Plays*, Penguin, 1963, pp. 15-16; for Stewart's plays, Rees, *Towards an Australian Drama*, ch. 11

41 Rees, pp. 108-10, 169-73

42 J. D. Pringle, *Australian Accent*, London, 1958, p. 130

43 *Ibid*

44 Kippax, Introduction to *Three Australian Plays*, p. 19

45 Kippax, *ibid*, pp. 19-20; Kippax, 'Drama', *Australian Society*, Davies and Encel ed., Melbourne, 1965, pp. 202-4

46 Hugh Hunt, *The Making of Australian Theatre*, p. 43

47 For drama in this period, see also Eunice Hanger, 'Australian Drama', *The Literature of Australia*, Dutton ed.; *Meanjin Quarterly*, 1964, no. 3 (Theatre Issue); *Southerly*, 1963, no. 2 (Drama Issue)

48 Tyrone Guthrie, *A Life in the Theatre*, London, 1960, p. 252

49 McLeod, *Pattern of Australian Culture*, p. 336; see also Pringle, *Australian Accent*, pp. 128-32

50 Hugh Hunt, *The Making of Australian Theatre*

51 H. G. Kippax, 'Drama', *Australian Society*, Davies and Encel ed., p. 201; see pp. 198-201 for his account of the early years of the Trust.

52 Covell, *Australia's Music*, pp. 242-68

53 Alan Brissenden, 'Present-Day Ballet in Australia', *Meanjin*, 1956, no. 4; Robin Grove, 'Ballet and Australia', *Meanjin Quarterly*, 1964, no. 3; Peggy van Praagh, *Ballet in Australia*, Melbourne, 1965

54 Arthur Jacobs, 'Report on Musical Australia', *Meanjin*, 1952, no. 4

55 Covell, *Australia's Music*, p. 278; pp. 111-32, 270-79 on the A.B.C. and music; my pp. 202-6 are largely based on Covell.

56 *Ibid*, pp. 132-40

57 Felix Werder, 'Composing in Australia', *Meanjin*, 1957, no. 2

58 Covell, pp. 145-7

59 *Ibid*, pp. 152, 154-7

60 *Ibid*, pp. 152-4; Margaret Sutherland, 'Young Days in Music', *Overland*, no. 40, Summer 1968-9

61 *Ibid*, pp. 161-3 (Le Gallienne), 182-91 (Werder), 178-82 (Banks), 168-79 (Williamson), 200-211 (Sculthorpe), 211-14 (Meale)

62 *Ibid*, pp. 191-5, (Dreyfus), 195-200 (Sitsky), 224-32 (Butterley)

63 *Ibid*, pp. 234, 269

64 On the A.B.C. in the 50s, see G. C. Bolton, *Dick Boyer. An Australian Humanist*, Canberra, 1967, chs. 6-12; John Thompson, 'Broadcasting and Australian Literature', *Literary Australia*, Clement Semmler and Derek Whitelock ed., Melbourne, 1966; articles on TV in *Overland*, no. 41, 1969

65 John Baxter, *The Australian Cinema*, Sydney, 1970; Craig McGregor, *Profile of Australia*, London, 1966, pp. 249-51

66 Freeland, *Architecture in Australia*, pp. 252-3

67 *Ibid*, p. 263

68 *Ibid*, pp. 279-81; Robin Boyd, *Artificial Australia* (A.B.C. Boyer Lectures, 1967), pp. 27-9

69 Robin Boyd, *Sunday Australian*, 12 September 1971

70 Freeland, p. 305

71 Boyd, *Artificial Australia*, p. 16; Freeland, pp. 291-3

72 S. M. Wadham, 'Science', *The Pattern of Australian Culture*, McLeod ed.; J. Gani, *The Condition of Science in Australian Universities*, Oxford, 1963; *Records of the Australian Academy of Science* (1967-); S. Encel, 'Science, Technology and the Australian Community', *Search*, vol. 1, 1970; Ann Mozley, 'A Check List of Publications on the History of Australian Science', *Australian Journal of Science*, vol. 25, no. 5, 1962, and Supplement, *ibid*, vol. 27, no. 1, 1964

73 Cf. A. Grenfell Price ed., *The Humanities in Australia*, Sydney, 1959

74 Cf. Vincent Buckley, 'Intellectuals', *Australian Civilization*, Peter Coleman ed., Melbourne, 1962; Donald Horne, *The Lucky Country*, Penguin, 1964, pp. 204-8, and *The Next Australia*, Sydney, 1970, ch. 7.

10 CONTEMPORARY CONCLUSION

1 Robin Boyd, *Artificial Australia* (A.B.C. Boyer Lectures, 1967), p. 4

2 Ian Turner, 'Intellectuals in Australian Life', *Overland*, no. 33, Summer, 1965-6; Richard Hofstadter, *Anti-Intellectualism in American Life*, New York, 1966; Jack Lindsay, 'The Alienated Australian Intellectual', *Meanjin Quarterly*, 1963, no. 1; Noel McLachlan, 'The Australian Intellectual', *ibid*, 1967, no. 1

3 Hofstadter, p. 34

4 Geoffrey Blainey, *The Rush That Never Ended*, Melbourne, 1963, pp. 65-6, 77, 292

5 A. G. Austin, 'Anti-intellectualism in Australian Life', *Australian Rationalist*, no. 1, 1969

6   J. D. Pringle, *Australian Accent*, London, 1958, p. 134

7   Donald Horne, *The Next Australia*, Sydney, 1970, p. 86

8   Craig McGregor, *Profile of Australia*, London, 1966, p. 254

9   Robin Boyd, *Artificial Australia*, pp. 3-5

10 Peter Coleman, *Obscenity Blasphemy Sedition. Censorship in Australia*, Brisbane, n.d., p. 19

11 Marjorie Barnard, 'How "Tomorrow and Tomorrow" Came to be Written', *Meanjin Quarterly*, 1970, no. 3. For a general review of censorship, *Overland*, nos. 27-8, 1963

12 James Gleeson, *William Dobell*, London, 1964, p. 145

13 Bernard Smith, *Australian Painting*, pp. 395-8

14 Submission by the Committee for an Enquiry into the Arts (Melbourne) to the Commonwealth Government, 1961

15 Allan Healy, 'The Alien Antipodes: Australia seen from England', *Meanjin Quarterly*, 1972, no. 2, p. 200

16 Robin Boyd, *Artificial Australia*, p. 49

17 Brian Kiernan, *Images of Society and Nature*, Melbourne, 1971, ch. 6

18 Introduction to Rodney Hall and Thomas W. Shapcott ed., *New Impulses in Australian Poetry*, St Lucia, 1968; Alec King, 'The Look of Australian Poetry in 1967', *Meanjin Quarterly*, 1968, no. 2; James Tulip, 'Contemporary Australian Poetry', *Southerly*, 1972, nos. 2-3

19 Carl Harrison-Ford, 'Poetics before Politics', *Meanjin Quarterly*, 1970, no. 2; Rodney Hall, 'Attitudes to Tradition in Contemporary Australian Poetry', *Poetry Australia*, no. 32, February 1970

20 David Williamson, *Australian*, 1972

21 *Bulletin*, 7 August 1971

22 Margaret Williams, 'Snakes and Ladders: New Australian Drama', *Meanjin Quarterly*, 1972, no. 2, p. 179

23 Programme notes, *The Feet of Daniel Mannix* (Australian Performing Group)

24 David Williamson, *Australian*, 28 August 1970. See also, Margaret Williams 'Mask and Cage: Stereotype in Recent Drama', *Meanjin Quarterly*, 1972, no. 3; Katharine Brisbane, *Australian*, 20 March 1971

25 H. G. Kippax, *The Entertainment Arts in Australia*, J. Allen ed., London 1968

26 Pp. 223-5 closely based on Bernard Smith, *Australian Painting*, chs. 10-12. A useful recent illustrated survey is James Gleeson, *Modern Painting 1931-1970*, Melbourne, 1971

27 Smith, p. 386
28 *Ibid*, p. 334
29 Franz Philipp, *Arthur Boyd*, London, 1967, p. 12
30 Smith, p. 342
31 *Ibid*, pp. 348, 351-2
32 *Ibid*, pp. 334-41
33 R. H. Morrison ed., *Australia's Russian Poets*, Melbourne, 1972
34 K. S. Inglis, 'The Daily Papers', *Australian Civilization*, Peter Coleman ed., Melbourne, 1972; John Douglas Pringle, 'Something to Write Home About', *Quadrant*, no. 73, 1971
35 Terry Smith, *The Review*, 11-17 March 1972
36 Robin Boyd, *Australia's Home*, pp. 223-5, *The Australian Ugliness, passim*
37 J. H. Davidson, 'Notes on a Nationalist: Donald Horne's "The Next Australia"', *Meanjin Quarterly*, 1971, no. 4, pp. 444-5
38 A. A. Phillips, 'Provincialism and Australian Culture', *Meanjin Quarterly*, 1966, no. 3
39 *Times Literary Supplement*, 8 May 1969
40 Hughes, *The Art of Australia*, pp. 311-15
41 A. D. Hope, 'Australian Literature and the Universities', *Meanjin*, 1954, no. 2, p. 167
42 An adaptation from Philip Rahv, 'The Native Bias', *Literature and the Sixth Sense*, London, 1970, p. 269

APPENDIX: A NOTE ON MELBOURNE AND SYDNEY

1 C. M. H. Clark, 'Faith', *Australian Civilization*, Peter Coleman ed., Melbourne, 1962, pp. 85-7
2 Vincent Buckley, *ibid*, p. 101
3 John Docker, 'Sydney Intellectual History and Sydney Libertarianism', *Politics*, 1972, no. 1

INDEX